OHR אור השחר
HaShachar

Torah, Kabbalah and Consciousness in the
Daily Morning Blessings

David Bar-Cohn

Urim Publications
Jerusalem • New York

Ohr HaShachar: Torah, Kabbalah and Consciousness
in the Daily Morning Blessings
by David Bar-Cohn

Book layout and cover design by D. Bar-Cohn.
Cover photo by Markus Gann/Dreamstime.
The author may be contacted at: www.barcohn.com.

Printed in Israel

First Edition
ISBN: 978-965-524-151-8

Urim Publications
P.O. Box 52287
Jerusalem 91521 Israel

www.UrimPublications.com

Library of Congress Cataloging-in-Publication Data

Bar-Cohn, David.
    Ohr hashachar : Torah, Kabbalah and consciousness in the daily morning
blessings / David Bar-Cohn. — First edition.
        p. cm.
    ISBN 978-965-524-151-8 (hardback)
    1. Judaism—Liturgy—Texts—History and criticism. 2. Jewish meditations.
3. Spiritual life—Judaism. I. Title.
BM660.B34 2014
296.4'5—dc23
                                                                    2014009147

To Kerry and the boys,

a source of so much life!

And in loving memory of my parents,

Peter and Charlotte Behrendt, *z"l*

אָז יִבָּקַע כַּשַּׁחַר אוֹרֶךְ

"THEN YOUR LIGHT WILL BREAK FORTH
LIKE THE DAWN"

(YESHAYAHU 58:8)

THE DAVID CARDOZO ACADEMY
Machon Ohr Aaron & Betsy Spijer
Rabbi Nathan Lopes Cardozo, Ph.D., Dean

מכון קרדוזו דוד
DAVID CARDOZO ACADEMY

May 20, 2013
י"א סיון תשע"ג

To pray properly as a Jew requires courage. Courage to confront oneself. To look carefully at the words of the *siddur* and dare to ask oneself the daunting questions of what exactly one is saying, and whether those words truly reflect one's heart, hopes, and aspirations. And if there is a disconnect between one's words and one's heart, if the prayer experience does not achieve a meaningful personal impact, what does one do then?

Unfortunately, these questions are too often avoided. The candor and vulnerability they require make us too uncomfortable. We lack the courage, and so we simply pray because we "ought to" be praying. We pretend that the prayer reflects our souls because that is what a Jew "ought to" believe. For those brave enough to confront the difficult questions, finding an adequate resolution is not a simple matter either. Some who struggle to find meaning in the *siddur* may choose to abandon prayer altogether. Others may decide to change the text of the *siddur* to be more in consonance with their hearts.

But there is another approach, which is adopted in the book *Ohr HaShachar*. That is to contend with the words of the *siddur*, to wrestle and strive with them until the point where one can now look at the same prayers in a new light. In his exploration of the morning *berakhoth*, David Bar-Cohn has artfully retained fidelity to traditional meanings and commentaries, while at the same time advancing novel explanations and new dimensions of meaning that speak to the heart of the modern, thinking individual.

To write a commentary on the *berakhoth* in the 21st Century is to recognize that the prayer book is not only meant for the simple believer, but also for the intellectual, the questioning individual, and even the skeptic. All have spiritual journeys worthy of addressing, and all deserve the opportunity to connect to the words of the *siddur*, and to the deeper concepts of Jewish tradition, in a way that provides intellectual nourishment, that truly speaks to them. The road to confront our own inner being is an art, and to be guided by a book like this is a great privilege.

7 Cassuto Street, Jerusalem, 9643307, Israel
T: +972.2.642.7272 * F: +972.72.240.0108 * E: office@cardozoacademy.org
www.cardozoacademy.org

9 Iyar 5773 / April 19, 2013

Dear Rabbi Bar-Cohn,

I have had the pleasure of examining the manuscript of your important work, "Ohr HaShachar."

As the word "Ohr" implies, your book indeed sheds fresh illumination on texts that are recited on a daily basis, and for that precise reason, run the risk of being said by rote, devoid of real engagement. As someone who has spent the last twenty-five years as a congregational rabbi and Torah educator, I appreciate to what a profound extent we are sorely in need of an "upgrade" of our typical prayer experience.

You have also successfully woven together historical, linguistic, philosophical and science-related observations in a highly readable form.

The amount of careful thought and detail you put into this work is evident, and is reflected in the hundreds of Torah insights one encounters throughout the book.

I unreservedly recommend "Ohr HaShachar" both for lay people and for rabbis and educators, for experienced "daveners" and for the newcomer to the siddur – any and all who would like to explore a fresh path for reinvigorating this so central element of our spiritual lives.

May you only go from strength to strength,

Joel Zeff

י"ב באייר, תשע"ג
April 22, 2013

Dear Rabbi Bar-Cohn,

Thank you for the opportunity to review your *sefer* **Ohr HaShachar**. In my opinion you have successfully presented important concepts in the *Mesorah* and *Kabalah* in a way that speaks to the thinking individual.

The *sefer* is a pleasure to read because your commentary is rooted in today's language which can be easily understood. It is of benefit whether one is new to Judaism or a long-time learner.

The result is that you deliver a unique set of tools to help start our day. This *sefer* is a manual for helping one heighten his or her awareness of the Creator, beginning from the moment one wakes and speaks the words *"Modeh Ani"* to the final morning blessing *"HaMa'avir Sheina."* One cannot help but feel invigorated after beginning the day with such a deep understanding. It has a cumulative effect.

This *sefer* is a tremendous aid for *tefilah*. It is a reflection of your commitment to Torah and your overwhelming desire to educate others. May you merit to see your *sefer*, **Ohr HaShachar**, warmly received and well circulated amongst *Klal Yisrael*.

With Torah blessings and warmest regards,

Rabbi Daniel Channen
Director, Issur V'Heter
Yeshiva Pirchei Shosanim

Contents

Preface

The Mixed Blessings of Targum

When looking at translations of traditional Jewish liturgy, I find it difficult to escape the feeling that something significant is missing—and perhaps even amiss. The words *"Blessed are You Lord/Hashem"* have a ring to them that is distinctly different, in a palpable, fundamental way, from the original Hebrew phrase *Baruch atah Hashem*. Even using the word "prayer" does not seem adequate to fully capture the meaning of the Hebrew term *tefila*.

This is the double-edged sword of *targum*, translation. On the one hand, translation enables many people to engage with Torah and *tefila* who would otherwise be unable to do so. However, translation also loses many key dimensions of the original Hebrew, including linguistic nuances, grammar, idiomatic expressions, the sound of the words as they roll off the tongue, their appearance on the page, and so on. Hebrew has its own "personality," which very much contributes to the content itself. We simply miss out on that in translation.

When the Torah was first translated into Greek, it was considered to be a terrible tragedy, a cause for national mourning. Part of the reason is that the Torah would now be filtered through Greek—not just the language, but the whole mindset and philosophy of Greek civilization. Certainly it is true that any societal influence is bound to impact the way we look at Torah. However, it is one thing to speak about and wrestle with Torah in light of those influences, and it is another to write it down as such with a sense of finality, and to deem the translation to be in any way "equivalent" to the original Hebrew text.

Yet at the same time, we *need* translation. This is true not only for those who do not know Hebrew, but even for fluent Hebrew speakers.

That is because *targum* is much more than just "translation." It is part of the process of gaining a greater *understanding* of the text, of the words and concepts that make up our tradition. Toward the end of the Torah, Moshe tells the people to write a copy of the Torah onto stone, "very clearly" (*ba'er heiteiv*). Rashi takes this phrasing to mean that the Torah should be written in seventy languages. In other words, translation is a vehicle for clarity. If we stay exclusively within the Hebrew but do not truly understand what we're saying, then essentially we are preserving the "scaffold" of the text, keeping it intact, but without developing an intimate connection to the material. The mark of such intimacy is the ability to explain and translate the texts and their underlying concepts.

Once we do this, we return to the original Hebrew, only now in a manner that is vastly enriched. That same Hebrew is now invested with new meaning and greater coherence. However, since we never arrive at the "perfect" translation, the process repeats itself, making *targum* an ongoing effort to refine our understanding and gain greater intimacy with Torah. It is a process that also extends, quite naturally, to *tefila*.

About the Book

Many of the translations typically given in the *siddur*—e.g., "blessed" and "holy"—have always left me with a distinct feeling of unease. That in turn has given rise to some real challenges: If *baruch* means something more than "blessed," what is it exactly? If *asher kideshanu* conveys something substantially different from "Who has made us holy," what translation would I suggest instead? This book is the result of my effort to address questions such as these. It is a work of "*iyun tefila*," a journey into the words of Jewish prayer in search of greater understanding.

My goals in this journey were to try to ascertain the *meaning* of the words, and at the same time to arrive at *meaningfulness*—which as I quickly discovered are two very different endeavors. The former entails objective research. The latter requires that one search *within* and listen to what resonates. But both of these aims are equally important in the context of the *siddur*. If we lack a proper understanding of the words we say, we are not genuinely engaging with the *tefila*. And if we understand the meaning of the words but have difficulty seeing the personal relevance, the *tefila* is not engaging with *us*. Either way, it constitutes a disconnect between the text and the reader.

The translations I adopt in the book, many of which may strike the reader as fairly novel, reflect my attempt to bridge that gap. I strive here for both objective *and* subjective meaning, to present translations that are accurate, and that are relevant to the thinking reader—perhaps even the reader whose approach leans decidedly toward the "rational."

A Rational and Holistic Approach to Torah

My methodology in this book is to take traditional Torah concepts, as they come up in the *brachot*, and explain them in a way that a rational, modern thinker would be able to appreciate. There are several reasons for this approach: For one, I believe that when we bring out dimensions of Torah that can be comprehended on rational grounds, without requiring undue leaps of faith, this makes for a stronger, more robust tradition. Secondly, there are a great many sincere individuals who are simply not moved by appeals to emotion or religious sentiment alone. They need a more rationally-oriented approach to Torah, and to the words of *tefila* as well. Furthermore, when we speak about Torah concepts in lofty, abstract, metaphysical terms, this can sometimes constitute a "pious cop-out" for not working to achieve a more in-depth understanding. By contrast, when we approach the same topics in rational, down-to-earth terms, we are forced to be "concrete," to try to pin down what these concepts truly convey. That is, after all, the very purpose of *targum*.

At the same time, this book is very much directed to the traditional Torah audience, who will find in it *chidushim* (new approaches) relating to a host of concepts: *kedusha* and *bracha*, *neshama* and *nefesh*, *tuma* and *tahara*, *cheit* and *kapara*, *shalom* and *tzedek*, *Etz HaChaim* and *Etz HaDa'at*, *Hashem* and *Elokim*, and so on. I also postulate a holistic approach to Torah built on what I call the "Life principle," as well as a "three-phase" model for describing the developmental process as understood in Torah (both of which I will explain in due course). I delve into the function of the *mitzvot*, the idea of *techiyat hametim*, and the age-old question of *tzadik v'ra lo* (the suffering of the righteous). My goals are to contribute to the world of Torah thought, and to give those interested in the larger concepts and "big picture" of Torah ample material on which to reflect.

The reader will also notice that I use the terminology of Kabbalah—e.g., the *sephirot*, the *tzimtzum*, *ohr* and *kli*, etc. To be clear: I am not a mystical thinker. I would instead refer to this as "Rational Kabbalah," an approach that borrows the language and systematics of Kabbalah to communicate aspects of human experience and creativity. As I explain in the pages ahead, it is a system focused on the interplay of two basic elements: "energy" and "consciousness." The approach again is holistic, offering a model for understanding the system as a whole.

Book Scope and Caveats

The book covers just a small section of *tefila*: the first set of *brachot* said in the morning, from *Modeh Ani* through *Birchot HaShachar*. The *nusach* (version) followed is *Ashkenaz*, only because that is the one with which I am personally most familiar. When arriving at translations, I endeavor to stay true to the Hebrew words and root meanings, and where possible to support my conclusions with *psukim* from Tanach, *divrei Chazal* (statements of the Talmudic sages) and classical Torah and *tefila* commentaries. References to these can be found in the footnotes. I encourage the reader to peruse these notes, since aside from the citations, they contain much additional material and elaboration to help elucidate the concepts presented in the main body of the book. Bear in mind, however, that this book is not a collection of commentaries. What I am offering here is my perspective on the morning *brachot*. When you read this book, you are getting my thoughts filtered through the *tefila* and other source material. I suppose this is true of most writing, i.e., that is as much a view into the author's mind as it is about the material itself, but I want the reader to know that I am very much cognizant of that fact.

As I said above, the process of *targum* is one of perpetual fine-tuning. In fact, this book has gone through many revisions and rewrites over the past several years, reflecting my continuing work and changes in perspective—to the point where I was reluctant to put it out at all! But I put my faith in the reader that you will take these caveats to heart, read the book for what it is, and even contribute to refining the concepts and translations presented here. After all, this book is part of a much larger conversation, one that has been ongoing for millennia—and we are all invited to join in.

With that, I wish the reader much enjoyment. If anyone is enriched or finds new personal relevance in *tefila* from the ideas presented here, I will consider it a great success!

Modeh Ani
מוֹדֶה אֲנִי

מוֹדֶה אֲנִי לְפָנֶיךָ מֶלֶךְ חַי וְקַיָּם שֶׁהֶחֱזַרְתָּ בִּי נִשְׁמָתִי בְּחֶמְלָה רַבָּה אֱמוּנָתֶךָ.

Modeh Ani is the first statement made upon awakening.[1] More than an expression of gratitude, it reflects the desire that our newly restored consciousness be enlightened, vitalized, as we embrace yet another day of life.

מוֹדֶה אֲנִי
I gratefully yield

Modeh – The Act of Yielding

Modeh ani is often translated "I am grateful." The word *modeh* (מודה) however stems from the root *yada* (ידה), which not only means "thank" but also "admit," "concede."[2] So for example, if two people are engaged in a debate, and one person says, "*Ani modeh*," this means, "I admit you are correct. I yield to your position."[3] *Modeh ani* thus implies *yielding*, opening oneself up to the *hashpa'a* (influence) of another. It is expressing the willingness to receive, thereby enabling the other to give/transmit.

Fig. 1   Modeh – yielding to another

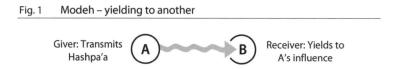

Giver: Transmits   (A) → (B)   Receiver: Yields to
Hashpa'a   A's influence

---

[1] Although the *Modeh Ani* prayer was added only after the time of the *Shulchan Aruch* (its first known appearance is in *Seder Hayom*, c. 1599), it is based on parts of the *bracha* of *Elokai Neshama* (see p. 117), which is sourced in the Talmud.

[2] As in מוֹדֶה וְעֹזֵב (*Mishlei* 28:13). *Modeh* is related to *vidui* (ידוי), admission or confession.

[3] See the entry for ידה in the *Dictionary of the Talmud*, M. Jastrow. The Talmud contains dozens of instances of *modeh* that imply conceding/yielding to another in a matter of law.

Netzach, Hod and Active Receptivity

Modeh is a term of *hoda'ah* (הודאה), yielding, conceding and acknowledg-ing. It is thought by some to be related to the concept of *hod* (הוד),[4] which in Kabbalah is understood as the quality of deference, giving way to an-other.[5] In the array of the Ten *Sephirot*,[6] the attribute of *hod* is placed across from *netzach* (נצח), which conveys the opposite quality—assertion and dominance. The word *menatze'ach* (מנצח) means a leader or director, in the sense of directing or asserting one's will. *Netzach* also implies "ever-lasting," continuing without end, and in that sense can mean asserting oneself continually, even unrelentingly. The attributes of *netzach* and *hod* constitute the two sides of a giver-receiver relationship. One side as-serts/gives/transmits, while the other yields/defers/receives.

This relationship can also be expressed physically in terms of exer-tion of force. If two sides press against one another with equal force, no movement takes place. There is no transfer, no giving or receiving. Only when one side exhibits *hod*, yields, lets down its guard, can anything be imparted from one party to the other.

Fig. 2   Netzach and Hod – giving and receiving

No transfer   Transfer

Both sides exert, neither yields | Netzach / Exerting   Hod / Yielding

---

[4] As in, הוד הוא מלשון להודות, "*Hod* is from the term *lehodot*" (Shelah, *Shevuot, Perek Torah Ohr*); also הוד הוא לשון שבח והודאה (R. Yehuda Leib Frenkel, *Likutei Maharil, Parshat Tazria*).

[5] This is as opposed to the word *hod* as used in Tanach, which connotes majesty and splendor. R. Aryeh Kaplan attempts to reconcile the Kabbalah and Tanach definitions, rendering *hod* to mean "submission and awe in the face of something that exhibits splen-dor and majesty." (See *Inner Space*, Ch. 4, Note 34.)

[6] There are ten *sephirot*, broken into three groups of three, plus one. The first group is *keter-chochma-bina* (or *chochma-bina-da'at*, depending on the context), followed by *chesed-gevura-tiferet*, then *netzach-hod-yesod*, and finally *malchut*. The *sephirot* are traditionally un-derstood to be channels or conduits for conducting the flow of energy/light into Creation, moving from the more abstract/ethereal to the more concrete/physical. The approach taken in this book regarding the *sephirot* is a non-mystical one, relating them to specific aspects of human experience and interaction.

In human relationship terms, *hod* is the act of granting another person the space to express his or her will. Of course *hod* is an expression of will in and of itself, since it requires the "willingness" to receive what the other has to offer. To be *modeh* means to defer, and to "admit" in the sense of creating a space for the other to enter.[7]

Modeh Ani thus connotes more than a passive "thank you" said upon receiving a gift. It conveys *active receptivity*, our desire to yield so as to receive more fully, more consciously. It is a decision to make ourselves participants in the gift-giving process and, in so doing, to "acquire" the gift. *Modeh ani* implies taking ownership of the lives we've been given and assuming accountability. With the words *modeh ani*, we embrace—with gratitude and resolve—the awesome responsibility that comes with being granted a new day of life.

לְפָנֶיךָ
to Your illuminating presence

Toward Vitality and Enlightenment

The word *lefanecha* (לפניך), "before you," stems from the word *panim* (פנים), meaning face or presence.[8] In this case, it is a reference to the presence of *Hashem*,[9] also known as the "*Shechina*," literally the "localization" of *Hashem*.[10] This *Shechina* or presence is characterized as that which illuminates, emits *ohr* (light), as it says:

---

[7] In the same way that the English word "admit" means to acknowledge/confess as well as to allow something or someone in, so too does *modeh* carry the same dual meaning.

[8] See the entry for לפני in the *Brown-Driver-Briggs Hebrew and English Lexicon*, which defines the word to mean "at the face of" or "in the presence of." Indeed, we find places in Tanach where לפניו is expressed by the phrase עַל פָּנָיו (see e.g., Radak on *Bereshit* 32:22).

[9] I use the word "*Hashem*" (lit., "the Name") throughout this book, rather than "God." One reason is that I feel the word God evokes a philosophical/theological discourse that is not the focus here. Additionally, the name *Hashem* (the four-letter name ה-ו-ה-י) is understood in the tradition to convey the concept of *rachamim* (compassion), and by extension *chaim* (life). The conceptual connotation of *Hashem* is in contrast to the name *Elokim*, which conveys *din* (judgment). The *Hashem-Elokim* distinction will be clarified further on.

[10] See *Torah and Existence*, R. Chaim Zimmerman, p. 111, which states: "Lifanav [*sic*], before Him, means the revelation of Shechina and kedusha."

יָאֵר ה' פָּנָיו אֵלֶיךָ
"May Hashem illuminate His presence upon you"[11]

The plain meaning of *ohr* is visible light, but as the above *pasuk* implies, *ohr* also connotes radiance, energy and vitality.[12] It suggests "enlightenment"—the *ohr hasechel*, illumination of the mind. *Lefanecha* is thus a reference to *ohr* and the vitalization of consciousness. But consciousness illuminated and vitalized by *what* exactly? The tradition understands the above *pasuk* to be referring to the light of Torah.[13] Elsewhere, Torah is explicitly likened to light/*ohr*:

כִּי נֵר מִצְוָה וְתוֹרָה אוֹר
"For a candle is a commandment and Torah is light"[14]

The idea of the *panim*/face emitting light is also exemplified by Moshe. The Torah tells us that when Moshe came down from Mount Sinai after receiving the second set of Tablets, his face shined.[15] Moshe was so "enlightened," so utterly imbued with the *ohr haTorah*, that he became an independent source of light and wisdom himself.[16] Just as the "face of *Hashem*" is said to radiate Torah, so too is Moshe's—so much so that the Torah is referred to as *Torat Hashem* as well as *Torat Moshe*.[17] Yet Moshe remained uniquely Moshe, an independent mind.

Perhaps then we can understand the phrase *modeh ani lefanecha* in a similar fashion: We yield to the light of knowledge and wisdom, to the *ohr haTorah*, and we wish to be so illuminated that we become beacons of enlightenment ourselves. It is to have one's unique and independent mind so invigorated, so lit up, that an aura of vitality radiates from one's face.

---

[11] *Bamidbar* 6:25

[12] As in, ואין 'יאר' אלא חיים (Rabbeinu Bachye on *Bamidbar* 6:25).

[13] As in, יאר זה מאור תורה (*Bamidbar Rabbah* 11:6). See also Abarbanel and Rabbeinu Bachye on *Bamidbar* 6:25.

[14] *Mishlei* 6:23

[15] See *Shemot* 34:29. This interpretation follows Rashi and others, whereby קרן עור is understood to mean a beam or ray (radiant light) emanating from the skin.

[16] The radiance issuing from Moshe is referred to in the Midrash as *"karna shel Torah"* (see *Midrash Rabbah* on *Eicha*, *Parsha* 2). Also see Rashi on *Bamidbar* 27:20: "The face of Moshe was like the sun; the face of Yehoshua was like the moon." Meaning, Moshe's face was a source of light, whereas Yehoshua's was a reflection of that light.

[17] Even further, the name Moshe (משה) is viewed as an anagram of "*Hashem*" (השם). (See R. Avraham Saba, *Tzror Hamor, Parshat Vezot HaBracha*: משה בהפוך אותיות הוא השם.)

מֶלֶךְ

Reigning Influence

When the Will for Life Reigns

In *Modeh Ani*, we refer to *Hashem* as *"melech,"* king.[18] A king is one whose will or influence (*hashpa'a*) reigns over the kingdom. When we invoke the concept of *Hashem* as king, it is to speak about the influence of the *retzon Hashem*, *Hashem*'s will. What is the primary manifestation of this will? It is the *retzon hachaim*, the will for Life,[19] as the *pasuk* says:

חַיִּים בִּרְצוֹנוֹ

"life is His will"[20]

Similarly, we say between Rosh Hashana and Yom Kippur:

זָכְרֵנוּ לְחַיִּים, מֶלֶךְ חָפֵץ בַּחַיִּים

"Remember us for life, King who desires life"[21]

To proclaim *Hashem* as *melech* is to accept the will for Life as the reigning influence in our consciousness. It is to make the desire for Life our guiding light—coloring our pursuits and interactions, shaping our understanding of Torah, and permeating our very being. As it says explicitly:

כִּי מֹצְאִי מָצָא חַיִּים

"For whoever finds Me has found life"[22]

---

[18] The word *melech* also functions in place of the *shem Hashem*. Because *Modeh Ani* does not contain the *shem Hashem*, it is generally accepted that one may say it immediately upon waking up, before washing one's hands. (See *Magen Avraham* 4:28.)

[19] You will notice that the word "Life" is capitalized in many instances throughout this book. This is done to intimate a definition of life that encompasses more than just the state of being alive, but also includes vitality, joy, energy, inspiration—all those things that denote "aliveness." It is also a reference to what we will call the "Life principle," the suggestion that the desire for life and aliveness be understood as the central organizing principle of the Torah system.

[20] *Tehilim* 30:6. This phrase is often translated, "His favor is for a lifetime" (paralleling the previous phrase in the *pasuk*, "His anger is for a moment"), or alternatively, "With His favor, there is life" (see e.g., Rashi and *Metzudat David*). However the word *ratzon* also connotes "will" or "desire," rendering the phrase to mean, "With His will, there is life," i.e., *Hashem*'s will is for life.

[21] From the *Bracha* of *Avot*, *Amida* for *Aseret Yemei Teshuva*. In the four brief additions to the *Amida* said during this time, the word *chaim* is mentioned no fewer than eight times.

[22] *Mishlei* 8:35

The King Transmits and the People Receive

Functionally speaking, a *melech* can be likened to a "transmitter," one whose influence transmits/flows to the people.[23] As such, we can understand the king-subject relationship as one of transmitter-receiver. The king broadcasts the signal. If the people yield to and receive that signal, if they are *modeh*, then the influence of the king is imparted. (Thus the *melech* exhibits *netzach* and the people *hod*.) If not, there is the concept of *ein melech belo am*—"there is no king without a people," i.e., a king is not a king unless someone accepts the kingship/*malchut*.[24]

Fig. 3   Melech as transmitter

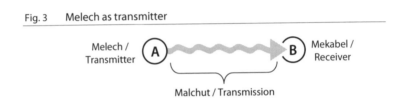

Although they come from two different linguistic roots, the word *melech* (מלך) is suggestively similar to the word *molich* (מוליך), meaning "lead" (lit., cause to go, move).[25] Indeed, the function of a *melech* is to be *molich*—to lead, to initiate motion, and to transmit and impart influence within the kingdom. So the word *melech* very much follows the idea of *modeh ani lefanecha*—yielding to allow an influence to reign within us. What is that influence? It is first and foremost the will for Life.

חַי וְקַיָּם

dynamic and firmly standing

Chai – Life and Motion

The word *chai* means "alive," although not merely in the sense of organic life. To be *chai* is to be dynamic, animated, possessing energy and

---

[23] As in, והמלך עיקרו להיות משפיע לעם והם מקבלים ממנו (R. Tzadok HaKohen, *Takanat HaShavin*).

[24] The concept of אין מלך בלא עם is referenced in many places, such as the Malbim's commentary (*Tehilim* 10), the *Meshech Chochma* (*Bamidbar* 20), the *Kedushat Levi* (*Parshat Beshalach*).

[25] As in, כי שם מלך הוא המוליך והמנהיג (*Haktav v'Hakabbalah*, *Bereshit* 14:22).

motion. Spring water, for instance, is referred to as *"mayim chaim."* It is alive in that the water is moving, flowing, as it says:

מַעְיַן גַּנִּים בְּאֵר מַיִם חַיִּים וְנֹזְלִים מִן לְבָנוֹן.

"A garden spring, a well of living waters that flow from Lebanon."[26]

Likewise, living creatures are *chai*, alive, when they display movement— mobility, respiration, blood flow, cellular and brainwave activity. When such movement slows down or ceases, life is diminished, slips away.

What does it mean to say that *Hashem*, as *melech*, is *"chai"*? On a very straightforward level, it means that so long as the influence/transmission of a *melech* is still active—i.e., the kingdom is affected by it, moved by it—the *melech* is effectively *"chai."* Regarding *Hashem*, the influence/*malchut* is will for Life itself. The "kingdom" is the entire universe. The transmission of life and movement is incessant and ever-present—as active or *"chai"* as anything could possibly be.

So not only is the *Hashem's* transmission *chai*, alive and ongoing, but the actual *content* of that transmission is *"chaim"*—it is life/energy itself. *Hashem* is called the *chei olamim*,[27] the "life of the worlds." All the energy and animating motion in the universe—from the spiraling of galaxies, to the daily functioning of every living creature, to the constant, frenzied molecular activity of ostensibly "inanimate" matter—is a manifestation of the will for Life, of the *malchut Hashem*.[28] It is this same energy, the same "will," which stirs us to life every waking morning.

Kayam – Enduring Transmission

The term *chai* goes together with *kayam*. *Kayam* means "standing," in the sense of being firmly established or enduring. Something that is *kayam* (e.g., a building, a theory or a leader) stands, endures, remains functioning. A *melech* who is *kayam* is one who currently reigns, whose influence is active, whose transmission is up and online. *Hashem* is the *melech chai vekayam*, meaning that the will for Life is firmly implanted throughout

---

[26] *Shir HaShirim* 4:15. See also Ibn Ezra on *Bereshit* 26:19, who defines *mayim chaim* as "continuously flowing."

[27] For instance, in the *Borei Nefashot bracha*, ending ברוך חי העולמים.

[28] As in, חי העולמים, מקור החיות של כל העולמות (R. Tzadok HaKohen, *Divrei Chalomot* 23).

the world, manifesting its influence continuously,[29] in the ceaseless movement of every particle, and in the energy that flows within every living being.

The phrase *chai vekayam* might also be understood to mirror the experience of a person waking up—being alive (*chai*) and standing up (*kayam*) to greet the new day. In addition, the word *kayam* can be thought of in relation to the concept of leverage. In order to stand up, one needs solid ground on which to push one's legs. Likewise, in order for kingship to be *kayam*, a *melech* must first have the throne, the formal mandate that provides the "leverage," so to speak, for the king to exert an influence. In Kabbalah, this is conceptualized as needing a *yesod* (base or foundation) as a prerequisite for *malchut* (reign, kingship).[30]

Ohr and Kli – Energy and Structure

Malchut and *yesod* are one set of terms corresponding to energy and structure, or to "*ohr*" and "*kli*" as they are referred to in the Kabbalah. *Ohr*, as we have discussed, is light/energy. A *kli* is the vessel/container used to hold, channel and conduct that energy. While it may sound esoteric, these can be understood as two basic components of everyday systems. One is the dynamic component, and the other is the static component. One is the content, and the other is the infrastructure designed to carry that content. Take a few down-to-earth examples: There is electricity, and there is the wiring used to conduct that electricity. There is water, and there is plumbing that directs the water where we want it to go. There is blood, and there are the blood vessels which carry it throughout the body. There are human drives and vitality, and there are societal rules and boundaries designed to hone/channel that vitality. These are all *ohr*-to-*kli* relations. The relationship is one of interdependence. One can have all the structure in the world, but without energy the system is dead, lifeless. And one can have boundless energy, but unless there is a structure to conduct it, the system is also effectively dead. *Both* energy and

---

[29] In the sense of, ודברך אמת וקיים לעד (*Rosh Hashana Amida*), and הדיבור של ה' יתברך חי וקיים לעד (R. Tzadok HaKohen, *Pri Tzadik, Parshat Tetzaveh*). The *davar* (word) of the *melech* is an expression of the *melech*'s *ratzon*/will.

[30] As in the phrase יסוד כסא ה' (*Orot Yisrael* 6:7, R. Avraham Yitzchak Kook).

structure, *ohr* and *kli,* are needed to produce a living system and for that system to continue to thrive.[31]

The phrase *chai vekayam* can be seen as a reference to both needed elements, energy and structure—*chai* referring to the energy and motion component,[32] and *kayam* referring to the structural component, the leverage or sound foundation from which energy may be transmitted.[33] *Yesod* and *malchut* thus have a *kli-ohr* relationship. *Yesod* is a *kli* for *malchut,* the structure and conduit required in order for influence to be imparted.[34]

Receiver Becomes Transmitter

We spoke earlier of Moshe receiving the *ohr haTorah,* to the point where he himself radiated, transmitted. One can think of this in terms of a *kli* (vessel) that receives and fills up to the point where it spills over to others. This is the trait of a *melech Yisrael* (King of Israel), who must first yield to and receive the *ohr haTorah* as a prerequisite for transmitting it to the people. Before the influence of the *melech* is worthy of reigning, the *melech* must first learn how to open up to the influence of another. *Malchut* thus ultimately stems from *hod/hoda'ah,* yielding and positioning oneself to receive.

The Torah identifies Yehuda as the tribe best suited to the function of kingship.[35] The name Yehuda (יהודה) is linked with *hoda'ah* (הודאה), the property of thanking/yielding.[36] Of all the tribes, Yehuda has a particular

---

[31] See p. 76, regarding *Hashem* and *Elokim* and the need for both energy and structure.

[32] As in the term אור החיים.

[33] As in the phrase יסוד קיים (e.g., אינו מוסד על יסוד קיים, *Meshech Chochma, Parshat Netzavim*).

[34] Note that the Kabbalah tradition often says the opposite, that *malchut* is a *kli* for *yesod.* One reason is that *malchut* is sometimes thought of as being a governing "structure," the context or *kli* that is set up, and within which a *yesod* (physical/societal foundation) is built. However, we have been speaking about *malchut* not as the formal structure of kingship, but as the actual *content* imparted by the king. Making *malchut* the content-component of the system leaves *yesod* as the structure-component, which is naturally more suited to the meaning of the word *yesod* itself. *Yesod* means "foundation," a base upon which something else rests or grows out from. It holds, contains, supports and conducts. It imparts form and direction. Thus, *yesod* is a structure, a *kli.* See also R. Tzadok HaKohen, who states: וידוע דשלום דרגא דיסוד שהוא כלי (*Dover Tzedek*).

[35] As it says, לֹא יָסוּר שֵׁבֶט מִיהוּדָה, "The scepter will not depart from Yehuda" (*Bereshit* 49:10).

[36] As it says, הַפַּעַם אוֹדֶה אֶת ה' עַל כֵּן קָרְאָה שְׁמוֹ יְהוּדָה, "'This time I will thank/yield to *Hashem*'; therefore she called his name Yehuda" (*Bereshit* 29:35).

capacity for yielding and admitting, for active receptivity. This is perhaps best illustrated in Yehuda's statement regarding Tamar:

צָדְקָה מִמֶּנִּי

"She is more righteous/correct than I am"[37]

This is an act of yielding, conceding. Yehuda effectively says *"modeh ani"* to Tamar.[38] It is his capacity to yield which gives Yehuda the ability to lead. Receptivity precipitates transmission—*hod* gives way to *malchut*. Thus the one who exercises *hod* is the same one who in time will transmit, and others will defer to them. The other tribes eventually yield to Yehuda, as the *pasuk* says:

יְהוּדָה אַתָּה יוֹדוּךָ אַחֶיךָ

"Yehuda, your brothers will yield to you"[39]

Giving and Receiving Localized in Ahava and Simcha

Transition from the role of receiver to that of giver can also be understood in the realm of emotions and everyday human relationships. Take as an example *simcha* (joy) and *ahava* (love). Joy is essentially a positive, high-energy state. When a person is filled with joy, the tendency is for that energy to spill over to others in the form of *ahava*, love. *Simcha* is the fullness of energy, and *ahava* is a means of giving, radiating that energy outward.[40]

Ideally, a relationship produces a continuous circuit of *simcha* and *ahava*. One person's *ahava* is radiated to the other, who experiences it as *simcha*. That *simcha* is then radiated back to the other as *ahava*, and so on. As it says in the *Sheva Brachot* (seven blessings) for a newlywed couple:

שַׂמֵּחַ תְּשַׂמַּח רֵעִים הָאֲהוּבִים

"Be joyous, beloved counterparts"

That is, when the couple rejoices, they become *re'im ahuvim*, mutually radiated by one another's love, transmitting love back and forth.

---

[37] *Bereshit* 38:26

[38] As it says in the Midrash, יהודה הודה במעשה תמר (*Sechel Tov Buber* on *Bereshit* 29:35).

[39] *Bereshit* 49:8

[40] Loving and giving are sometimes described as related concepts in Torah, since the roots *ahav* (אהב, love) and *yahav* (יהב, give) bear a suggestive similarity.

Netzach and Hod – Volume Control

We have discussed *hod* as a prerequisite for *malchut*, a "yielding to receive" which then leads to becoming a giver, a transmitter. However, *hod* is also necessary once one becomes a giver. In order to transmit effectively, the giver must defer/yield, at least to some extent, to the needs of the receiver. If one were to unload the full extent of their transmission, it could very well overwhelm or damage the receiver. Alternatively, the transmission could simply go ignored, being perceived as inaccessible.

Transmission without *hod* would be pure *netzach,* assertive and overpowering. Therefore, *hod* is necessary in order to turn down the flow, such that the transmission will enliven the receiver, not overwhelm or shatter them. The dynamic of *netzach* and *hod* can thus be conceptualized as a sort of "volume control," whereby the strength of the signal is adjusted to facilitate transmission.

Fig. 4   Hod used in transmission

A Foundation of Trust

The self-assuredness of *netzach* is an attractive quality, a sign of leadership. But that alone does not engender *trust*. That trust comes when the leader's self-confident pursuit of their will is tempered by, and channeled through, an awareness of other people's needs. That is *hod*. So a *melech* must also exercise *hod*—they must be aware of, empathize with, and yield to the people's specific needs and limitations.[41] It is the fine-tuning of *netzach* and *hod* which generates *yesod*. Knowing how to carefully balance asserting one's will on the one hand, and empathizing with the receiver on the other, is what creates the stable foundation, the basis, for meaningful communication/transmission, one person to the other. A balanced *yesod* serves as the basis and mandate for *malchut*. That is to say,

---

[41] This explains why the property of *hod* is sometimes referred to as "empathy." (See e.g., *Inner Space* by R. Aryeh Kaplan, p. 42.) The giver needs to know the receiver.

confidence coupled with attentiveness forms the trust that is the basis for leadership.

Moshe and Aharon – Netzach and Hod

The attributes of *netzach* and *hod* are embodied in the relationship between Moshe and Aharon. Moshe is revered by the people for his intense transmission of Torah—unadulterated and unfiltered. His brother Aharon is beloved because he is able to modulate the intensity of that transmission and make Torah accessible to the people. As such, the trait of *netzach* is attributed to Moshe and the trait of *hod* to Aharon.[42] Similarly, Moshe is characterized by *emet* (unfiltered, exacting truth), while Aharon is known for *shalom* (peace, equilibrium),[43] providing the interface between Moshe and the people.[44] Functioning together, they create an effective, life-imbuing transmission system for Torah.

So too in *Modeh Ani*, when we yield to the *ohr haTorah*, to the light of knowledge and understanding, it is not meant to overwhelm or dominate over us. Rather, it should be vitalizing, harmonizing, of the highest personal meaning and relevance. Torah embodies the will for Life, and its *malchut*/influence should be a source of Life for us.

שֶׁהֶחֱזַרְתָּ בִּי נִשְׁמָתִי בְּחֶמְלָה
*that You returned my consciousness within me,
out of the desire to spare/keep alive*

Neshama – the Return of Consciousness

The *neshama* is said to return to us upon awakening. "*Neshama*" (נשמה) is typically translated as "soul," though in Tanach the word is used to mean *neshima* (נשימה), "breath,"[45] or sometimes "breathing being."[46]

---

[42] Each of the seven so-called "lower *sephirot*" is associated with a figure in Tanach who is said to embody that characteristic. (See p. 64, Fig. 11.)

[43] As the Talmud states: משה היה אומר ׳יקוב הדין את ההר׳ אבל אהרן אוהב שלום ורודף שלום, "Moshe used to say, 'Let the *din*/law pierce the mountain,' whereas Aharon loves *shalom* and pursues *shalom*" (*Sanhedrin* 6b).

[44] See *Shemot* 4:16 and 7:1, where Aharon is designated as an interpreter/go-between for Moshe.

[45] As in, הָאָדָם אֲשֶׁר נְשָׁמָה בְּאַפּוֹ (*Yeshayahu* 2:22).

[46] As in, כֹּל הַנְּשָׁמָה תְּהַלֵּל יָ-הּ (*Tehilim* 150:6).

Clearly though, the word *neshama* in *Modeh Ani* cannot be referring to breath, since our breath is not taken from us when we sleep (i.e., we do not stop breathing during sleep), nor is it returned to us when we awaken. Rather, *neshama* can be better understood in this context as relating to "consciousness." It is our consciousness that is restored upon awakening.[47]

So when we go to sleep and become unconscious, deprived temporarily of our faculties of awareness and reasoning, our *neshama* "leaves" us in the sense of being inaccessible, offline. When we awaken, our conscious awareness is restored—the *neshama* is "returned," so to speak, comes back online.

Chemla and the Will for Life

The return of the *neshama* is done with "*chemla*." *Chemla* (חמלה) is usually translated as pity or mercy. It comes from the word *chamal* (חמל), meaning to spare, keep alive, maintain existence, not destroy or use up. *Chemla* therefore means acting purely out of one's desire that something not be destroyed, gone from the world, wasted, damaged or otherwise condemned to suffer. It is acting for *life*, irrespective of deservingness. The added word *chemla* underscores the fact that the restoration of life and consciousness is in no way "owed" to us. We are not entitled to an additional day of life. Our waking up is simply a gift, a pure expression of the will for Life.

When we say "*modeh ani... shehechezarta bi nishmati bechemla*," in the straightforward sense we are expressing thanks for the gift of renewed consciousness. However, it can also be understood to mean: Now that our consciousness has been restored—a reflection of the overarching desire for life—we can yield to the light of knowledge, embrace the *ohr haTorah*, which itself embodies the will for Life. Thus, in addition to this statement expressing gratitude/*hoda'ah* "for" the *neshama*, it is saying that we express it "because" of the *neshama*.[48] The *neshama* gives us the ability to be *modeh*. Being conscious allows us to take in the light and vitality of the new day.

---

[47] The connection between *neshama* and consciousness will be explored in greater depth in the chapter on *Elokai Neshama*, p. 117.

[48] This is in fact stated explicitly in the statement, כל זמן שהנשמה בקרבי מודה אני לפניך (*Elokai Neshama bracha*, see p. 135).

רַבָּה אֱמוּנָתֶךָ
Your unwavering-reliability is tremendous

Emuna – Reliability, Not Existential Belief

The word *"emuna"* is often understood in the sense of a belief that something *exists*, that it is objectively real, despite our inability to prove it to be so. But in Tanach, *emuna* carries a more pragmatic connotation—namely, having faith in another, deeming them to be dependable, reliable.[49] As such, *emuna* can refer to anything that is faithful and reliable, that holds steady, as the Torah says about Moshe's hands during the battle with Amalek:

וַיְהִי יָדָיו אֱמוּנָה עַד בֹּא הַשָּׁמֶשׁ
"and his hands were [held] steady until the sun went down"[50]

There is a linguistic relationship between the words *emuna* (אמונה) and *emet* (אמת, truth).[51] Both are ways of referring to faithfulness. As with *emuna*, the concept of *emet* in the Torah is a more pragmatic term than it is typically understood. Rather than conveying "absolute truth," *emet* means staying "true to" someone or something, remaining faithful to them. For instance, when the Torah uses the phrase, "do for me *chesed* and *emet*,"[52] it is speaking about *emet* not in terms of ultimate truth, but rather in the sense of being true or faithful in the context of a *brit*, a covenant or contract between two parties.[53] A statement is *emet* when it faithfully, accurately describes something or recounts past events. It is like when we refer to a "true" right angle, we are saying that it faithfully, exactingly turns upward at ninety degrees. Both *emet* and *emuna* connote

---

[49] As in the *pasuk*: וַיַּאֲמִינוּ בַּה' וּבְמֹשֶׁה עַבְדּוֹ (*Shemot* 14:31). Clearly this does not mean that the people believed that Moshe "existed." Rather, they had faith in Moshe, relied on him. One can use the phrase "believed in" as a translation here, but only in the sense of belief as conveying confidence and trust.

[50] *Shemot* 17:12. The Torah says in the previous *pasuk*, "As Moshe lifted his hand, *Yisrael* overpowered, and as he rested his hand, Amalek overpowered."

[51] See the *Brown-Driver-Briggs Lexicon*, where the two entries are cross-referenced. Also see *How the Hebrew Language Grew*, Edward Horowitz, p. 36, which posits that the word אמת was originally אמנת, but that the *nun* eventually dropped out.

[52] See *Bereshit* 47:29; also 24:49 and *Shemot* 34:6.

[53] On the phrase *chesed ve'emet* in *Bereshit* 47:29, Ibn Ezra states that the word *emet* is from *emuna* (being faithful to uphold one's commitment), and that the letter *tav* makes it a feminine form.

being faithful, holding steady, not wavering, and therefore imply continuity and staying power. Hence, *sheker*—understood as the opposite of *emet*—is compared to *hevel*, "vapor,"[54] that which is without substance, which is fleeting, quickly dissolves, has no *"kiyum"* (does not stand) and leaves no lasting trace.[55] If something does not last, it is not "true" in the sense of *emet*.

Moshe – Ne'eman and Emet

A form of the word *emuna* is *"ne'eman"* (נאמן), an adjective describing one who is steady and trustworthy. The Torah says regarding Moshe:

לֹא כֵן עַבְדִּי מֹשֶׁה בְּכָל בֵּיתִי נֶאֱמָן הוּא.

"Not so is My servant Moshe; in all My house he is trustworthy."[56]

The context here is about distinguishing Moshe from the other *nevi'im* (prophets). Whereas others have *nevua* only during limited times and circumstances, i.e., in visions and dreams, Moshe is called *"ne'eman,"* reliable and trustworthy, like a trusted servant who can speak to the master of the house at any time.[57] What is it about Moshe that makes him the most trusted, so able to be relied upon? The Midrash explains: *Moshe vetorato emet*—"Moshe and his Torah are true."[58] The word *"emet"* here is not speaking in a philosophical or factual sense. Rather, it implies that Moshe is able to relay the Torah transmitted to him faithfully and exactly. His teaching is "true to" the original transmission. Therefore he is *ne'eman*, trustworthy. Likewise, when the Torah is called *"Torat emet,"* it means that the Torah is faithful, has staying power,

---

[54] As in, שֶׁקֶר הַחֵן וְהֶבֶל הַיֹּפִי (*Mishlei* 31:30).

[55] The idea that *emet* and *sheker* relate to permanence is echoed in the Midrash. *Yalkut Shimoni* (*Parshat Bereshit* 1:3) states that the letters that make up the word *emet* (א-מ-ת) each have two "legs." They are stable, they stand. This is in contrast to the letters that make up *sheker* (ש-ק-ר), which have only one leg each. They are unstable, destined to fall. The Midrash states further that the letters א-מ-ת span the entire Hebrew alphabet, beginning, middle and end. *Emet* thus has staying power. The letters ש-ק-ר however are only one letter apart from one another. *Sheker* is momentary, fleeting.

[56] *Bamidbar* 12:7

[57] See Ibn Ezra on *Bamidbar* 12:7.

[58] *Bamidbar Rabbah* 18:20

is true-to-life in the sense of having the capacity to remain relevant and life-imbuing over time.[59]

Robust and Faithful Flow

The phrase *"rabba emunatecha"* is taken from a *pasuk* speaking about the renewal that takes place each morning:

חֲדָשִׁים לַבְּקָרִים רַבָּה אֱמוּנָתֶךָ.

"[Hashem's kindness and compassion] are new every morning; abundant is Your faithfulness."[60]

Rabba emunatecha reflects the faithfulness and dependability with which the *neshama*, conscious awareness, is restored each and every day when we awaken. It is *"rabba"* (great, abundant, vast), suggesting the tremendously robust and pervasive flow of life, the transmission of energy and animating movement, that is delivered throughout the world, day after day, without faltering or wavering. To the great gifts of renewed life and consciousness, we gratefully yield, without any sense of entitlement. To the ongoing transmission of *ohr*, the light of knowledge and Torah, we open ourselves up, joyfully, and with a sense of responsibility.

An additional understanding could render *rabba emunatecha* as relating to *Hashem's* faith, as it were, in the human being. Meaning, to grant us yet another day of life is a show of remarkable faith that, despite our track record until now, today may be the day when we truly embrace and internalize the will for Life. Despite our having relied until now on pure *"chemla"* to gain another day of life, perhaps today we will truly earn our place in this world.

Modeh Ani is a statement, not a *bracha* (blessing) per se. In the next two chapters, we will discuss the distinct nature and function of a *bracha*—starting with the concept of *bracha* and its relation to *kedusha*, followed by the specific *bracha* formula *"Baruch atah Hashem…"*

---

[59] As in, תורת אמת שהיא אחרית ונצחית (Shelah, *Tamid, Perek Ner Mitzva*), and תורת אמת נצחית וקיימת לעולמי עולמים (R. Moshe Chaim Ephraim of Sudilkov, *Degel Machaneh Ephraim, Parshat Ki Tisa*).

[60] *Eicha* 3:23; the bracketed phrase *"Hashem's* kindness and compassion" reflects the previous *pasuk*: חַסְדֵי ה' כִּי לֹא תָמְנוּ כִּי לֹא כָלוּ רַחֲמָיו.

Bracha and Kedusha
ברכה וקדושה

Bracha and *kedusha*, commonly translated as "blessing" and "holiness" respectively, are frequently invoked within *tefila* (prayer) and are
among the most central concepts in the Torah system. We will now
explore the meaning of each term and see how the two concepts inter-
relate.

Bracha – Expansion and Proliferation

The word *bracha* (ברכה) comes from the root *barach* (ברך), to "bless" or
"kneel." The first *bracha* mentioned in the Torah comes in the Creation
story, on the day that fish and birds are introduced:

וַיְבָרֶךְ אֹתָם אֱ-לֹהִים לֵאמֹר פְּרוּ וּרְבוּ
וּמִלְאוּ אֶת הַמַּיִם בַּיַּמִּים וְהָעוֹף יִרֶב בָּאָרֶץ.
"Elokim[1] blessed them, saying: Bear fruit and multiply,
and fill the water in the seas, and the birds should multiply on the earth."[2]

A similar *bracha* is issued for human beings, that they should multiply
and fill the earth—implying an expansion in number as well as volume,
spreading out to occupy more space.[3] But it is not that the blessing of
expansion and multiplicity is simply one "category" of *bracha*—rather,

---

[1] The correct pronunciation is "*Elo-him,*" but we will use the transliteration "*Elokim,*" as
commonly adopted for conversational purposes. The exception is where the word is used
to refer to judges or gods, in which case we will transliterate it as "*elohim.*"

[2] *Bereshit* 1:22

[3] The *bracha* of abundant offspring is also given to various individuals in the book of
Bereshit, such as Noach (*Bereshit* 9:1), Avraham (12:2), Sarah (17:16), Yishmael (17:20),
Rivka (24:60), Yitzchak (26:3, 26:24) and Ya'akov (28:3). See also the *pasuk,* וּבֵרַכְךָ וְהִרְבֶּךָ
(*Devarim* 7:13).

multiplicity is implied in the very concept of *bracha* itself.[4] Rashi[5] in fact calls *bracha* a "*lashon ribui*," a term denoting multiplicity:

כל 'ברכה' שבמקרא לשון ריבוי הוא
דבר המרבה ומצוי בו שובע.

"Every 'bracha' in Scripture [Tanach] is a term of multiplicity;
it is something that increases, and fullness is found in it."[6]

In Tanach, we find *bracha* explicitly linked with the idea of "increase":

יְבָרֵךְ אֶת בֵּית יִשְׂרָאֵל...
יֹסֵף ה' עֲלֵיכֶם עֲלֵיכֶם וְעַל בְּנֵיכֶם.

"He will bless the House of Israel...
Hashem will increase upon you, upon you and upon your children."[7]

Bracha and Doubling

A well-known *drash* (homiletic interpretation) relating to the word *bracha* is that the concept of multiplicity—particularly "doubling"—is carried by the numerical values of its root letters (ברך, whereby ב=2, ר=200, כ=20), and by its overall value (222).[8] The word *bracha* is also related to *berech* (ברך, "knee"), the joint that essentially "doubles" the leg, bending it into two distinct segments.[9] Furthermore, the growth and proliferation of living systems is essentially a product of doubling, down to the cellular level itself. In mitosis, one cell divides in two, each of those new cells divide in two, and so on. Thus, the cell division that occurs within our bodies at every moment is a true "*bracha*" in the literal sense of the word.

---

[4] See e.g., R. Tzadok HaKohen who cites the above *pasuk* regarding fish and birds to show that *bracha* implies multiplicity and increase (*Pri Tzadik, Parshat Bereshit*).

[5] R. Shlomo Yitzchaki (1040–1105), the foremost commentator on Tanach and Talmud.

[6] *Rashi* on *Sota* 10a. The idea of *bracha* as ריבוי and תוספת is well-established throughout the tradition—see e.g., Rashba, *Teshuvot* 5:51; Ramban on *Bereshit* 27:28; Rabbeinu Bachye on *Bamidbar* 6:24, *Devarim* 8:10; Maharal, *Derech Chaim* 1:2; and R. Chaim of Volozhin, *Nefesh Hachaim* 2:2.

[7] *Tehilim* 115:12–15. The *pasuk* then continues with the words "ברוכים אתם."

[8] See Maharal, *Tiferet Yisrael, Perek* 34. See also *Netzach Yisrael, Perek* 15, where he uses the same numerical reasoning to support the idea that the *bechor*/firstborn (בְּכֹר, same letters as ברך) receives a double portion.

[9] This is likewise a *drash*. The straightforward connection between *berech* and *bracha* is in the sense of kneeling before another in order to petition them for a *bracha*. See e.g., *II Divrei HaYamim* 6:13 (kneeling), followed by 6:16 (petitioning).

Bracha and Breicha — Pooling and Expanding

The *Parsha* of *Ki Tavo* lists an array of *brachot* that are contingent upon observance of the *mitzvot*.[10] These include *brachot* for abundant offspring as well as overall material abundance—increase of cattle and produce of the field, plentiful rain, etc. In addition however, there are *brachot* that seem not to relate to "abundance" per se, but rather to general success and fortune, such as being "the head and not the tail," being "above and not below," having our enemies fall before us in war, being blessed in our coming and in our going, etc. The question is, how do examples of general success fit the definition of *bracha* as expansion and multiplicity?

We can think about it the following way: What success really implies is the idea of "flow," where our will and activities pour forth, without being disrupted, harmed or otherwise impeded. It is in this sense that *bracha* (בְּרָכָה) relates to *breicha* (בְּרֵכָה, pool), a place where water flows, literally "pools," increases, fills up a space. So too where we succeed, there is flow, and the success pools up—our material possessions increase, our joy wells up, our sphere of influence expands, and our will and desire bear fruit. Success brings expansion, proliferation and growth. It is therefore a *"bracha."*

Bracha and Klala – Growth vs. Atrophy

The idea of "blessing," the wish for another's success, is sometimes brought in the Torah in contradistinction to "curse," the desire for another's downfall. While *bracha* implies growth, expansion and proliferation, *klala* (קללה, curse) connotes just the opposite—that which not only holds back or stifles growth, but reverses the process. Instead of the system expanding and gaining strength, it atrophies, abates, becomes smaller, weaker, less significant. Similarly, whereas a *breicha* refers to the pooling of water, expanding and filling a space, the verb *kalal* (קלל, to "lighten") is employed in the story of the Flood to describe the abating or diminishing of water, as it says:

וַיֵּדַע נֹחַ כִּי קַלּוּ הַמַּיִם מֵעַל הָאָרֶץ

"and Noach knew that the waters had abated from upon the land"[11]

---

[10] See *Devarim* 28:1–14.
[11] *Bereshit* 8:11

Bracha and Klala as States of Health

Regarding *bracha* and *klala* in the Torah, the Midrash states as follows:

> "'See, I place before you today, blessing and curse' (Devarim 11:26). Rabbi
> Elazar said: When the Holy One made this statement at Sinai, at that point
> [the following verse began to apply]: 'From the mouth of the Most High will
> come out neither bad nor good' (Eicha 3:38). Rather, bad comes of its own ac-
> cord upon those who do bad, and good comes upon those who do good."[12]

According to the above *midrash*, good and bad, blessing and curse, come
of their own accord, as consequences of our actions, not as something
imposed from the outside. The Netziv[13] elaborates on this *midrash*:

> "This is the reward and punishment of the doctor. The doctor does not in any
> way willingly punish someone who transgresses his warning. Rather, [the
> patient] is punished by himself. This is not like the punishment of a king, be-
> cause such punishment comes only by the will and action of the punisher."[14]

In other words, it would be erroneous to think of the blessings and curses in the Torah in the sense of rewards and punishments being doled out
by a monarch. Rather, the model is one of health, where *bracha* and *klala*
are realities we create for ourselves based on the choices we make. The
Torah is thus intended to help guide us in making healthy choices, to
steer us toward *bracha* and away from *klala*.[15]

Bracha and Diffusion – the Pressure to Expand

Aside from *bracha* implying an increase in number, as we saw above it
also carries the directive to "fill the earth," to occupy more space. In
terms of physical mechanics, we know that something under pressure
will tend to expand to take up additional space. For instance, if we blow
into a balloon, the air puts pressure against the elastic latex and causes

---

[12] *Devarim Rabbah* 4:3

[13] R. Naftali Tzvi Yehuda Berlin (1816–1893).

[14] *Ha'emek Davar*, toward the beginning of *Parshat Bechukotai*.

[15] The Netziv goes on to describe *teshuva* ("repentance") in similar health terms: "Thus,
teshuva is effective not through forgiveness but rather as a medicine. It is like the doctor
who prescribes medicine to eliminate the pain and illness that was caused by the person's
carelessness. This medicine does not constitute the doctor's forgiveness for [the patient]
not listening to him; rather it is naturally created to heal. So too, *teshuva* is medicine, as it
says, 'He repented and was healed' (Yeshayahu 6:10)."

the balloon to expand, which alleviates that pressure. On the human experiential or psychological level, when a room becomes too crowded, there is a tendency for people to alleviate this people-pressure by spilling over into the next room. This constitutes a more tolerable, more *stable* situation. Similarly, when an organization has too much work, it will expand its staff in order to take some of the pressure off. Regarding the *bracha* of fish and birds, "multiplying" leads quite naturally to "filling" the seas and skies, since only so many individuals can comfortably occupy the same territory.

In a range of different contexts, there is a tendency for a system under high pressure to expand outward, diffuse and/or increase itself, so as to alleviate that pressure. When this happens, the system depressurizes, reaches equilibrium. So besides having the property of multiplicity and increase, *bracha* can also be understood as a release of pressure, whereby boundaries are extended and the system is spread across a wider area.

Fig. 5   Bracha – Expansion, release of pressure

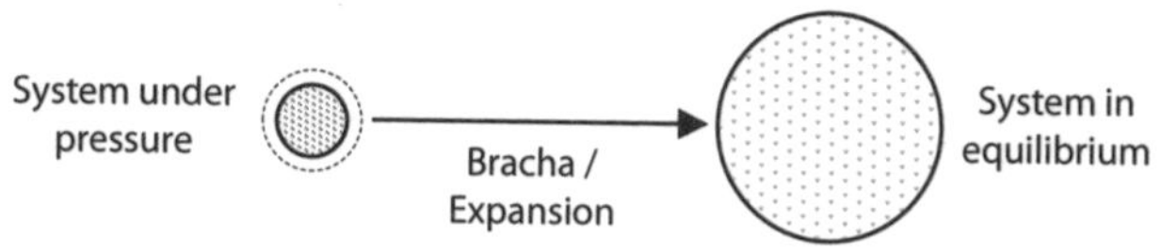

System under pressure — Bracha / Expansion → System in equilibrium

Kedusha – Defining the Concept

The words *kadosh* and *kodesh*[16] (from the family of words relating to *kedusha*) are routinely translated as "consecrated," "sanctified," "holy," or alternatively, "set apart," "separate," "prepared," "purified," "elevated" or "special." The variety of translations testifies to the fact that it is exceedingly difficult to find one translation that works in all contexts, and that indeed *kedusha* is a concept that has been challenging to adequately understand.

What's more, some of the definitions themselves require further definition and clarification. For instance, what does it mean exactly to be elevated, holy or special? Special in what sense? And if we define *kadosh* as "separate," does this imply that separation and detachment represent some sort of ideal state?

---

[16] *Kadosh* is the adjective form. *Kodesh* is a noun, referring to the thing itself that is *kadosh*.

Against this backdrop, we will now explore a definition of *kedusha* that in a way relates to all the above definitions and offers a unifying explanation.

Intensification by way of Restriction

In short, *kedusha* can be understood as the dual action of restriction and intensification. That is to say, it connotes becoming more restricted[17] and therefore more intense, more constricted and therefore more concentrated, more limited in scope and therefore more focused. When something is "*kadosh*," it is intensified by being constrained to specific, designated borders.

This is why *kedusha* is sometimes seen as implying "separation." When something becomes more focused, restricted, concentrated into a particular area, this by definition implies a separation from other areas. But while *kedusha* typically involves an act of separation, it is by no means *equivalent* to separation, whereby separating is seen as the goal, an end unto itself. Rather, it is the intensity/focus that is the goal and separation simply the means.

In this way, *kedusha* can also be conceptualized as "withdrawing into oneself," thereby concentrating, focusing. As opposed to *bracha*, which is a movement outward, *kedusha* is a movement inward. *Bracha* reduces pressure and intensity, whereas *kedusha* increases pressure and intensity.[18]

---

[17] As an example, consider the seemingly strange admonition regarding *kilayim*, forbidden mixtures. The Torah says not to plant two different crops together, פֶּן תִּקְדַּשׁ, "lest its fruit become *kodesh*" (*Devarim* 22:9). Given the context, this cannot mean "lest it become sanctified," which implies attaining a "higher" state. So the phrase is generally taken to mean, "lest it become 'like' *kodesh*," i.e., like a sanctified item that is forbidden to consume. As Rashi says, תקדש לשון הקדש (*Kiddushin* 38a)—it is the language of *hekdesh*, restricted property from which we are prohibited to derive personal benefit. However, if we understand *kodesh* to mean "restricted," then we can simply give the phrase פֶּן תִּקְדַּשׁ the straightforward translation, "lest it become restricted."

[18] This may help to explain the meaning of the *pasuk*: הִתְקַדְּשׁוּ לְמָחָר וַאֲכַלְתֶּם בָּשָׂר (*Bamidbar* 11:18), where *Bnei Yisrael* are promised meat after staging a protest in the desert. The question is why were they told "sanctify yourselves" before eating the meat? Rashi quotes the *Sifri*, which understands הִתְקַדְּשׁוּ to mean "prepare yourselves" to be punished. But perhaps we can understand this more specifically to mean "brace yourselves." To brace oneself is to tighten, become clenched, constrict oneself to a smaller space so as to defend from a blow. This accords with the understanding of *kedusha* as a movement inward, becoming more compacted, concentrated, feeling a sense of intensity and pressure.

Fig. 6   Kedusha – Concentration, increase of pressure

In the Torah, there is *kedusha* as it relates to persons, objects, places, times, and to *Hashem*. We will now look at examples of each and see how the definition of *kedusha* as restriction/intensification applies.

Kedusha of Am Yisrael

Am Yisrael (the Jewish people) is called upon to be *kadosh*, as it says:

דַּבֵּר אֶל כָּל עֲדַת בְּנֵי יִשְׂרָאֵל וְאָמַרְתָּ אֲלֵהֶם קְדשִׁים תִּהְיוּ
*"Speak to all the assembly of the Children of Israel
and say to them: You shall be kadosh"[19]*

Rashi explains here that *kedoshim* (pl., of *kadosh*) means maintaining restrictions, especially as it pertains to the sexual domain. He mentions *kohanim* (priests), who are likewise told to be *"kedoshim"* and are given even further restrictions. Indeed, there is a connection between *kedusha* and *kehuna* (priesthood), as the Torah says explicitly:

וְאַתֶּם תִּהְיוּ לִי מַמְלֶכֶת כֹּהֲנִים וְגוֹי קָדוֹשׁ
"And you will be to me a kingdom of priests and a holy nation"[20]

Am Yisrael and the *kohanim* are *kadosh* in that they live a "restricted" and focused lifestyle. But it is not restriction for restriction's sake, nor is it restriction to the "nth" degree, as in self-denial or total asceticism. And the purpose is not to achieve just *any* kind of focus or intensity, since one can be intense and focused in a way that is highly constructive, or in a way that is very much destructive. Rather it is being *kadosh laShem*, "to *Hashem*,"[21] meaning it is a restriction wherein we bind ourselves to Torah,

---

[19] *Vayikra* 19:2

[20] *Shemot* 19:6

[21] *Kadosh* without *"laShem,"* strictly speaking, connotes being restricted, intensely focused, dedicated, but without saying to *what*. Indeed, the root קדש is found in other ancient Near Eastern languages in connection with their religions. (See the entry for קדש in the *Brown-Driver-Briggs Lexicon*.) For instance, the word *kadesha* (prostitute) may have

to the *retzon hachaim*, the will for Life. Torah enjoins us to focus our energies (physical, mental, financial, and so on) in a way that is life-imbuing, that imparts vitality to ourselves, to others and to the society at large. That focus on and commitment to Life is our *kedusha*.

Thus, *too much* restriction, or restriction that undermines *simcha* or has a deadening effect on a person or the community, is entirely counter to the idea of *Am Yisrael* being a "*goy kadosh.*" For instance, when we focus so intensely that we shut out all outside input, living a completely insular life, this actually has a *weakening* effect. By attempting to be ultra-pure, ultra-clean, without any adulteration whatsoever, we become hypersensitive, less robust. It is like someone who is so health-conscious that they refuse to allow even a single morsel of food to pass into their mouth that is not the purest, healthiest, most organic—or someone who is so germ-conscious that they wash their hands constantly and sterilize surfaces they contact out of the fear of exposing themselves to harmful microbes. If anything, behaviors like these tend to precipitate a more *delicate* state of health, where the person is continually staving off illness.

That is not to say we shouldn't try to employ better health practices regarding diet and disease prevention—certainly that is a *good* thing! However, attempting to live *too* pure a lifestyle, whether pertaining to food or anything else, can actually lower our immunity, our tolerance to "foreign" elements, such that the slightest exposure to anything that does not fit the most narrow definition of acceptability elicits a severe negative reaction. Therefore, we need to balance the intensity of *kedusha* with a wider exposure.[22] It makes us a more robust, healthy, versatile, flexible, adaptable, well-rounded, "alive" people—one that is capable of maintaining a relationship with the rest of the world.

There is an idea that the *kedusha* of *Am Yisrael* relates primarily to "separateness," in the sense of distinctiveness from other nations, as is seemingly implied in the *pasuk*:

---

originated from the practice of sacred prostitution, done in pagan temples as a fertility cult rite. A *kadesha* was a restricted/dedicated prostitute. When the Torah speaks about the *kedusha* of *Am Yisrael*, the specification "*laShem*" is assumed, even if it isn't stated explicitly. So too here, we will use the words *kadosh/kodesh/kedusha* taking as a given that it is *laShem*.

[22] Indeed there are six days in the week of *chol* for every one day of *kodesh*.

כִּי עַם קָדוֹשׁ אַתָּה לַה׳ אֱ-לֹהֶיךָ וּבְךָ בָּחַר ה׳
לִהְיוֹת לוֹ לְעַם סְגֻלָּה מִכֹּל הָעַמִּים

*"For you are a holy people to Hashem Elokecha, and Hashem selected you
to be, for Him, a people of prized-possession, out of all the peoples"*[23]

But it is not merely being "separate," either in physical location or in the
way we act, which makes *Am Yisrael* "kadosh." As the above *pasuk* states,
it is being *kadosh* "to *Hashem*." It is separating from those activities that
impair, dim or diminish our vitality, that contravene the will for Life,
which makes *Am Yisrael* "kadosh" as a people. It is restricting in order to
intensify and focus our vitality in productive ways.

Kedusha of Objects, Places and Time

The word *kodesh* (קודש, pl., *kadashim*) refers to "restricted property,"
something belonging to *Hashem* as it were, to the *Mikdash* (Temple) or
the "*Klal*," the public domain/national collective. Access to *kodesh* is restricted to specific people at specific times, as it says regarding the
Mishkan (the Tabernacle used in the desert):

וְאַל יָבֹא בְכָל עֵת אֶל הַקֹּדֶשׁ

"and [Aharon] may not come at all times to the Kodesh"[24]

וְהַזָּר הַקָּרֵב יוּמָת

"and the outsider who approaches [the Mishkan] will die"[25]

Likewise, outsiders are restricted from eating *kodesh*, certain meats that
were brought as *korbanot* (sacrifices), as it says:

וְכָל זָר לֹא יֹאכַל קֹדֶשׁ, תּוֹשַׁב כֹּהֵן וְשָׂכִיר לֹא יֹאכַל קֹדֶשׁ.

*"And no outsider may eat kodesh;
a tenant of a kohen and a hired worker may not eat kodesh."*[26]

Regarding time, Shabbat is called "*kodesh laShem*"[27] and has *melacha*
(work-related) restrictions attached to it, as the *pasuk* says:

---

[23] *Devarim* 14:2; see also 7:6. Regarding the translation "prized-possession" for *segula*,
see p. 151.

[24] *Vayikra* 16:2, "the *Kodesh*" referring the *Kodesh Kedoshim* of the *Mishkan*.

[25] *Bamidbar* 1:51; see also 3:10, 3:38, 18:7.

[26] *Vayikra* 22:10

[27] As it says, וּבַיּוֹם הַשְּׁבִיעִי שַׁבַּת שַׁבָּתוֹן קֹדֶשׁ לַה׳ (*Shemot* 31:15).

וּבַיּוֹם הַשְּׁבִיעִי שַׁבַּת שַׁבָּתוֹן מִקְרָא קֹדֶשׁ,
כָּל מְלָאכָה לֹא תַעֲשׂוּ, שַׁבָּת הִוא לַה' בְּכֹל מוֹשְׁבֹתֵיכֶם
*"And on the seventh day is a Shabbat Shabbaton, a mikra kodesh;
you must not do any work—it is a Shabbat laShem in all your dwellings"*[28]

Kedusha of Shabbat

Out of the hundreds of instances of the term *kedusha* (in its numerous grammatical variants) throughout the Torah, only once does it appear in the book of *Bereshit*, and it is in relation to time. The Torah says regarding the seventh day of Creation, "He made it *kodesh*" (וַיְקַדֵּשׁ אֹתוֹ).[29] Once again, the definition of restricted/intensified applies. The seventh day is "*kodesh laShem*," meaning it is "restricted," not free for us to use except within certain confines. In this sense, Shabbat is like "*hekdesh*," an item donated to the *Mikdash*, whose use is now restricted. In fact, the connection to the *Mikdash* is even more direct, since the restrictions of Shabbat are tied directly to the thirty-nine *melachot* (creative work activities) involved in the construction of the *Mishkan*.

Why is it this work in particular which is prohibited? Because the *Mishkan* is considered to be *Am Yisrael*'s "Act of Creation." Just as the world, according to the Torah tradition, is created as a space in which to propagate the *ohr hachaim* (energy, vitality, the will for Life), so too the *Mikdash* is created as a space for bringing *ohr* into the world,[30] as a beacon of light and wisdom. And just as the Creator desists from the work of creation on Shabbat, so too does *Am Yisrael* desist from its work of creation on Shabbat.

---

[28] *Vayikra* 23:3. Like other types of *kodesh*, Shabbat is also "restricted" in its being exclusively for *Am Yisrael*, meaning that others are theoretically forbidden from adhering to all the Shabbat-related restrictions. (See *Sanhedrin* 58b, also *Yalkut Shimoni, Parshat Noach*.) This is in the same sense of וְהַזָּר הַקָּרֵב יוּמָת.

[29] *Bereshit* 2:3

[30] See *Midrash Tanchuma, Parshat Tetzaveh* (quoted by *Kli Yakar* on *Bereshit* 28:11), which asks why the windows of the *Mikdash* were narrow toward the inside and wide facing the outside. The answer given is: שיהא האור יוצא מבית המקדש ומאיר לעולם, "So that the light should go out from the *Beit HaMikdash* and illuminate the world." Other sources speak about the *Mikdash* as a source of *ohr*, e.g., ממקום בית המקדש נבראת האורה (*Bereshit Rabbah* 3:4). These references can also be understood in the sense of כִּי מִצִּיּוֹן תֵּצֵא תוֹרָה (*Micha* 4:2), whereby *ohr* is a metaphor for Torah.

Mikdash and Creation Parallels

The tradition draws numerous parallels between the *ma'aseh bereshit* (act of Creation) and the *ma'aseh haMishkan* (act of building the *Mishkan*). One instance regards the *pasuk*:

בְּיוֹם כַּלּוֹת מֹשֶׁה לְהָקִים אֶת הַמִּשְׁכָּן
"On the day Moshe finished erecting the Mishkan"[31]

Chazal (the Talmudic Sages) say about this verse that the word *et* (את) is written to include the creation of the world (as in אֵת הַשָּׁמַיִם וְאֵת הָאָרֶץ).[32] The Midrash also states:

מצינו שהיה המשכן שקול כנגד מעשה בראשית.
"We find that the Mishkan was weighed against the act of Creation."[33]

Regarding Betzalel, who was placed in charge of designing the *Mishkan*, the Talmud states:

יודע היה בצלאל לצרף אותיות
שנבראו בהן שמים וארץ.
*"Betzalel knew how to arrange the letters
through which the heavens and earth were created."*[34]

Additionally, the Midrash explains in one place: "Worlds were created and destroyed repeatedly, until finally ours was created and allowed to stand."[35] And separately it states: "Moshe set up the *Mishkan* and took it apart seven times [on each of the seven days of inauguration] until finally he set it up and allowed it to stand."[36] Furthermore, the six days of Creation bear a suggestive similarity to the first six items listed in the building of the *Mishkan*.[37]

---

[31] *Bamidbar* 7:1

[32] See *Midrash Tanchuma, Parshat Naso* 19.

[33] *Yalkut Shimoni, Parshat Beha'alotcha* 8. Meaning there is an equivalence, a correspondence, between the two.

[34] *Brachot* 55a

[35] See *Bereshit Rabbah* 3:7, 9:2.

[36] See *Bamidbar Rabbah* 13:2.

[37] Several *midrashim* list correspondences between components of the *Mishkan* and the Creation narrative. (See e.g., *Yalkut Shimoni, Parshat Beha'alotcha* 8, and *Tanchuma Buber, Parshat Pekudei, Perek* 38.) Note that each comes up with a different set of correspondences. What I am presenting is an original alternative *drash*, whose strength is that it not only provides a conceptual match between the days of Creation and the components of the *Mishkan*

Day One/Item One is the *ohr* and the *Aron*, the first "light" (of "let there be light") and the Ark of the Covenant. The word *aron* (ארון) itself is understood in the tradition as stemming from the word *ohr* (אור).[38] In terms of function, both the *ohr* of Day One and the *Aron* are considered to be the primary sources of light/power/vitality in their respective systems. All else is seen as being built around, and drawing from, the *ohr* and the *Aron*.

Day Two/Item Two is the *rakia* and the *Kaporet*, the "firmament" and the Ark Cover. The *rakia* acts as a separator between the lower water (seas) and upper water (clouds). Likewise, the *Kaporet* (with its *Keruvim*) acts as the separator between the *Aron* below and the *Anan* (cloud) above. In fact, the empty space above the *Kaporet* is explicitly referred to in Tanach as "*rakia*":

וָאֶרְאֶה וְהִנֵּה אֶל הָרָקִיעַ אֲשֶׁר עַל רֹאשׁ הַכְּרֻבִים

"I saw, and behold—toward the rakia that is above the head of the Keruvim"[39]

Day Three/Item Three is the *eretz* and *desheh*, and the *Shulchan* and *Lechem HaPanim*—the land and produce, and the Table and Showbread.[40] The land houses the produce, just as the Table houses the Showbread. Also, it is the *desheh*, the produce of the land, which is used to make the *Lechem HaPanim*, the Showbread.

Day Four/Item Four is the *me'orot* and the *Menorah*, the celestial luminaries and the Lamp.[41] Both provide visible light in the everyday usable sense, as opposed to the "light" of Day One/Item One. There are seven branches in the *Menorah*, and the tradition recognizes seven primary celes-

---

(as the Midrash does), but it also matches them in precise sequential order (according to *Bereshit* 1 and *Shemot* 37). As it happens, several of these correspondences do coincide with the Midrash (which I will note), but others do not.

[38] See *Yerushalmi Yoma* 5:3, brought by Rabbeinu Bachye on *Shemot* 25:10.

[39] *Yechezkel* 10:1. Several *psukim* later (10:15), Yechezkel recognizes the *Keruvim* to be the "*Chaya*" that he saw at the Kevar river, i.e., in his first vision. Chapter 1 is Yechezkel's vision of the *Kisei HaKavod* of Creation, and Chapter 10 is a similar vision, this time regarding the *Mikdash*. This itself is another example of the linkage between the Creation and the *Mishkan*. See Rabbeinu Bachye on *Shemot* 25:18 (the instruction to make the *Keruvim*), who discusses Yechezkel's parallel visions.

[40] This follows the Midrash: ביום השלישי בראת מזונות שנאמר 'תדשא' ואף אנו עשינו לשמך שלחן ועליו לחם הפנים (*Midrash Tanchuma Buber, Parshat Pekudei, Perek* 38).

[41] Again, this matches the Midrash: שנאמר 'ויעש א-להים את שני המאורות וגו'' וכנגדן עשינו לך מנורה (Ibid.).

tial luminaries.[42] Additionally, just as the *ohr* of Day One fuels the visible light of Day Four, so too the "*ohr*" of the *Aron* (i.e., the *Shechina*) is understood to fuel the light of the *Menorah*.[43]

Day Five/Item Five is the fish and birds, and the Incense Altar. The fish and birds relate back to Day Two, occupying the lower and upper *mayim* respectively. Likewise, the Incense Altar relates back to Item Two, the smoke from the *ketoret* (incense) being used to cover the *Kaporet* on Yom Kippur. This was done to protect the *Kohen Gadol* from the *Anan* (cloud) which rested on the *Kaporet*.[44]

Day Six/Item Six is the land animals and humans, and the Outer Altar. It is the land animals which provide the primary *korbanot* (sacrifices) which humans bring to the Altar. Also, both the Altar and humans/land animals are associated with earth, soil. The Altar in the *Mishkan* is filled with earth.[45] Day Six describes the "earth" bringing forth creatures. The name Adam (אדם, lit. "earthling") itself comes from the word *adama* (אדמה, earth), as well as *dam* (דם, blood). In the *korban* procedure, blood is sprinkled on the Altar.

---

[42] These being the sun, the moon and the five planets easily visible to the naked eye: Mercury, Venus, Mars, Jupiter and Saturn. See the Midrash, ibid., which mentions the correspondence between the seven branches of the *Menorah* and the seven major luminaries.

[43] The Talmud (*Megila* 21b) says of the seven lamps of the *Menorah* that the outer six (i.e., their wicks) faced the center "western" lamp, and the western lamp faced the *Shechina*. As such, it was thought to draw from the *Shechina*. Whereas the other lamps burned out overnight, the western lamp is said to have stayed lit until the following afternoon, with the same amount of oil (see *Shabbat* 22b).

[44] Aharon is told not to enter the *Kodesh Kedoshim* lest he be killed, כִּי בֶּעָנָן אֵרָאֶה עַל הַכַּפֹּרֶת, "because in the Cloud I will appear above the *Kaporet*" (*Vayikra* 16:1–2). Only on Yom Kippur is the *Kohen Gadol* allowed to enter, and in order to protect himself he is instructed to burn incense: וְכִסָּה עֲנַן הַקְּטֹרֶת אֶת הַכַּפֹּרֶת אֲשֶׁר עַל הָעֵדוּת וְלֹא יָמוּת, "And the cloud of the incense should cover the *Kaporet* that is above the Testimony, so he will not die" (16:13). This rule was enacted to preempt another tragedy of the sort that occurred with Nadav and Avihu, who were killed while burning incense in the *Mishkan*. Presumably they were inside the *Kodesh Kedoshim* without the smoke of the *ketoret* properly covering the *Kaporet* and thus lacked that vital protection. It is unclear whether their lethal mistake stemmed from using coals taken from outside the *Mishkan* (as in, וַיַּקְרִיבוּ לִפְנֵי ה' אֵשׁ זָרָה, *Vayikra* 10:1; see *Sifri, Parshat Shemini* 1:32), using a combination of incense ingredients outside of what was specified (as in, לֹא תַעֲלוּ עָלָיו קְטֹרֶת זָרָה, *Shemot* 30:9), drinking alcohol before entering the *Kodesh Kedoshim* (as in, יַיִן וְשֵׁכָר אַל תֵּשְׁתְּ, *Vayikra* 10:9), or a combination of these or other factors.

[45] As in, מִזְבַּח אֲדָמָה תַּעֲשֶׂה לִּי (*Shemot* 20:20).

Moreover, both the work of the Creation and the work of the *Mishkan* are described as "*melacha*," and the Torah uses similar language with regard to the completion of that work:

וַיְכַל אֱ-לֹהִים בַּיּוֹם הַשְּׁבִיעִי מְלַאכְתּוֹ אֲשֶׁר עָשָׂה

"And Elokim completed, on the seventh day, the melacha that He produced"[46]

וַיְכַל מֹשֶׁה אֶת הַמְּלָאכָה

"And Moshe completed the melacha"[47]

Day Seven is Shabbat, which corresponds not with any particular component of the *Mishkan*, but with the *Shechina* (the *kevod Hashem*, the "glory" of *Hashem*) entering into the *Mishkan*.[48] As soon as Moshe completes the *melacha*, the *Mishkan* is filled with the *kevod Hashem*, imparting it with *kedusha*.[49] In the same way, as soon as the work of Creation is completed, the seventh day is imbued with *kedusha*. Sources in the tradition also speak of the *Shechina* as entering on Shabbat.[50]

In addition, each of the seven Days/Items can be understood as corresponding to one of the seven so-called "lower *sephirot*."[51] *Chesed* (1) is pure outflow of energy. *Gevura* (2) is the strength of restraint, separation, holding back, delineating borders. *Tiferet* (3) is the splendor and radiance of life which results from the focus of energy, a balance of outflow and restraint. *Netzach* (4) is asserting, shining forth brightly, unremittingly. *Hod* (5) is yielding, mitigating, protecting. *Yesod* (6) is foundation, the grounded balance between assertion and yielding. It is the system (the Creation/*Mishkan*) in its final form, fine-tuned and ready for use. *Malchut* (7) is when the system goes into operation, when life and vitality reign.

---

[46] *Bereshit* 2:2

[47] *Shemot* 40:33

[48] As the Midrash states, בשביעי היה כולו אור ובמשכן כיון שנכנס הא-להים לתוכו התחיל מבהיק מן השכינה, "On the Seventh Day, everything was *ohr*/light; and in the *Mishkan*, since *Ha'elokim* entered inside it, it began to shine from the *Shechina*" (*Yalkut Shimoni, Parshat Beha'alotcha* 8).

[49] As it says, וַיְכַס הֶעָנָן אֶת אֹהֶל מוֹעֵד וּכְבוֹד ה' מָלֵא אֶת הַמִּשְׁכָּן (*Shemot* 40:34).

[50] As in, ושבת הוא זיו השכינה ואור ה' יתברך הממלא את המשכן (R. Tzadok HaKohen, *Likutei Ma'amarim*, p. 43). See also ahead, Note 52.

[51] "Lower" meaning that in the usual diagram of the Ten *Sephirot* they are placed below the three "upper *sephirot*," keter-chochma-bina (or alternatively *chochma-bina-da'at*). Also, the term "lower" relates to human attributes that are more concrete and down-to-earth, as compared to the "higher," mind-oriented human functions, which are more abstract.

Fig. 7   Creation/Mishkan/Sephirot correspondences

Unit	Work of Creation	Work of Mishkan	Sephira
1	Ohr	Aron	Chesed
2	Rakia	Kaporet	Gevura
3	Eretz/Desheh	Shulchan/Lechem	Tiferet
4	Me'orot	Menorah	Netzach
5	Fish/Birds	Incense Altar	Hod
6	Land animals/Humans	Outer Altar	Yesod
7	Shabbat/Kedusha	Shechina/Kedusha	Malchut

Shabbat and Shechina

Just as the *Shechina* is described as entering into the space of the *Mishkan*, so too is it considered as having entered the world when Shabbat comes in.[52] This *Shechina* might be thought of as the intensity, the amplified *ohra* and *simcha*, the heightened sense of awareness and aliveness, which is experienced as a result of *kedusha*, of focusing our energies effectively. We engage in our *melacha* during the week, build our "*Mikdash*" so to speak, and then as Shabbat comes in, we "power up" the system, experience the flow of vitality and illumination that enters, filling the space we've created. This is the great light and joy that is possible to attain on Shabbat, as well as the joy the tradition describes *Am Yisrael* as having when unified in the space of the *Mikdash*.

The visage of the *Shechina* ("*pnei haShechina*") can thus be understood as a reflection of ourselves.[53] We see it, experience it—what is known as the "revealed" *Shechina*—when we have done the work of successfully cultivating *kedusha*. When we have not, this is called *hester panim*, literally the "hidden face." The *Shechina* is hidden in as much as our own presence lacks vitality and light.

---

[52] The analogy between Shabbat and the *Shechina* is made, among other places, within the *piyut* "*Lecha Dodi*" of *Kabalat Shabbat*. The preliminary verses speak about receiving the presence of the "bride"/*pnei Shabbat*, and in subsequent verses the theme transitions to the idea of *Am Yisrael* receiving the *kevod Hashem/pnei haShechina* in the *Mikdash*, in Jerusalem.

[53] As in, אור השכינה הוא כנסת ישראל (R. Avraham Yitzchak Kook, *Orot Yisrael* 1:8), wherein the *Shechina* is explicitly identified with *Am Yisrael*.

Shamor and Zachor

The two presentations of the *Aseret Hadibrot* (Ten Commandments) in the Torah famously include two versions of the commandment to observe Shabbat:

זָכוֹר אֶת יוֹם הַשַּׁבָּת לְקַדְּשׁוֹ

"Remember the day of Shabbat to sanctify it"[54]

שָׁמוֹר אֶת יוֹם הַשַּׁבָּת לְקַדְּשׁוֹ

"Guard the day of Shabbat to sanctify it"[55]

Shabbat is spoken about in terms of *"zachor,"* the command to remember it, as well as *"shamor,"* the command to guard it. Both *zachor* and *shamor* are done *"lekadesho,"* to impart Shabbat with *kedusha*. That is, both are understood to restrict/intensify the day. *Zachor* is a restriction that takes place primarily in consciousness. To remember Shabbat is to focus one's mental energies on matters of the day, restricting them from dwelling on weekday concerns.[56] *Shamor* is the restriction of one's actions and refers to safeguarding the prohibition from engaging in the thirty-nine *melachot*. *Zachor* and *Shamor* together make Shabbat *kodesh*, give it its energy and intensity.

Vayvarech and Vaykadesh – Bracha and Kedusha

Regarding the seventh day of Creation, the Torah states:

וַיְבָרֶךְ אֱ-לֹהִים אֶת יוֹם הַשְּׁבִיעִי וַיְקַדֵּשׁ אֹתוֹ

"And Elokim blessed/expanded the seventh day, and He sanctified/intensified it"[57]

The first action taken in relation to the Seventh Day is *"vayvarech."* Shabbat is given a *bracha*—it is expanded, imbued with multiplicity. Materially, this takes the form of abundance and plentitude.[58] The Torah speaks of the double portion of manna that fell before Shabbat, which we hint to

---

[54] *Shemot* 20:7

[55] *Devarim* 5:11

[56] In Halacha, the *mitzva* of *"zachor"* is associated with making *Kiddush* (see Rambam *Hilchot Shabbat* 29:1), i.e., focusing our thoughts on what the day is about.

[57] *Bereshit* 2:3

[58] The Ibn Ezra understands the word ויברך as "תוספת טובה." Likewise, the Rashbam says that Shabbat was given a *bracha* "מכל טוב," due to the fact that all the needs and nourishment of living creatures had already been created in the previous days.

Bracha and Kedusha | 53

with the two loaves of challah eaten at Shabbat meals.[59] There is also a corresponding "conscious expansion" associated with Shabbat, a sense of broadening one's potential for enlightenment.[60] Furthermore, time itself is understood to "expand" on Shabbat. We do not prepare on Shabbat for the next day, implying that Shabbat is timeless, never-ending relative to the week. Likewise, Shabbat is called *me'ein olam haba* (similar to the world to come), the era we envision when life continues indefinitely.

The next action is "*vaykadesh.*" Shabbat is given *kedusha*—it is restricted (by abstaining from *melacha*) and intensified (through focus on the day, and through *simcha*). Together, *vayvarech* and *vaykadesh* comprise an expansion and contraction, multiplicity and intensity. Shabbat is "blessed" with a sense of outward expansion, proliferation and abundance. We then take that abundance and draw inward, focus it, condense it, by restricting our thoughts and actions on matters of the day at hand. The idea is that the abundance of Shabbat be experienced more potently, and that our enjoyment (*oneg*) should be intensified.

Hashem as Kadosh

A number of verses in the Torah call on *Am Yisrael* to be *kadosh*, and to be as such on the basis of *Hashem* being called "*kadosh*," as in:

וִהְיִיתֶם קְדֹשִׁים כִּי קָדוֹשׁ אָנִי

"and you shall be kadosh, for I am kadosh"[61]

The verses where this concept is cited focus either on restricting oneself from becoming *tamei* (impure), or in general on restricting oneself to a higher standard of conduct. All this is suggestive of maintaining a certain focus in life, an intensity, whose goal is to hone the vitality of the individual and society. It is *kedusha* in the life-affirming sense. But what does the verse mean, "*ki kadosh ani*," that we conduct ourselves as such because *Hashem* is "*kadosh*"? Does *Hashem* maintain restrictions, withdraw from *tamei* items, adhere to the specific set of standards in which human

---

[59] The double portion of manna is the explanation Rashi offers (citing *Bereshit Rabbah* 11:2) for the term ויברך (as well as ויקדש, being that no manna fell on Shabbat, i.e., it was "restricted," withheld).

[60] The Ibn Ezra speaks about ויברך as also referring to the "כח ההכרה והשכל."

[61] *Vayikra* 11:44; see also 11:45, 19:2 and 20:26 (and 21:8, which enjoins Aharon HaKohen to be *kadosh*, "*ki kadosh ani*").

beings are commanded? No, rather it is that *Hashem signifies* this higher mode of conduct. *Hashem* is *"kadosh"* in the sense of evoking the very Life principle that we are asked to live by, in being associated with the *Torat chaim*, the Torah of Life. We emulate the *"kedusha of Hashem,"* as it were, by striving to embody the will for Life.[62]

That is one way *Hashem* can be described as *"kadosh."* There is also the way the prophets conceptualize it, as in:

קָדוֹשׁ קָדוֹשׁ קָדוֹשׁ ה' צְבָא-וֹת מְלֹא כָל הָאָרֶץ כְּבוֹדוֹ

"Kadosh, kadosh, kadosh is Hashem [commander] of legions,
all the earth is filled with His kavod"[63]

That is, the entire created world is filled with life/*chiyut*, all matter teeming with movement and vitality, coursing with energy. The special emphasis of *"kadosh"* here suggests unparalleled intensity on the greatest conceivable scale.[64] The phrase *"melo kol ha'aretz kevodo"* implies the utter pervasiveness of life-energy within the Creation, where all that intense *kedusha* localizes. The world is the will for Life incarnate, realized and manifested in all its fullness and awesome grandeur.

Additionally, there is *Hashem* referred to as *"kadosh"* when being identified with the vitality/intensity/power of the *Mikdash*.[65] *Hashem* is understood as *kadosh* in the sense of being "restricted/concentrated," as it were, in the space of the *Mikdash*, manifesting intensely in the form of the *Shechina/kevod Hashem*.

---

[62] Thus, in the story of Moshe "hitting the rock" (*Bamidbar* 20:1–13), where Moshe chastises the people and gives them water only begrudgingly, the *pasuk* says: לֹא הֶאֱמַנְתֶּם בִּי לְהַקְדִּישֵׁנִי לְעֵינֵי בְּנֵי יִשְׂרָאֵל, "You did not have faith in Me to sanctify Me in the eyes of the Children of Israel." Meaning, Moshe did not stay true to the Life principle, to show the people that his primary focus, in keeping with the *Torat chaim*, was their life and welfare. As a result, he became unfit to be the leader who would bring them into the Land of Israel, the ארץ החיים. It was not Moshe but the water itself that saved the people and through which the Life principle was sanctified/magnified, as it says: הֵמָּה מֵי מְרִיבָה...וַיִּקָּדֵשׁ בָּם. (See also Note 45, p. 221.)

[63] *Yeshayahu* 6:3

[64] The Vilna Gaon (*Bi'ur Hagra*) says regarding the triple expression of *"kadosh"*: ג' פעמים להגדיל העניין, that it is done to "amplify/enlarge the matter," to express something on a massive scale.

[65] In fact the *psukim* before and after *"kadosh, kadosh, kadosh"* (*Yeshayahu* 6:3) refer explicitly to the *Mikdash*.

The Power and Volatility of Kedusha

The picture that emerges in the Torah concept of *kedusha* is often rather analogous to energy or power. This is particularly so regarding the *Mishkan/Mikdash*. For instance, the *Aron* (Ark of the Covenant) which functions as the seat of the *Shechina*, which sits as the centerpiece of the *Mikdash* inside the *Kodesh Kedoshim*, is described in relation to "power":

קוּמָה ה' לִמְנוּחָתֶךָ אַתָּה וַאֲרוֹן עֻזֶּךָ.

"*Arise, Hashem, to Your resting place, You and the Ark of Your power.*"[66]

Only it is not merely power in the sense of authority or majesty. The Torah seems to describe a tangible and potentially lethal power associated with the *Aron* and with the *Mishkan* in general.[67] Indeed, the Israelites protested to Moshe about it being deadly to come in proximity to the *Mishkan*:

כֹּל הַקָּרֵב הַקָּרֵב אֶל מִשְׁכַּן ה' יָמוּת

"*Each and every one who approaches the Mishkan of Hashem dies!*"[68]

For that reason, the Levites were set up to shield the *Mishkan*, so that people would not approach too near and be killed:

וּשְׁמַרְתֶּם אֵת מִשְׁמֶרֶת הַקֹּדֶשׁ וְאֵת מִשְׁמֶרֶת הַמִּזְבֵּחַ
וְלֹא יִהְיֶה עוֹד קֶצֶף עַל בְּנֵי יִשְׂרָאֵל.

"*And guard the safeguard of the Kodesh, and the safeguard of the Altar, so there will not be any more violent-outburst upon the Children of Israel.*"[69]

The *Mishkan* is described in ways that one might describe a power plant. It requires highly specialized handling and protocols for self-protection—what to touch and what not to touch, what to wear and what not to wear, where to go and where not to go. It contains various

---

[66] *Tehilim* 132:8

[67] See e.g., the story of Nadav and Avihu (*Vayikra* 9:24), where "a fire came out from before *Hashem* and consumed them." The Rashbam notes that the fire came out "from inside the *Kodesh HaKedoshim*." Also note the many instances of the phrase ולא ימות/ולא תמותו in the Torah relating to the *Mishkan*, and *psukim* such as: לֹא אֶעֱלֶה בְּקִרְבְּךָ...פֶּן אֲכֶלְךָ בַּדָּרֶךְ (*Shemot* 33:3) and פֶּן יִפְרֹץ בָּהֶם ה' (*Shemot* 19:22) regarding the danger of being in proximity to the *Shechina*. See also *II Shmuel* 6:7, where Uza touches the *Aron* and is killed.

[68] *Bamidbar* 17:28

[69] *Bamidbar* 18:5. This command is also stated earlier (1:53), that the Levites should be stationed around the *Mishkan* as a shield to prevent the death of those trying to enter.

spaces that are designated off limits except to authorized personnel who are familiar with the specific procedures. It is volatile and dangerous, and shielding is put in place to protect the surrounding public from harm. Yet despite the danger, it is seen as being vital to the community, a source of energy, vitality.

So the "intensity" of *kedusha*, from the perspective of the Torah, is taken as something entirely real and tangible, and something to be handled very cautiously. This is done to protect the people, as well as to prevent *chilul* ("defilement," i.e., draining of) *kedusha*.

Kodesh and Chol – Concentration and Vacuum

The Torah sets up the concepts of *"kodesh"* and *"chol"* as opposites:

וּלֲהַבְדִּיל בֵּין הַקֹּדֶשׁ וּבֵין הַחֹל

"and to distinguish between the kodesh and the chol"[70]

The word *chol* (חול) is typically translated as "secular" or "mundane." It comes from the root *chalal* (חלל), which carries a broad range of meanings: "profane" or "defile," "begin," also "pierce through" (as in "slay") and "make a hole."[71] The common thread among these varied meanings, as we will see, is the connotation of emptiness, absence, void or vacuum. *Chol/chalal* describes that which lacks substance or has been drained of vitality/energy.

For instance, a *chalal* (חלל) refers to a corpse. A *"chalal cherev"* is a person slain by the sword. This person is not only left with a physical hole but has been emptied of blood/life-energy. The same word *chalal* can likewise refer to an empty space or vacuum. Also in the family of meanings is the word *choleh* (חולה), a sick person, one who is weak, lacking vital energy.[72] A *chalon* (חלון), a "window," refers to an empty space in the wall. *Techila* (תחילה) means "beginning" in the sense of starting

---

[70] *Vayikra* 10:10

[71] Note that the root חלל meaning "defile" or "begin" may actually be a different root than חלל meaning "pierce," with one word originally containing a "soft *chet*" and the other a "hard *chet*"—a distinction that was lost over time. (See *How the Hebrew Language Grew*, Edward Horowitz, p. 105.) However, Torah tradition recognizes only one letter *chet*, and that will guide our methodology for purposes of this book.

[72] For instance, the Talmud speaks about making oneself into a *"choleh"* by means of fasting (see *Brachot* 12b), i.e., depleting one's energy by denying oneself food and drink.

from a blank slate, empty, void of any prior events. Thus *chol* (חול) can be understood as absence or lack. To be *mechalel* (מחלל) is to induce such a lack. A *chilul* (חילול) is an act that evacuates, creates a void, drains something of its energy or substance. The *pasuk* says:

וּמִן הַמִּקְדָּשׁ לֹא יֵצֵא וְלֹא יְחַלֵּל אֵת מִקְדַּשׁ...

*"[The Kohen] should not exit from the Mikdash,
so that he should not defile/drain the Mikdash..."*[73]

The Torah warns here and in many other places against *chilul kedusha*, generally taken to mean "defilement of holiness." In light of the meaning discussed above, it might be more precisely understood as an act that "drains" or "depletes" *kedusha*. It dilutes the concentration, downgrades the intensity, blurs the focus, and diminishes/wastes the life-energy and vitality that had previously been cultivated. So the analogy to energy and power applies here as well. The Torah's concern to safeguard *kedusha*, particularly as it concerns the *Mikdash*, might be analogous to what today we would call "energy conservation." It is the desire not to drain or waste a precious, vital resource.

The clarification of the concept of *"chol"* therefore provides additional confirmation regarding our understanding of *"kodesh."* *Chol* is characterized by a relative lack, vacuum, low concentration. *Kodesh* is characterized by just the opposite—having a relatively *high* concentration, a high level of intensity.

Chalal and Creation

According to Kabbalah, the famous introduction "In the beginning"[74] is not quite the beginning of the story. There is a state which is thought to

---

[73] *Vayikra* 21:12, prohibiting the *Kohen Gadol* from leaving the *Mishkan* in order to bury a close relative. This is to avoid his returning in a state of *tuma* and causing a *chilul*/depletion in the *kedusha* of the *Mishkan*. (See p. 90, on the connection between *tuma* and *chilul*.)

[74] This phrase, or "In the beginning of" (i.e., rendering it in the construct state), is the classical translation of the word בראשית. A more accurate translation however might be "in the first phase [of]" or possibly "as the foremost event [of]." The word ראשית means "first/top portion," referring either to that which is sequentially first, or to the top, best, choicest portion, irrespective of time. Unlike "in the beginning," which denotes a starting point *before* any events (and which would be better conveyed by the word תחילה, as we discussed earlier), ראשית is the first "portion," part, phase, period, chunk of time—which *includes* the first set of events. For example, the *pasuk* בְּרֵאשִׁית מַלְכוּת צִדְקִיָּה (*Yirmiyahu* 49:34)

exist prior to that, before Creation.[75] In this primordial state, all is *ohr*, a formless, indistinguishable "light."[76] But being entirely uniform, without any distinction whatsoever—no "otherness," no space of non-light for that light to radiate within and be perceived—the term *ohr*, "light," is really just a placeholder to describe something which utterly defies description.[77]

Creation thus begins by producing the first *distinction*. In Kabbalah, this is called the "*tzimtzum*," the "constriction," where *ohr* is consciously compressed, pulled back, leaving in its wake a *chalal panui*, an empty space or vacuum. Before Creation, there is only uniformly distributed *ohr*. After the *tzimtzum*, we now have two distinct areas adjacent to one another: that of high-concentration (*ohr*) and that of low concentration (*chalal*/vacuum).[78] This is the initial distinction, an empty space amidst a sea of *ohr*. It is a space devoid of any content, without a "world."

Fig. 8   Compression – Creation, Part 1

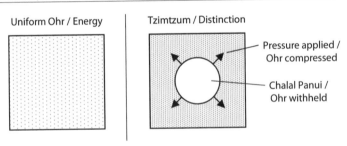

Uniform Ohr / Energy   Tzimtzum / Distinction

Pressure applied / Ohr compressed

Chalal Panui / Ohr withheld

means "in the first part of Tzidkiyahu's reign," not "at the very start," as in when he was being anointed or first put on the crown. So too, בראשית ברא א-להים refers to the "first part" of history, of the world as we know it—or possibly the "top/foremost event." In this all-important first phase, as the foremost event, the ראשית, *Elokim* created the שמים וארץ.

[75] All references to "Creation" in this book should be understood as relating to a specific concept within the framework of Torah, not as making any assertions about universal cosmology. Torah is concerned with the human world, and especially human conscious processes. The concept of Creation, especially as understood in Kabbalah, can likewise be interpreted in that light.

[76] This initial *ohr* is not the one the Torah refers to in the phrase ויהי אור, "and there was light." Rather, it is the "light" that is understood to preexist the Creation, referred to in Kabbalah as the *ohr ein sof*, the endless (i.e., uniform, all-pervasive) light.

[77] See p. 103, where this concept is connected to the idea of *yesh me'ayin*.

[78] The question of the theoretical impossibility of "compressing" *ohr ein sof* (something that is infinite) is a philosophical one, like the idea of deriving finite from infinite, or something from nothing. That is why in the previous note I define *ein sof* as "uniform" and "all-pervasive," rather than "infinite."

The pre-Creation state represents total equilibrium. It is perfectly stable, and perfectly static. With the introduction of distinction however, tension is introduced. This tension is the key to pumping *life*—energy and movement—into the Creation. Tension means that high-pressure wants to flow into low-pressure. The *ohr* naturally seeks to decompress, diffuse into the adjacent vacuum. In order to maintain the distinction, *ohr* must be consciously held back. However, in order to produce a Creation and not leave it as an empty void, *some* of this pressure is released, allowing a limited, focused stream or ray (a "*kav*") of *ohr* to flow into the *chalal*.[79] Thus we have "*Vayehi ohr*" ("And there was light").[80]

Fig. 9   Decompression – Creation, Part 2

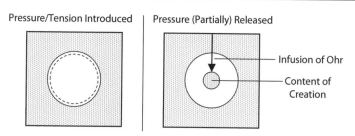

The primordial, static *ohr* has now been converted into usable *ohr*, energy. Within that *ohr*, finer distinctions are continually made. New vacant spaces are carved out, new *kelim* (conduits) created, with *ohr* flowing into them, generating ever greater complexity. Eventually we have the fullness of Creation, a world which can be used, inhabited.

Creation and Human Creativity

The Creation might be understood as a "thought" within the conscious space of the Creator. As such, it can be taken as a metaphor for human consciousness. Every time we open up the mind to a new question or idea, it is in effect an act of *tzimtzum*. When we illuminate the matter with knowledge and insight, it is drawing *ohr* into the *chalal*, building a

---

[79] This is a simplified version of the Kabbalistic model of Creation as described by the Arizal (R. Yitzchak Luria) and others. (See the Arizal's *Etz Chaim* 1:1.)

[80] *Vayehi ohr* takes place only once *ohr* can be perceived, once it is distinguishable against the backdrop of non-*ohr*. See p. 103 for further discussion of "*yehi ohr/vayehi ohr*."

world.[81] And when we continue to make distinctions and further refine our thinking, we participate in the ongoing act of creation, in the sense of:

מְחַדֵּשׁ בְּכָל יוֹם תָּמִיד מַעֲשֵׂה בְרֵאשִׁית

"He renews, each day, continuously, the act of Creation"[82]

Bracha and Kedusha in Creation

The sequence of compression and decompression, creating a space and then infusing *ohr*/energy into that space, can be understood as *kedusha* and *bracha* respectively. The *tzimtzum* is an act of restricting, withdrawing into and compressing oneself, becoming more intense, concentrated. That precisely matches the concept of *kedusha* we spoke of earlier.[83] The release of *ohr* into the *chalal* is an act of decompression, expanding and filling a space. This is the concept of *bracha*.

Note however that this is only from one perspective, from the point of view "inside the *ohr*" as it were. From the perspective of the *chalal*, the experience is just the opposite. First, the space expands and opens outward, constituting *bracha*, and then the space is infused with *ohr*/energy, becoming more intensified and concentrated, constituting *kedusha*.

Holidays – the Mikra'ei Kodesh

We spoke about Shabbat as "*kodesh*." It is the first of what the Torah calls the "*mikra'ei kodesh*,"[84] times when *Am Yisrael* is "called together for restriction/intensification." The Torah holidays of Pesach, Shavuot, Rosh Hashana, Yom Kippur, Sukkot and Shemini Atzeret, like Shabbat, have restrictions on *melacha*. The holidays are also imbued with a corresponding intensity, each one differing in quality and content according to the nature of the day.

We will focus for a moment on Pesach and Sukkot, the pair of week-long holidays, which illustrate the cycle of *bracha* and *kedusha* we have been discussing. Pesach is a season of growth and outward movement—

---

[81] See also p. 182, on the concept of *she'eila*, a "question," as a space of creation.

[82] From the *Yotzer Ohr bracha* in *Shacharit*.

[83] Thus we have another entry to understanding *Hashem* as "*kadosh*"—as the Creator restricting, withdrawing and compressing, so as to create a space for Creation.

[84] As in, וּבַיּוֹם הַשְּׁבִיעִי שַׁבַּת שַׁבָּתוֹן מִקְרָא קֹדֶשׁ (*Vayikra* 23:3).

bracha. Sukkot, which comes exactly half a year later, is a season of aggregation, inward movement—*kedusha.*

Pesach and Expansion

The first holiday mentioned in the Torah is Pesach, which commemorates the idea of the Exodus from Egypt, and consequently the birth of *Am Yisrael* as a national entity. The theme of Pesach is one of *bracha*—expansion and proliferation. To begin with, the Israelites in Egypt are described as experiencing a tremendous population explosion, as the *pasuk* says:

וּבְנֵי יִשְׂרָאֵל פָּרוּ וַיִּשְׁרְצוּ וַיִּרְבּוּ וַיַּעַצְמוּ בִּמְאֹד מְאֹד

*"The Children of Israel bore fruit and teemed and multiplied
and strengthened very, very much"*[85]

Then, after being subjected to years of slavery and great pressure in *Mitzraim* (the word מצרים from צר, literally a tight, compressed space), *Am Yisrael* is finally liberated, the pressure released, as it bursts forth from Egypt.[86] Pesach is called the *"zman cheruteinu,"* the "time of our freedom." Freedom is a movement of outward expansion, where one was oppressed (in the sense of pressed down), held back, and is now opened up, let free. *Cherut* (freedom), in this sense, is really an expression of *bracha*, a movement outward.[87]

Additionally, the Torah states that Pesach must be celebrated in the springtime.[88] Springtime is the season of birth. Animals and plants reproduce and proliferate, crops burst forth from the ground. So not only from

---

[85] *Shemot* 1:7

[86] In this sense, the continual "hardening of Pharaoh's heart" can be understood conceptually as a way of building up the pressure on *Mitzraim*, both to its own destruction and to pave the way for a more explosive/decisive exit from *Mitzraim* by *Am Yisrael*.

[87] The word חרות (freedom) does not appear in Tanach, and its origins are unclear. However, it bears a suggestive similarity to the root חרה, which generally means "flare with anger." Perhaps in the same way the English word "flare" connotes both "burning" as well as "opening outward," we can say the same for חרה. Thus, the expression חרון אף, aside from meaning "burning anger," would translate more literally to "flaring nostril," as in a person's nostrils opening outward in the heat of rage. In the same sense, חרות can be conceptualized as the movement of "opening outward," being freed up from a state of closedness, confinement.

[88] As it says, שָׁמוֹר אֶת חֹדֶשׁ הָאָבִיב וְעָשִׂיתָ פֶּסַח לַה' אֱ-לֹהֶיךָ (*Devarim* 16:1). See also *Shemot* 13:4, 23:15, 34:18.

the standpoint of the Exodus narrative but also in terms of cycles in nature and agriculture, Pesach is a time of *bracha*, expansion.

Sukkot and Aggregation

Sukkot is on the exact opposite end of the calendar. It is a time not of proliferation and spreading outward, but of concentration, aggregation, drawing inward. Whereas Pesach is characterized by *bracha*, Sukkot is characterized by *kedusha*. The word *sukkah* (lit., covering or shelter) is in fact used to refer to the *Mikdash* (the locus of *kedusha*), as it says:

בַּיּוֹם הַהוּא אָקִים אֶת סֻכַּת דָּוִיד הַנֹּפֶלֶת

"On that day, I will erect the fallen Sukkah of David"[89]

Why is the *Mikdash* likened to a *sukkah*? The Talmud cites an opinion that the *sukkot* (shelters) that protected the Israelites in the desert were actually the *Ananei HaKavod* (clouds of glory).[90] And the *Anan* (cloud) is said to rest on the *Mishkan*:

וּבְיוֹם הָקִים אֶת הַמִּשְׁכָּן כִּסָּה הֶעָנָן אֶת הַמִּשְׁכָּן

"On the day the Mishkan was erected, the cloud covered the Mishkan."[91]

In other words, when the *Mikdash* is referred to as a "*sukkah*," it can be taken as a reference to the *Anan HaKavod*, which is described as covering the *Mikdash* and imparting it with *kedusha*.[92] Likewise, the *sukkot* we

---

[89] *Amos* 9:11, referring to the Temple that had been destroyed.

[90] See *Sukkah* 11b. This opinion is supported by *Yeshayahu* 4:5–6, which explicitly refers to the *Ananei HaKavod* as a "*sukkah*". The other opinion says that they were literal shelters, booths. Rashi and Ramban are among those who choose the *Ananei HaKavod* explanation (see their comments on *Vayikra* 23:42). A straightforward connection between *sukkot* and *Ananei HaKavod* is that both clouds and booths serve to provide shelter from the sun, a welcome relief from the brutal desert heat. Indeed, the holiday of Sukkot comes at a time of the year when clouds reemerge and the invigorating cool of autumn returns.

[91] *Bamidbar* 9:15. The Torah itself refers not to "*ananei hakavod*" (in the plural) but to a single "*amud he'anan*," a "column of cloud" that appears as a cloud by day and fire by night (perhaps similar to a wildfire, where during the day the flames are obscured by smoke, and at night the flames are prominent and the smoke is obscured). This cloud is described as protecting the Israelites from the Egyptians, leading the way through the desert, and resting on the *Mishkan*. The Midrash however refers to multiple *ananei hakavod*, several clouds that served separate functions, one of which rested on the *Mishkan*. (See *Bamidbar Rabbah* 1:2, and *Mechilta d'Rashbi* 13.)

[92] As it says, וְנִקְדַּשׁ בִּכְבֹדִי (*Shemot* 29:43).

build and reside in today are seen in Kabbalah as reproducing the effect of the *Ananei HaKavod*, creating a focused, high-intensity space of *kedusha*.[93]

Furthermore, Sukkot is called the *"zman simchateinu,"* the "time of our joy." *Simcha* is a state of concentrated positive energy, intense joy. Also, Sukkot comes in the fall, the season of aggregation. It is called the *chag ha'asif* (holiday of ingathering).[94] We gather in the harvest, take in the food that will carry us through the winter. Autumn is when leaves and seeds fall from the trees, drawn back into the ground to start the process of growth once again. So from a Torah-thematic point of view, as well as from the perspectives of nature and agriculture, Sukkot is seen as a time of coalescing, drawing inward, becoming more focused, more intense. It is a time of *kedusha*.

Cycling Between Bracha and Kedusha

The seasonal movement between Pesach and Sukkot is a continuous cycle of *bracha* and *kedusha*. Pesach is the time of peak expansiveness, proliferation and movement outward. After the Pesach period, the process of compression and drawing inward begins. This process culminates in Sukkot, a time of peak concentration, aggregation and intensity. Following the Sukkot period, the process of expansion begins once again, culminating in Pesach, and so on. It might be thought of as a sort of national "respiration," cycling between a breath in and breath out, inspiration and expiration.

Fig. 10   Pesach / Sukkot cycle – Bracha and Kedusha

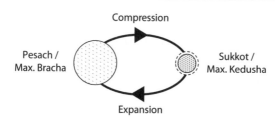

---

[93] See the Arizal's *Sha'ar HaKavanot*, glosses on *Chag HaSukkot*.
[94] See *Shemot* 34:22.

Expansion and Contraction of Time and Sephirot

Although we typically speak about the "three pilgrimages" (*shalosh regalim*) as encompassing three holidays—Pesach, Shavuot and Sukkot—in fact it is four holidays, the fourth being Shemini Atzeret. The reason it is not called the "*arba* (four) *regalim*" is that Sukkot runs immediately into Shemini Atzeret, so there is no need for an additional pilgrimage—the person is already on site, in Jerusalem. So really it is four holidays in two primary cycles. One cycle begins with Pesach and culminates in Shavuot. The other begins with Sukkot and culminates in Shemini Atzeret. The Pesach cycle is expanded, comprised of seven weeks followed by a *moed* (holiday), and the Sukkot cycle is compressed, consisting of seven days followed by a *moed*.[95]

This contrast of expansion and contraction is also apparent in the *sephirot* correspondences within each cycle. On each of the seven days of Sukkot, we invite into the *sukkah* one of the seven "guests" (*ushpizin*), and each guest is associated with one of the seven "lower *sephirot*," as follows:

Fig. 11   Sukkot/Sephirot correspondences

Day	Guest	Sephira
1	Avraham Avinu	Chesed
2	Yitzchak Avinu	Gevura
3	Ya'akov Avinu	Tiferet
4	Moshe Rabbeinu	Netzach
5	Aharon HaKohen	Hod
6	Yosef HaTzadik	Yesod
7	David HaMelech	Malchut
8	(Shemini Atzeret)	

During the Omer, between Pesach and Shavuot, this time is expanded, multiplied to the power of two. Rather than seven days, the

---

[95] There is an additional *yom tov* on the seventh day of Pesach, but it is not a separate *moed*/holiday. It is the only *yom tov* when the "*Shehechianu*" *bracha* is not recited. The seventh day of Pesach is a *yom tov* to "cap" the end of Pesach with *kedusha*. The end of Sukkot has no similar cap, since Shemini Atzeret already serves that function.

period is seven days times seven—forty-nine days.[96] The *sephirot* expand correspondingly. Each week is associated with a primary *sephira*, and each day within that week is associated with a secondary *sephira*, as follows:

Fig. 12   Omer/Sephirot correspondences

Week	Sephira	Day	Sephira Expansion
1	Chesed	1	Chesed
		2	Gevura
		3	Tiferet
		4	Netzach
		5	Hod
		6	Yesod
		7	Malchut
2	Gevura	8	Chesed
		9	Gevura
		10	Tiferet
		11	Netzach
		12	Hod
		13	Yesod
		14	Malchut
...week 3=Tiferet, 4=Netzach, etc...			
8	(Shavuot)	50	

The period from Pesach to Shavuot is again exemplified as one of *bracha*, multiplicity, shown by the expansion of time (7x7) and expansion of the number of *sephirot* (7x7). By contrast, the period between Sukkot and Shemini Atzeret is one of *kedusha*, concentration. The holiday is compressed into seven days, and the number of *sephirot* is correspondingly condensed.

[96] See Ramban on *Vayikra* 23:36, who refers to the forty-nine days leading up to Shavuot as being כחולו של מועד בין הראשון והשמיני בחג, like the *chol hamoed* of Sukkot leading up to Shmini Atzeret.

Kedusha and Bracha – Intensity and Release

The cycling back and forth of *kedusha* and *bracha* echoes what we spoke about in the first chapter regarding the dynamics of *simcha* and *ahava*, where the intensity of joy is radiated and projected outward in the form of love, and where that love is experienced by the other as joy, and so on.[97] When something is *kadosh*, concentrated and brimming with life-energy, it can—and often needs to—spill over in order to alleviate the pressure and intensity. This spilling over, expansion, dissemination of one's "energy" outward, is the action of *bracha*.

Bracha and Kedusha as a Wave

We might look at a wave as a metaphor for expressing the concepts of *bracha* and *kedusha*. *Bracha* would correspond to amplitude, the size (expanse) of the wave crest or wave trough. The more *bracha*, the greater the volume or range of influence the wave possesses. *Kedusha* would correspond to wavelength, the distance between crests. The more the wavelength is restricted, compressed, the more *kedusha*, the greater the frequency (cycles per second), and the more energy is carried by the wave.

Fig. 13   Bracha and Kedusha expressed as a wave

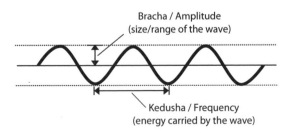

Bracha / Amplitude
(size/range of the wave)

Kedusha / Frequency
(energy carried by the wave)

We will now move on to examining the *bracha* formula, *"Baruch atah Hashem...,"* as recited in the morning *brachot* and elsewhere.

---

[97] See p. 30.

Baruch Atah Hashem
ברוך אתה ה׳

בָּרוּךְ אַתָּה ה׳ אֱ-לֹהֵינוּ מֶלֶךְ הָעוֹלָם, אֲשֶׁר קִדְּשָׁנוּ בְּמִצְוֹתָיו...

Every *bracha* we recite contains the formula *"Baruch atah Hashem."* These words are what make it a *"bracha"* per se, as opposed to any other *tefila* (prayer). The question is, what exactly does the phrase *baruch atah Hashem* mean? What is a *bracha* intended to convey?

בָּרוּךְ אַתָּה ה׳
Be expanded, You Hashem

Baruch – Description or Action?

The words *baruch atah* are typically translated "blessed are you." In the previous chapter, we discussed the concept of *bracha* (blessing) in terms of expansion, proliferation, dissemination and multiplicity. Accordingly, this could yield translations such as "expanded are you" or "multiplied/bountiful are you." But whether "blessed are you" or "expanded are you," the translation assumes the word *baruch* to be a descriptive term, i.e., characterizing *Hashem* as being inherently blessed or expanded.[1] The question is, does the term *baruch* connote a description, or does it convey an action? Does it *describe* that which already has *bracha*, or is it intended to *confer* a *bracha*, bring about a new state of *bracha*? Should it be "blessed *are* you, or does "blessed *be* you" better convey the concept?

---

[1] The phrase "inherently blessed" is important to note here. Ibn Ezra (on *Shemot* 18:10) makes the point that where the word ברוך is used in Tanach to refer to *Hashem*, it should be understood as an adjective, describing the inherent quality of *Hashem*, as "blessed," and not as a passive participle, meaning "blessed by another," as ברוך is sometimes used to imply. Abudraham (R. David Abu Dirham, commentary on *Birchot HaShachar*) expresses a similar idea about ברוך, and adds: שהוא עצמו הוא מקור הברכות ואינו מקבלם מאחרים, "because He Himself is the source of *brachot* and does not receive from others."

There are cases in Tanach where the word *baruch* clearly connotes a description, "*is* blessed," as in the *pasuk*:

לֹא תָאֹר אֶת הָעָם כִּי בָרוּךְ הוּא

"You will not curse the people, because it is blessed"[2]

However, some instances of *baruch*—notably including the phrase "*baruch atah*"—may also imply the more active "*be* blessed," as in:

בָּרוּךְ אַתָּה בְּנִי דָוִד, גַּם עָשֹׂה תַעֲשֶׂה וְגַם יָכֹל תּוּכָל

*"Blessed be you, my son David—you will surely do it
and you will also surely succeed"*[3]

Here, the phrase *baruch atah* can either be understood as Shaul HaMelech (King Saul) reassuring David, "You *are* blessed," or alternatively it can be taken as Shaul giving a *bracha* to David: "May you *be* blessed." The latter interpretation of *baruch atah* is strongly implied in other *psukim*, such as:

בָּרוּךְ אַתָּה בָּעִיר וּבָרוּךְ אַתָּה בַּשָּׂדֶה.

"Blessed be you be in the city, and blessed be you be in the field."[4]

This is one of many blessings promised to *Bnei Yisrael* contingent upon their following the commandments. Moreover, they are still in the desert, having no cities and no fields. So it cannot be saying "blessed *are* you," describing *Bnei Yisrael* in the present. Rather, the statement refers to the future and is meant to *confer* a blessing, as in "may you be blessed" or "blessed shall you be" (i.e., equivalent to the expression "*baruch tihyeh*").[5]

So there is strong precedent in Tanach for the phrase *baruch atah* to refer not to the description "blessed are you" but rather to the actual conferring of a blessing. This of course begs the question: If "*baruch atah*" commonly connotes "may you be blessed," how then do we regard the expression "*baruch atah Hashem*"? Is there such a thing as "conveying a *bracha*" to *Hashem*? Classical sources seem to imply that there is.

---

[2] *Bamidbar* 22:12
[3] *I Shmuel* 26:25
[4] *Devarim* 28:3
[5] Jewish English translations generally render "*baruch atah*" here as "blessed shall you be" or similar. See e.g., JPS Tanach, Koren Tanach, Artscroll *Stone Edition* Tanach, and *The Living Torah* (R. Aryeh Kaplan).

The Talmud relates the story of Rabbi Yishmael ben Elisha, *Kohen Gadol* (High Priest), who enters the Temple on Yom Kippur and encounters *Hashem*.[6] *Hashem* then asks Rabbi Yishmael for a *bracha*:

ואמר לי, ישמעאל בני ברכני, אמרתי לו, יהי רצון מלפניך
שיכבשו רחמיך את כעסך ויגולו רחמיך על מדותיך

"And He said to me: 'Yishmael my son, bless Me.'
I said to Him: 'May it be Your will that Your rachamim extinguishes Your anger,
and may Your rachamim prevail over Your [other] attributes'."[7]

The *bracha* given by Rabbi Yishmael is not a statement praising *Hashem* as being "inherently blessed." It is clearly intended to *impart* a *bracha*.

Traditional sources view the phrase *baruch atah Hashem*, like the above *bracha*, to be more than a statement of praise or thanks. It is intended to convey multiplicity and increase.[8] Yet classical commentators also reject the notion that a *bracha* serves to "add to" *Hashem*.[9] *Hashem* is called the "source of *bracha*," which cannot itself be increased. How then do we understand "multiplicity" where it comes to giving a *bracha* to *Hashem*?

Looking more carefully at the above quote, we see that Rabbi Yishmael's *bracha* expresses the desire that *Hashem* be manifested in the world with *rachamim*/compassion. It is in effect saying: "May *rachamim* be multiplied." The answer then is that giving a *bracha* to *Hashem* is not understood as adding *to* the source but rather drawing *from* the source and thereby adding to the world. The Zohar states this concept explicitly:

דברכאן דבריך בר נש לקב"ה, לאמשכא חיין ממקורא דחיי

"When a person blesses Hashem, [it is] to draw life from the source of life"[10]

The Zohar explains that this "life" is drawn to *Hashem*'s name, then rests on the person making the *bracha*, and from there spreads throughout the world. We might think of it as a visualization, whose purpose is to bring

[6] The text describes R. Yishmael as seeing "*Achatriel Kah Hashem Tzva-ot*," a name that suggests the "crown of *Hashem*," i.e., a vision of *Hashem*'s majesty (see Maharsha, *Brachot* 7a).

[7] *Brachot* 7a. *Hashem* then nods in affirmation of the *bracha*, which Rashi says is the equivalent of saying "*Amen*."

[8] As in, אינה הודאה בלבד אבל הוא לשון תוספת ורבוי (Rabbeinu Bachye on *Devarim* 8:10), and אינו לשון הודיה בעלמא אלא לשון תוספת השפעה (*Ha'emek Davar, Bereshit* 24:27, see *Harchev Davar*).

[9] As in, אין המשמעות לפי הדזומה להוסיף ברכה במי שאיננו צריך לשום תוספת חלילה (*Sefer Hachinuch, Parshat Eikev, Mitzva* 430). Also, אין הכוונה לעצמות אדון יחיד ב"ה חלילה (*Nefesh Hachaim* 2:2).

[10] *Zohar, Raya Mehemna, Parshat Ekev*; also quoted in *Nefesh Hachaim* 2:2.

the will for Life into our consciousness, and to instill within us a sense of responsibility to ensure that life prevails in the world.[11]

Thus, the words *baruch atah Hashem* can be understood not only in the descriptive sense of *Hashem* being the source of *bracha*, but also in the active sense of imparting a *bracha*. To say "*baruch atah Hashem*" is to evoke expansion and propagation—"Be expanded, You *Hashem*," i.e., "May life be expanded," may *chaim* be proliferated and the Life principle be amplified, and directed toward all those places in need of enlivening.[12]

Rachamim and Rechem – Nurturing Life

We have spoken about *Hashem* as the source of life, the vital/animating force which permeates all living creatures and all matter. This quality is particularly carried by the name "*Hashem*," the *shem Hashem* or Tetragrammaton (י-ה-ו-ה), also called the "*Shem Havaya*" (lit., the "name of being"). The *shem Hashem* is understood in the Torah tradition to be associated with *rachamim* (רחמים), "compassion."[13] *Rachamim* is generally thought to derive from the word *rechem* (רחם), meaning "womb."[14] Just as a fetus in the womb is continually nourished by the input of life-giving energy, without consideration as to "deservingness" but simply

---

[11] See also Rabbeinu Bachye, who says that when we make a *bracha*, יתברכו כל בריותיו ממנו (commentary on *Devarim* 8:10) and יהיה העולם שבע רצון ומלא ברכת ה' (*Kad Hakemach*). Also see R. Chaim Vital, *Pri Etz Chaim, Sha'ar Habrachot* Ch. 3, who explains the phrase *baruch atah Hashem* as initiating a flow of *shefa* (bounty, abundance) into the world.

[12] The above connotation of *baruch* has implications for a number of related expressions. For instance, the phrase ברוך ה' (typically rendered "Blessed is *Hashem*") can be understood to mean, "May *Hashem* (life/vitality) be propagated." Likewise, the term הקדוש ברוך הוא (generally translated "The Holy One, Blessed Is He") could more precisely mean: "The intensely concentrated life-energy (הקדוש)—may it be propagated (ברוך הוא)." The same can be said of the central statement in *Kaddish*, יהא שמיה רבא מברך, such that it translates to: "May His great name/legacy be propagated." The term שמה רבה, the "great name," refers to the *shem Hashem*, the name that bears the legacy and will for Life. Thus, *Kaddish* can be understood as expressing the desire that Life be propagated (making it all the more apt for a mourner to recite). Likewise, after the first *pasuk* of *Shema*, we say: ברוך שם כבוד מלכותו, "May the *shem kevod malchuto* be propagated." The "*shem kevod malchuto*" again refers to the *shem Hashem*, the life-legacy, which when imparted brings about כבוד מלכות, the glorious aura of the reign of Life.

[13] As stated in the Midrash: כל מקום שנאמר ה' זו מדת הרחמים שנאמר ה' ה' א-ל רחום וחנון (*Sifri Devarim, Parshat Va'etchanan* 26, quoting *Shemot* 34:6). Also: אין ה' אלא מדת הרחמים (*Tanchuma Buber, Parshat Tazria* 11).

[14] See the entry for רחמים, *Brown-Driver-Briggs Lexicon*.

to nurture life, so too is the world constantly nourished, sustained and enlivened. This enlivening *rachamim* is intimated by the *shem Hashem*. Thus, the phrase *"Baruch atah Hashem"* expresses the desire that *rachamim* be proliferated, that life-giving energy should flow throughout the world, nourish us, vitalize us and satisfy our needs—as if we were a fetus in the womb, i.e., without consideration as to whether or not we are "deserving."

Baruch Atah Hashem as an Act of Creation

The phrase *baruch atah Hashem* conceptually speaking replicates the act of Creation. It conveys the desire to have life-energy expand, propagate and fill otherwise lifeless space. That "space" also refers to human consciousness, infusing the will for Life into our mindset and our thoughts, so that we do more to make life manifest in the world.

We might say then that a *bracha* from the Creator equals *kedusha* for the Creation. When we make a *bracha*, expressing the desire for life-energy to propagate outward, the intended result is *kedusha*, an infusion of life-energy inward—upon us, as individuals and as a society.

Fig. 14   Baruch Atah Hashem – Invoking Bracha and Kedusha

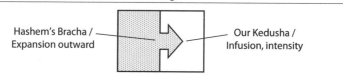

Hashem's Bracha / Expansion outward — Our Kedusha / Infusion, intensity

Know however that the idea of the words *"baruch atah Hashem"* imparting *kedusha* to the world is not intended to suggest a direct cause-and-effect relationship. While some may assert just that, i.e., that the very act of pronouncing a *bracha* creates an "effect" in the world, what is being intimated here is merely (but also significantly) that the *brachot* we say have the capacity to positively impact our *consciousness*.[15] The extent to which saying *brachot* leads to greater life-energy and *kedusha* "in the world" depends ultimately—and indeed *solely*—on whether our think-

---

[15] As such, the descriptions given in Kabbalah of what the words *baruch atah Hashem* "do" might be thought of not as assertions regarding unseen metaphysical processes, but rather as tools of visualization and *kavana* to help focus our thoughts constructively.

ing translates into positive action and interaction in the world. It is a task that requires an ongoing effort—not simply a formulaic recitation.

אֱ-לֹהֵינוּ
Our Conscious Guide

Elokim as a Template for the Mind

The word *Elokim*[16] is generally translated "God." However, given the various contexts in which the word "*elohim*" is used in the Torah (referring not just to "gods" but also to judges and leaders), and given the traditional interpretation of the name "*Elokim*" (as expressing *din*, the function of judgment and distinction), the word begs a more precise definition.

Elokim is that which provides conscious input, analysis and judgment, which renders decisions, dictates morality and generates a mental map for us to follow. In short, *Elokim* is what one might call a "conscious guide." This is, in any case, what people often look to God for—to guide their conscience, clarify notions of good and bad, what to do and what not to do. The concept of *Elokim/elohim* connotes a filter on the mind, a template for good/bad ethics and judgment. It also conveys the ability to delineate and analyze.

Din – Judgment and Distinction

The name *Elokim* is understood in the Torah tradition as evoking *din*, the judgment-making function.[17] In fact the Torah explicitly refers to human judges as *elohim*:

אֲשֶׁר יַרְשִׁיעֻן אֱלֹהִים יְשַׁלֵּם שְׁנַיִם לְרֵעֵהוּ
"[The litigant] whom the judges deem liable will pay double to his fellow."[18]

A "judge" is one who has the knowledge/ability to weigh and calculate a number of factors relevant to a given case, and to compute a precise result in accordance with the rules of the law. When we speak about the "judgment" of *din*, in theory this is a quantitative, analytical process,

---

[16] See p. 37, Note 1, regarding the transliteration "*Elokim*."

[17] As stated in the Midrash, כל מקום שנאמר א-להים זו מדת הדין שנאמר עד האלהים יבוא דבר שניהם (*Sifri Devarim, Parshat Va'etchanan* 26, quoting *Shemot* 22:8).

[18] *Shemot* 22:8. See also 22:7, and 21:6 where Rashi interprets *ha'elohim* as "*beit din*."

weighing the factors of the case, and having nothing to do with praise or condemnation of the litigants. (Indeed, judges are enjoined to be impartial, showing no favoritism to litigants based on factors such as social standing or wealth.[19]) Likewise, the word *dinim* (judgments) in some contexts is technically defined as "quantitative distinctions" or "discrete gradations."[20] So not only do the terms *din* and *Elokim* evoke ethics, judgment of good and bad, but they also imply analysis and distinction.

Left, Right and Middle

In the *sephirot* map, *din* is sometimes brought in place of *"gevura"* —the strength of restraint, withholding and delineation (which is the opposite of *"chesed"* —giving, flowing and allowing). The function of *din* is to draw a hard line between two things, or two litigants, to create a distinction between them. *Din* and *gevura* are the strength or energy required to generate and maintain borders, distinctions, to work against the natural tendency toward entropy and chaos, against allowing things to simply run their default course. Both are attributes of structure, organization and delineation—conscious intervention.

As a general rule, the *sephirot* on the "left" side of the map (*bina, gevura* and *hod*) have the function of separating, distinguishing and mitigating—defining limits. The *sephirot* on the "right" (*chochma, chesed* and *netzach*) by contrast convey unbridled vitality and flow. The left side acts to process/channel the right side so as to produce a usable result.[21] That result is found in the middle set of *sephirot* (*da'at, tiferet* and *yesod*, and ultimately *malchut*[22]). The left set relationally corresponds to *Elokim* and the right set to *Hashem*.[23] To put it in more down-to-earth terms, the goal

---

[19] As it says, לא תכירו פנים במשפט (*Devarim* 1:17), that a judge may not favor a litigant. (See also 16:19.)

[20] See e.g., *Sulam* (R. Yehuda Ashlag) on *Zohar* 1:1, which speaks of *"dinim"* as gradations, and the *"ko'ach hadin"* as that which creates *tzimtzum*/distinction.

[21] In this sense, the middle set of *sephirot* is less of a "balance" or "harmony" of right and left than it is a product generated by left processing right. As an analogy, the flow of water through a pipe is not a "balance" of water and pipe. Rather, it is the useful result of a pipe channeling and conducting water.

[22] *Malchut* is the result of the entire working system rather than the product of any particular pair of *sephirot*.

[23] In the Kabbalah tradition, each of the *sephirot* corresponds to a different *shem*. In general, the left-set of *sephirot* is associated with formulations of the name *Elokim*, con-

is for our various energies (intellectual, emotional, etc.) to be channeled and focused such that they yield maximum vitality.

Elokim and Hashem – Etz HaDa'at and Etz HaChaim

In the *chochma-bina-da'at* group, *chochma* (thought/wisdom) is a right-side/*Hashem* function. *Bina* (discernment) is a left-side/*Elokim* function. *Da'at* (awareness/knowledge) is the product of right and left. However, that distinction holds only when the three *sephirot* are looked at relative to one another. When the entire mental domain is discussed relative to other domains of life (emotions, actions, etc.), all three *sephirot*—*chochma*, *bina* and *da'at*—fall under the *Elokim* category, as the *pasuk* implies:

וָאֲמַלֵּא אֹתוֹ רוּחַ אֱ-לֹהִים בְּחָכְמָה וּבִתְבוּנָה וּבְדַעַת

"and I will fill him with the spirit of Elokim—
with chochma, tevuna [bina] and da'at"[24]

The name *Elokim* is associated with any weighing and considering, justifying and reasoning, and any moral judgment of good and bad. This definition is first given in the Garden of Eden story. The double name *Hashem-Elokim* is used throughout the Eden narrative, with the exception of one *pasuk*:

וִהְיִיתֶם כֵּא-לֹהִים יֹדְעֵי טוֹב וָרָע

"and you will be like Elokim, knowing good and bad"[25]

The Torah specifically makes the point of associating the name *Elokim* with *da'at tov vara* (awareness of good and bad). That is to say, *Elokim* relates to the faculty of *da'at*, conscious awareness. This consciousness—having within it the component of *bina* (discernment)—is binary, built on plurality, the ability to distinguish between one thing and the next. The word *Elokim* itself is in the plural, intimating that the mind, the function of judgment, operates in the frame of pluralities and distinctions.

By defining *Elokim*, we also back into a definition of *Hashem*. Since the name *Elokim* is explicitly linked with *da'at* and the *Etz HaDa'at* (the Tree of Knowledge), by implication the name *Hashem* is linked with

---

veying delineation and distinction, whereas the right-set is associated with formulations of *Hashem* (the *shem Havaya* and *E-l*), connoting power and flow.

[24] *Shemot* 31:3; see also 35:31.
[25] *Bereshit* 3:5

chaim and the *Etz HaChaim* (the Tree of Life).[26] *Elokim* relates to the binary model of judgment, conscious distinction, plurality, comparison, self-consciousness and reflection. *Hashem* by contrast is *"echad"* (one), evoking a holistic picture—flow of life and energy, simply "being," experiencing, without any judgment or analysis. The *shem Hashem* is also called the *"shem Havaya," havaya* meaning "being," existing.

In sum, *Elokim* connotes consciousness, judgment and analysis. *Hashem* connotes energy, life and being. One is *da'at* and *din*, the other *chaim* and *rachamim*.[27] And by extension, whereas *Elokim* is associated with processes that are linear, logical and largely predictable, *Hashem* is associated with that which is non-linear, chaotic, entropic and largely unpredictable. We see this lack of predictability exemplified in the famous response to Moshe, who is unsure of what he should say when the people inquire about *Hashem*, "What is His name?":

אֶהְיֶה אֲשֶׁר אֶהְיֶה, וַיֹּאמֶר כֹּה תֹאמַר
לִבְנֵי יִשְׂרָאֵל, אֶהְיֶה שְׁלָחַנִי אֲלֵיכֶם

*"I will be whatever I will be; and He said: Thus will you say
to the Children of Israel—I-Will-Be sent me to you"*[28]

---

[26] The *Etz HaChaim* and the *Etz HaDa'at* are the two trees singled out by name in the Garden of Eden narrative. Both play a central role in the story of humankind, and indeed both are described as being located "in the center of the garden" (see *Bereshit* 2:9 and 3:3).

[27] We have been discussing *rachamim* and *din* as opposites. Indeed they are explicitly referred to as הפכים ("opposites") in classical sources (see e.g., Alshich, *Devarim* 3; and Shelah, *Toldot Adam, Beit Yisrael*). Likewise, the Midrash frequently employs the phrase מהפכין מדת הדין למדת הרחמים (and vice-versa). In Kabbalah however, particularly in the *sephirot* model, *din* is often depicted not as the opposite of *rachamim* but as the opposite of *chesed*. *Rachamim*, in this picture, is viewed as the *product* of *din* and *chesed*. It is the end result, where judgment has been tempered and softened with kindness. But this difference does not pose a conceptual contradiction. Rather, these are simply two different models with two systems of terminology. In both models, there is a process that is concerned solely with what a person "deserves," whose focus is on the notion of "good and bad." This is referred to in both cases as *"din."* And in both models, there is a process that involves stepping outside of the mindset of "deservingness," beyond delineations of good and bad—to simply act for Life. In one system this process is referred to as *"rachamim,"* and in the other system the term used is *"chesed."* But the concept is the same.

[28] *Shemot* 3:14. The future tense rendering of *ehyeh* ("I will be") follows Rashi. Alternatively, *ehyeh* might be understood to mean "let me be" (in the jussive mood, as in יהי, "let there be"), so that *ehyeh asher ehyeh* translates to "Let Me be whatever I will be."

Unlike *Elokim*, which implies exactitude, certainty, and mathematical predictability, *Ehyeh Asher Eyheh* ("I will be whatever I will be") implies lack of certainty, a future deliberately left open. This factor of unpredictability and indeterminacy, spontaneity and surprise, is characteristic of *chaim*/Life. It is the property of *Hashem*, as distinct from *Elokim*.

Interdependence of Hashem and Elokim

In strict conceptual terms, *Elokim* without the vitality and spontaneity of *Hashem* is empty, devoid of life-input. *Hashem* without the conscious input of *Elokim* is directionless, chaotic. An overdominance of the *Elokim*-attribute, when localized within a person, might be characterized by someone who is overly rules-oriented, so obsessed with the need for structure and predictability that it stifles the person's vitality. An overdominance of the *Hashem*-attribute within a person could be characterized by one who is so spontaneous as to be unreliable, overlooking rules of basic civility, lacking boundaries and self-control. (The irony is that despite *Hashem* connoting life-energy and vitality, any such energy not channeled properly has the capacity to become destructive, an *anti-life* force.) The double name *Hashem-Elokim* implies life-energy being filtered and directed through consciousness. It is vitality and spontaneity expressed fully, but within distinct bounds, allowing it to be channeled constructively.

The phrase *Hashem Elokeinu* (lit., "*Hashem* is our *Elokim*") can thus be understood to mean that Life is our conscious guide, our mental template. To say this phrase in *tefila* is to declare our thoughts and actions, our will and ethical norms, to be *meshubad* (beholden, linked) to the singular organizing principle of protecting, maintaining, amplifying and propagating Life. The phrase *Hashem Elokeinu* therefore reflects our desire and commitment to be instruments of the will for Life.

Elokim and Creation in the Mind

We described *Elokim* as being associated with consciousness, and in particular with using the mind to create distinctions. Indeed the name *Elokim* is the one used in the Creation narrative, which is characterized by distinction-making—between *shamayim* and *eretz*, *ohr* and *choshech*, sea and land, and so on. In addition, we discussed the idea of the *tzimtzum* (the initial distinction between *ohr* and non-*ohr*) as the first act of Creation, and as a process occurring within consciousness.[29] What all this suggests is a concept of Creation that sees the world not only as being built *with* consciousness, but also as residing *within* the "mind-space" of the Creator.

The Ramban[30] in fact proposes that the first phrase of the Torah, "*Bereshit bara Elokim*" (בראשית ברא א-להים), can alternatively be read as "*Barosh yitbarei Elokim*" (בראש יתברא א-להים).[31] *Barosh* connotes "at first" or more literally "with (or within) the head," i.e., the "mind." The word *yitbarei* might best translate to: "it began to create itself."[32] Thus the full phrase, parsed according to the Ramban, could be translated as follows: "With(in) the mind, *Elokim* began to create itself."

This effectively renders *Elokim* as the "producer" of Creation, as well as the "product" of Creation. As strange as it sounds, we might say it could be no other way. No initial distinction—no *tzimtzum*—is possible without the distinction-making ability. No Creation is possible without *Elokim*, consciousness. Yet at the same time, without an initial distinction, if all we have is an utterly uniform "*ohr*," there is no consciousness whatsoever. Without the *tzimtzum*, there is no *Elokim*, no capacity for distinction. Thus, in this model, *Elokim* and the *tzimtzum* seem to emerge *simultaneously*. But emerge from what? Perhaps this is what the Kabbalah refers to as "*ratzon*," the spontaneous "will" for existence.[33] Following a singular burst of *ratzon*, *Elokim*/consciousness "began to create itself." It "began" in the sense that the process of Creation was initiated with the *tzimtzum*, but it is a process that is ongoing, continuing even now, in our own consciousness, with every distinction we make.

---

[29] See p. 57, regarding Creation, *tzimtzum* and drawing distinctions in consciousness.

[30] R. Moshe ben Nachman (1194–1270), preeminent Torah commentator.

[31] See Ramban's introduction to *Sefer Bereshit*, where he references this parsing of the *pasuk* as an example of the possible letter/word permutations throughout the Torah text.

[32] The word יִתְבָּרֵא is a theoretical construction. No reflexive verb להתברא ("to create oneself") exists in Biblical or modern Hebrew. The translation "began to create" renders יִתְבָּרֵא in the "incipient past imperfect" tense, implying an action that began and is ongoing. (See *Biblical Hebrew Syntax*, Waltke & O'Connor, p. 503.) In this context, יִתְבָּרֵא suggests an ongoing, open-ended process of creation.

[33] In Kabbalah, *ratzon* is equated with the *sephira* of *keter* ("crown"). Just as a crown rests above the head, so too *ratzon/keter* is "above the mind," i.e., pre-conscious. It is pure spontaneity, meaning it is a will that is not "caused" by anything preexisting within the mind. This is the theoretical *ratzon* that we may understand as precipitating Creation according to this model.

Tzelem Elokim and the Distinctiveness of Humans

The Torah states regarding human beings:

וַיִּבְרָא אֱ-לֹהִים אֶת הָאָדָם בְּצַלְמוֹ בְּצֶלֶם אֱ-לֹהִים בָּרָא אֹתוֹ

"and Elokim created the human in His image;
in the image of Elokim He created him"[34]

The translation most of us are familiar with has human beings created "in the image of God." However, the phrase is more precisely translated "in the image of *Elokim*," which has a different connotation. To be created in the image of *Elokim* implies the capacity for abstract conscious thought.[35] That includes the distinction-making faculty of *din*, the awareness of "self vs. other"—and "good vs. bad"—associated with *da'at*, and ultimately the ability to use the mind to *create*.

That is to say, whereas countless living creatures on Earth have brains, human beings possess the distinctive ability to use the brain to weigh and analyze, calculate and reason, and to reflect prior to acting—as opposed to operating purely out of instinctive, action-reaction, stimulus-response mechanisms. All creatures are built in the *"tzelem Hashem"*—all are living, breathing, moving, filled with energy and vitality. They are *ba'alei chaim*, "possessors of life." But humans also have the *tzelem Elokim*, the capacity to think abstractly and create worlds with the mind, and indeed *within* the mind. Human beings are *ba'alei chaim vada'at*, possessors of life and consciousness.[36]

Elohim Acherim – Other Forms of Consciousness

When we refer to *Hashem* as *"Elokeinu,"* we are designating/affirming *"Hashem*-consciousness" (in the form of the *Torat chaim*, the Life principle in all its instructions) as *our* consciousness. This is the lens through which we choose to filter life experience and allow to shape our thinking and our actions. At the same time, we are by implication speaking about this consciousness as distinct from *elohim acherim*, "other gods."

The Torah forbids idolatry in no uncertain terms. But aside from the plain meaning of *avoda zara* (idolatry, lit., "foreign worship") as re-

---

[34] *Bereshit* 1:27

[35] See Rabbeinu Bachye on *Bereshit* 3:5, who says, הצלם הוא השכל. Also see Sforno on *Bereshit* 1:26, יעשה בצלמנו שהוא עצם שכלי ונצחי; and Abarbanel on *Bereshit* 1, הצלם השכלי.

[36] See also p. 167, regarding the *tzelem Elokim* vs. the *tzelem Hashem*.

ferring to following other "deities," we might understand it more conceptually as adopting external influences, "conscious guides" that contravene the Torah's Life principle, that negatively impact our thinking and actions. From that perspective, when the Torah speaks about exercising "judgment" against other *elohim*,[37] as *Hashem* being "greater" than them,[38] and as having none of them come "before" *Hashem*[39] (and we may find it odd that the Torah should speak about such "gods" as if they exist), we can think of it as the attempt to prevent foreign, negative, anti-Life influences from exerting a pull on *Am Yisrael*. That is to say, *Hashem/chaim*, the will for Life, must reign supreme in our consciousness above other influences and pulls, above other ideologies and values.[40] So we say "*Hashem Elokeinu*," and similarly we declare: "*Hashem hu HaElokim*" —*Hashem* is the *Elokim*.[41] Life alone is the ultimate organizing principle for human consciousness.

מֶלֶךְ הָעוֹלָם
Reigning-influence of space/time

Influencing the Unseen Farthest Reaches

The word *olam* (עולם) has both a *spatial* connotation, "world," that which stretches out seemingly without end in all directions, as well as a *temporal* connotation, referring to the "furthest reaches of time" in the past or future.[42] *Olam* is related to the verb *alam* (עלם), to hide or conceal, perhaps suggesting that something which exists in a far distant time or place is "unseen," concealed from us.

---

[37] See *Shemot* 12:12, וּבְכָל אֱלֹהֵי מִצְרַיִם אֶעֱשֶׂה שְׁפָטִים.

[38] See *Shemot* 18:11, עַתָּה יָדַעְתִּי כִּי גָדוֹל ה' מִכָּל הָאֱלֹהִים.

[39] See *Shemot* 20:2, לֹא יִהְיֶה לְךָ אֱלֹהִים אֲחֵרִים עַל פָּנָי.

[40] See p. 221, for further elaboration on the Life principle vs. other values.

[41] Said seven times at the culmination of the Yom Kippur *Ne'ila* service. It is our final—and arguably our ultimate—expression of *teshuva*, in the sense of affirming and rededicating ourselves to the first and highest principle of the Torah system.

[42] Biblical use of עולם almost exclusively regards time, not space in the sense of "world." A possible exception might be the *pasuk*, גַּם אֶת הָעֹלָם נָתַן בְּלִבָּם (*Kohelet* 3:11). However, given the existence of words such as קדם and לפני, both of which are used in Biblical Hebrew to imply "fore" in the sense of "before" (in time) as well as "forward" (directionally)—whereby time is visualized, like space, in three dimensions—there is arguably a linguistic precedent for עולם as well to convey maximal distance of both time and space.

Hashem is the *melech ha'olam*, transmitting influence within the *olam*. According to the *drash* brought earlier, we might say that *Hashem* is "*molich ha'olam*," puts the *olam* into motion, imparts life to the Creation.[43] The picture here is one of animating-energy and vitality permeating the farthest reaches of the world, including all those places that are hidden from our eyes, where no human has ever stepped, corners of Creation yet unseen by any telescope or microscope. This all-pervasive transmission of movement, activity and life has been ongoing since the most remote beginnings of time and will continue into a future far too distant to envision.

The *bracha* until this point (*Baruch atah Hashem Elokeinu melech ha'olam*) is termed "*shem umalchut*." It presents a picture of expansiveness (*baruch*), whereby *chaim* and the will for Life (*Hashem*) propagate inward, impacting and shaping our consciousness (*Elokeinu*), as well as outward, being a dominant influence (*melech*) throughout space and time (*olam*).

אֲשֶׁר קִדְּשָׁנוּ בְּמִצְוֹתָיו
Who has restricted/intensified us through His commands

When a *bracha* is made regarding a *mitzva*, the phrase is added: *asher kideshanu bemitzvotav*, "Who has made us *kadosh* with His *mitzvot*." We spoke earlier about the idea of *Am Yisrael* as an "*am kadosh*," whereby we restrict ourselves in an effort to intensify, focus on and be vehicles for the will for Life—to come alive as individuals, as communities and as a nation. The idea of the *mitzvot* (commandments) is to help us achieve this focus, to assist us in channeling our energies effectively, toward productive, enlivening ends. We can conceptualize this in terms of pressure.

Mitzvot as Addressing Inward and Outward Pressures

Every living system has a metabolism, wherein energy or nutrients are taken in, digested, and waste-products are expelled—a process of input and output. Input to the system is triggered by what we might call "inward pressure," the sensation of lack. Output from the system is initiated by "outward pressure," a feeling of high concentration or excess.

---

[43] See p. 26.

Fig. 15   Inward and outward pressure states

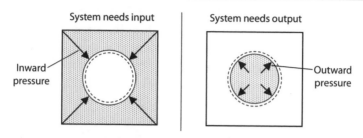

These inward/outward pressures comprise much of our human experience, pervading every area of life: food, emotions, intellect, sexuality, money and so on. Here are just a few examples:

Fig. 16   Human input and output as a function of pressure

Category	Inward pressure	Input	Outward pressure	Output
Food	Hunger	Eating	Fullness	Waste elimination
Money	Poverty	Income	Wealth	Spending/Giving
Intellect	Curiosity	Learning	Ideas	Teaching/Creating
Emotions	Loneliness	Connection	Joy	Love/Kindness
Sexuality	Desire	Intimacy	Excitement	Consummation

Mitzvot and Regulation of Pressure

Just as blood pressure must be maintained within a healthy range—not too high and not too low, so too pressures in all areas of life must be kept within bounds in order for one's energies to flow optimally. Where there is too little pressure, there is stasis, lack of movement, lack of life. Without the pressure of hunger, we would not eat. Without the pressure of the sexual drive, we would stop procreating. Without financial pressure and motivation, we would have no economy. Without emotional pressure, people would not connect with each other. Without intellectual pressure, the mind would stagnate—we could never advance or innovate. *Too much* pressure on the other hand puts undue stress on the system and ultimately wreaks destruction. Hunger that is extreme or prolonged equals starvation. Severe financial lack equals poverty, destitution. Too much sexual impulse makes for preoccupation and unhealthy promiscuity.[44] Joy that builds up with no outlet for love and giving makes for frustration, as do ideas that build up with no outlet for creating or teaching. The Talmud says regarding the need to teach, "More than the calf wants to nurse, the cow wants to give its milk."[45]

Many of the *mitzvot* can be understood as regulating inward and outward pressures. To reduce monetary pressures, we have the *mitzva* of giving *tzedaka*. To reduce sexual pressures, we have *mitzvot* that define relational boundaries as well as limit the amount of sexual stimuli to which we are exposed. To reduce interpersonal emotional pressures, we have *mitzvot* prohibiting us from bearing a grudge, commanding us to ask for and grant forgiveness. Some of these are positive *mitzvot* (to do), some negative (to avoid). Some are preventative and others corrective. By regulating such pressures, we enable proper flow, healthy movement at every level of life—individual, interpersonal, communal and societal. In short, the *mitzvot* are designed to contribute to our overall state of *shalom*. As the *pasuk* says:

לוּא הִקְשַׁבְתָּ לְמִצְוֹתָי וַיְהִי כַנָּהָר שְׁלוֹמֶךָ

"If only you listened to My commands, your shalom would be like a river"[46]

Shalom – Dynamic Equilibrium

The word *shalom* (שלום) is often spoken of as "peace," implying lack of conflict or war. But more generally, *shalom* refers to "soundness," stability, an even-keel state characterized by the experience of well-being and wholeness (as in שָׁלֵם, that which is complete or whole).[47] Indeed, when we inquire as to a person's *shalom*, we are not asking whether the person

---

[44] Note that regarding sexuality, Chazal's suggestion is to "starve it" (see *Sukkah* 52b). But this "starvation" should not be compared to food-related starvation. The latter involves extreme inward pressure—a desperate feeling of lack. When Chazal speak about limiting one's sexual activity, the purpose is to have the exact opposite effect—to *reduce* the sensation of too much inward pressure, to alleviate the feeling of lack (in their words, "מרעיבו שבע"). Their understanding is that in the sexual domain, the more one satisfies it, the more the sensation of hunger is perpetuated ("משביעו רעב"). The same principle can be said for all things that have the capacity for addiction—i.e., that limiting one's exposure helps to minimize the unwanted "pull" that those things exert on a person.

[45] *Pesachim* 112a. The picture is precisely one of built-up pressure, the need for output.

[46] *Yeshayahu* 48:18

[47] See the entries for שלום and שלם in the *Brown-Driver-Briggs Lexicon*.

is at peace or war—we want to know about the person's welfare and well-being, i.e., "Is everything well/stable?"

Shalom can thus be understood as a state of equilibrium. When a system is under pressure, it is "out of *shalom*." When that pressure is released and the system returns to equilibrium, *shalom* is restored.

Fig. 17   Shalom and equilibrium

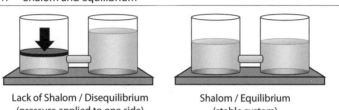

Lack of Shalom / Disequilibrium
(pressure applied to one side)

Shalom / Equilibrium
(stable system)

However, we must fine-tune what we mean by stability, because for living systems, something that is utterly and entirely stable is not in the state of *shalom* either. Total stability equals zero pressure, zero movement, and zero flow of energy. It is completely lifeless.[48] *Shalom* is thus characterized not by total stasis but by a *stable flow*, as we quoted previously, "your *shalom* would be like a river."

When we speak about the stability of *shalom*, we are talking about stabilized movement or "dynamic equilibrium." Meaning, *shalom* is not total equilibrium but rather an oscillation around equilibrium, from a low-pressure state to a high-pressure state, back to low, and so on. We have a sense of lack, then satisfy that lack, then become "filled" to the point where we feel the need to give or expel, and soon we feel the lack once again. It is this oscillation and self-regulation that vitalizes us, keeps us moving.

Lack of *shalom* can therefore be understood as either the state of *excess* pressure (inward or outward), or a dangerous *lack* of pressure.

---

[48] Perhaps this can help distinguish between the words שלום and השלום. Whereas שלום is characteristic of things that are alive, healthy, dynamic, whose pressures are stabilized, השלום ("the" *shalom*) constitutes complete stasis, a total and absolute release of pressure, a state that is characteristic of death, of no longer being in this world. Thus we respond to a person's greeting by saying "עליכם שלום," but when we speak of someone who died, we say "עליו/עליה השלום."

Fig. 18 Shalom and excess pressure

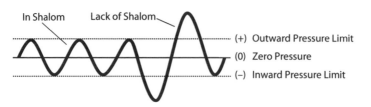

Fig. 19 Shalom and lack of pressure

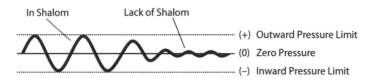

When we maintain a healthy range of pressure, when there is movement within reasonable boundaries, we have *shalom* (in the sense of dynamic equilibrium) and *kedusha* (in the sense of restriction that is optimally conducive to vitality). *Shalom* is a manifestation of *Hashem-Elokim*, energy and life-flow within bounds.

Tzedek, Mishpat and Equilibrium

The concept of *shalom* is associated with structural stability. As such, it is related to *yesod* (foundation)[49] as well as to *tzedek/tzedaka* (justice):

וְהָיָה מַעֲשֵׂה הַצְּדָקָה שָׁלוֹם

"And the product of tzedaka will be shalom"[50]

We have spoken about *shalom* as implying equilibrium. *Tzedek* certainly denotes equilibrium—the word "equilibrium" literally means "equal weight" (*equal libra*), referring to a scale or balance, as in the iconic "scales of justice" symbol. That is to say, when *tzedek*/justice is lacking,

---

[49] As in, שלום הוא מדת היסוד (R. Tzadok HaKohen, *Pri Tzadik*, *Parshat Miketz*, also *Parshat Bo* and other places).

[50] *Yeshayahu* 32:17. *Tzedaka* is a type of giving based on the principle of *tzedek*, "justice" to the downtrodden (as opposed to a *matana*, a "gift," which is given out of the desire to give, not because it is "right" or "deserved"). See also, צֶדֶק וְשָׁלוֹם נָשָׁקוּ (*Tehilim* 85:11), where *Metzudat David* comments, כשנעשה צדק תבוא שלום, "When *tzedek* is done, *shalom* will come."

the scales are out of balance and the system is in "disequilibrium," a state of high pressure. When justice is restored, the scales are balanced out, the system returns to equilibrium, and pressure is equalized.

The Torah says to judge the people with a "just judgment," a *mishpat tzedek*.[51] A *mishpat* (judgment, ruling)—when carried out properly, fairly—restores *tzedek*, societal/interpersonal equilibrium. Thus, *mishpat* brings *tzedek*, and *tzedek* is a form of *shalom*, equilibrium.

Fig. 20   Dynamics of Mishpat and Tzedek

| Lack of Tzedek
(system under pressure) | Mishpat
(proper judgment applied) | Tzedek
(system in equilibrium) |

Mishpat and *din* are vehicles for *teshuva*—they help a society "return" to equilibrium, to *tzedek* and *shalom*, by working to resolve interpersonal pressures. As the *pasuk* says:

עַד צֶדֶק יָשׁוּב מִשְׁפָּט

"unto just-equilibrium will judgment return"[52]

In sum, the idea of the *mitzvot* is to help us to be *kadosh*—to intensify our vitality via restriction, i.e., to focus our energies optimally. They do so in part by regulating the pressures we bear as individuals and as a society, so that those pressures are maintained within a healthy range.

Mitzvot and the "Chai Bahem" Principle

The above discourse notwithstanding, there are certainly many types of *mitzvot* that appear to have nothing whatsoever to do with equilibrium or the regulation of pressure. Significantly, this list would include many of the *mitzvot* for which a *bracha* is said, such as lighting Shabbat candles, hearing the *shofar*, shaking the *lulav*, separating *challah*, putting on a *talit*

---

[51] See *Devarim* 16:18.

[52] *Tehilim* 94:15

and *tefilin*, and many others. However, *all* of the *mitzvot* ultimately fall under the principle of *"chai bahem,"* that a person should "live" through them, as it says:

וּשְׁמַרְתֶּם אֶת חֻקֹּתַי וְאֶת מִשְׁפָּטַי
אֲשֶׁר יַעֲשֶׂה אֹתָם הָאָדָם וָחַי בָּהֶם, אֲנִי ה'.

*"And guard My statutes and My rules, so that a person
should do them and live through them—I am Hashem."*[53]

That is to say, the *mitzvot* are commands through which we are intended to derive Life. First and foremost, as the Talmud says, we are not to die as a result of doing a *mitzva*,[54] so for example we refrain from fasting on Yom Kippur when doing so would pose a danger to life. But in a more general sense, the *mitzvot* are to be used as vehicles for enhancing and elevating life[55]—cultivating vitality and joy, developing positive interrelations, promoting mindfulness, nurturing a sense of mutual responsibility, and invigorating the mind. When the *mitzvot* are done begrudgingly, or in a manner that deadens or saps vitality, this runs counter to the Life principle, contrary to the *kedusha* that the *mitzvot* are intended to achieve. It is a clear sign that the way we relate to the *mitzvot* is in need of a substantial upgrade.

The above *"chai bahem"* pasuk is punctuated with the phrase *ani Hashem*, "I am Hashem." That is to say, the *chai bahem* principle regarding the *mitzvot* is itself expressed by the axiom of *"Hashem/chaim"*—which generates and sustains the entire system.[56]

With an understanding of the *bracha* formula *"Baruch atah Hashem..."* in mind, we now begin the order of the morning *brachot*, starting with *Netilat Yadayim.*

---

[53] *Vayikra* 18:5

[54] As it says, וחי בהם, ולא שימות בהם, "Live through them, and not die through them" (*Yoma* 85b, *Sanhedrin* 74a, *Avoda Zara* 27b, 54a).

[55] As in, יוחי בהם' היינו שיעשה לשמה ויהיה נעשה לו סם חיים (*Degel Machaneh Efraim, Parshat Acharei Mot*).

[56] As in, וזהו אני ה', ויעשה אמת וחיים, והבן (Ibid.).

Netilat Yadayim
נְטִילַת יָדַיִם

בָּרוּךְ אַתָּה ה' אֱ-לֹהֵינוּ מֶלֶךְ הָעוֹלָם, אֲשֶׁר קִדְּשָׁנוּ בְּמִצְוֹתָיו וְצִוָּנוּ עַל נְטִילַת יָדָיִם.

Waking up and saying *Modeh Ani* are followed by *netilat yadayim* (lit., "taking/lifting the hands"), where water is poured from a cup three times over each hand (alternating right and left), and the above *bracha* is said.

Tuma and Washing Hands

There are a number of different reasons the tradition gives for *netilat yadayim* in the morning.[1] These include:

- **Briya Chadasha** – A person is like a "new creation" in the morning and washes his/her hands to inaugurate them for use.

- **Avoda** – A person prepares for "service" (i.e., prayer) similar to the way a *kohen* prepares for service in the *Mikdash*, by washing the hands.

- **Nekiyut** – A person washes out of "cleanliness" because it is assumed he/she touched an unclean or sweaty part of the body during sleep.

- **Ruach Ra'ah** – A "harmful spirit/force" is thought to rest on the hands during the night's sleep, which is removed by washing.

- **Tuma** – A person washes his/her hands to eliminate "ritual impurity."

We will focus here primarily on the reason of *tuma*. The Torah itself mentions washing the hands and cites *tuma* as the rationale, as it says:

וְכֹל אֲשֶׁר יִגַּע בּוֹ הַזָּב וְיָדָיו לֹא שָׁטַף בַּמָּיִם
וְכִבֶּס בְּגָדָיו וְרָחַץ בַּמַּיִם וְטָמֵא עַד הָעָרֶב.

"And anyone whom a zav touches, and [the zav] did not rinse his hands in water, he will launder his clothes and bathe in water and will be tamei until the evening."[2]

---

[1] See *Orach Chaim* 4, including the *Mishna Berura*.

[2] *Vayikra* 15:11. A *zav* (fem., *zava*) is one who has had an abnormal genital discharge and is considered to be *tamei* (impure).

The plain meaning of the verse is that a *zav* who did not wash his hands will impart that *tuma* to others on touch. The traditional interpretation however is that despite the phrase "rinse his hands," really a *zav* must immerse his entire body in water before touching someone.[3] In any case, throughout the Torah various instances of *tuma* are said to require some type of immersion in water. The question is, what exactly is *tuma*, and how is water considered a remedy?

Understanding Tuma

Tuma is typically defined as spiritual or ritual impurity,[4] uncleanness, a form of contamination or pollution. But impure in what sense? Contaminated by what?

In the Torah itself, *tuma* largely relates to contact with dead animals and humans, genital discharges of various types including blood (as in childbirth and menstruation), and *tzara'at*, an affliction of the skin, clothing or walls of one's house. Dead things, discharges and afflictions of the skin are all fairly suggestive of concerns over *disease*. Also, the presumption of contagion, contamination by touch, and remedies prescribed in the Torah such as purging one's body and clothing in water, or being quarantined, separated from others, would also seem to relate to stemming the spread of disease.

Yet there are examples of *tuma* in the Torah that do not appear to have disease or physical health as the rationale. For instance, *tuma* is the reason given for not eating non-kosher animals. If this were purely a question of health, why does the Torah not also list other foods that are potentially hazardous, such as certain species of berries or mushrooms? Also, the ancient Israelites surely saw other people eat animals like pig and hare without necessarily incurring any physical harm. Furthermore,

---

[3] Brought by Rashi and others, and sourced in *Chulin* 106a. The Ramban suggests that the word "hands" simply refers to the part of the body that typically does the touching.

[4] I say "spiritual or ritual," but the reader should understand that these words describe potentially very different approaches. The idea of "spiritual" impurity generally implies the belief in *tuma* as an unseen negative force, a nonphysical presence that is damaging to the *nefesh*/soul. This might be termed the more "mystical" approach. The idea of "ritual" impurity however, does not necessitate the existence of any unseen, nonphysical forces. Rather, it is to say that the Torah system has designated certain things as "impure" for purposes of religious life, whereby *tuma* is understood as having social, psychological and/or symbolic significance. *Tuma* is seen as a status, not a "thing" per se.

the Torah states regarding non-kosher animals, *"tamei hu lachem,"* that they are *tamei* "for you," implying that they are *not tamei* for other people.[5] This does not sound like a health warning, but rather a prohibition/restriction that applies only and specifically to *Am Yisrael*.[6]

Another example where disease is clearly not the concern is idolatrous worship, which the Torah associates with *tuma*:

כִּי מִזַּרְעוֹ נָתַן לַמֹּלֶךְ לְמַעַן טַמֵּא אֶת מִקְדָּשִׁי

"because he gave of his progeny to the Molech, to contaminate My Mikdash"[7]

Sacrificing one's child "to the Molech," via fire, was seen as bringing *tuma* to the *Mikdash*. It stands to reason that the designation *"tuma"* here indicates *not* that the practice was viewed as transmitting a "disease" per se, but rather that it was deemed antithetical to everything *Am Yisrael* stood for. This type of *tuma* was cleansed on the holiday of Yom Kippur:

וְכִפֶּר עַל הַקֹּדֶשׁ מִטֻּמְאֹת בְּנֵי יִשְׂרָאֵל וּמִפִּשְׁעֵיהֶם לְכָל חַטֹּאתָם

"and [Aharon] will atone for the Kodesh, from the impurities of the Children of Israel and from their transgressions, for all their sins"[8]

Indeed, the fact that the above verse speaks about *tuma* in the same breath as *cheit* (sin), and as requiring *kapara* (atonement), strongly suggests that *tuma* was not understood strictly in terms of physical health and disease.

Moreover, *netilat yadayim* in the morning (done in a prescribed manner—from a cup, alternating hands, etc.) hardly seems designed to combat disease. Nonetheless, given the volume of ink the Torah devotes to *tuma* by way of skin afflictions, discharges, contact with dead animals and people, and to rules regarding contamination, quarantine and so on, it is difficult to argue that physical health plays no role whatsoever.

---

[5] See multiple instances of the phrase *tamei hu lachem* in *Vayikra* 11 and *Devarim* 14.

[6] Again, the "spiritual" vs. "ritual" divide comes into play when interpreting the phrase *tamei hu lachem*. The idea that there are certain animals that are *"tamei* for you" could indicate that there is something about the spiritual makeup of *Am Yisrael* wherein animals without cloven hooves, or that do not chew their cud, pose a danger to the *nefesh*/soul. Alternatively, it could be understood that there is something about consuming such animals that ritually (symbolically, morally, etc.) runs contrary to the ideal of *Am Yisrael* conducting itself in a more elevated manner.

[7] *Vayikra* 20:3

[8] Ibid., 16:16

Tuma and Chol

Perhaps the difficulty relates to how one defines health and illness. Take for example the word *machala* (from *chol*), meaning "illness." As we discussed earlier, the family of words relating to *chol* convey "lack," as in being drained of energy, evacuated of life-force, either partially or completely.[9] So while in etiological terms, illness may stem from microbes or some other agent, what makes someone a "*choleh*" per se is the negative impact the illness has on that person's vitality and life-force. It is an empirical observation, not a diagnosis. Being a *choleh* is to be in a diminished state, weakened, lacking energy as a result of an illness.

In the same way, while *tuma* is not equivalent to "disease" as such, it can be understood as bringing about "*chol*," a lack or diminishment of life-force, vitality. That *chol* can manifest either as *machala*, being drained of physical energy, or as *chilul*, being drained of *kedusha*. Indeed we find that the Torah connects the two states, *chol* and *tamei*, setting them up in opposition to *kodesh* and *tahor* respectively:

וּלֲהַבְדִּיל בֵּין הַקֹּדֶשׁ וּבֵין הַחֹל
וּבֵין הַטָּמֵא וּבֵין הַטָּהוֹר.

*"And to distinguish between the kodesh and the chol
and between the tamei and the tahor."*[10]

Meaning, just as *tahara* and *kedusha* are related concepts, so too are *tuma* and *chol*. *Tahara* leads to *kedusha*, and *tuma* leads to *chol*—it depletes *kedusha*, drains it of its intensity. The draining and weakening effect of *tuma* is "*chilul*." We see that *tuma* and *chilul* also go hand-in-hand:

לְמַעַן טַמֵּא אֶת מִקְדָּשִׁי וּלְחַלֵּל אֶת שֵׁם קָדְשִׁי

"so as to contaminate My Mikdash and defile/deplete My kodesh name"[11]

That is, damage to *kedusha* is described in terms of both *tuma* and *chilul*. Likewise, when a *kohen* is exposed to a corpse, the *tuma* incurred is said to constitute *chilul*:

---

[9] See p. 56.

[10] *Vayikra* 10:10

[11] Ibid., 20:3. This is the end of the *pasuk* quoted earlier, relating to the "Molech."

לֹא יִטַּמָּא בַּעַל בְּעַמָּיו לְהֵחַלּוֹ

*"He shall not become tamei, a master among his people,
to defile/deplete himself."[12]*

In addition, *tuma* and *chilul* are both used in Torah narratives involving sexual impropriety.[13]

So we see that *tuma* is associated with *chol* and *chilul*, depletion of life-energy and *kedusha*. What this implies, and which some classical Torah thinkers indeed suggest, is that *tuma* is not a contaminant, nor is it a "thing" per se, but rather it is the name we give to those phenomena or activities which induce a loss of *nefesh* (life-force), a depletion of *chiyut* (vitality).[14] If we understand *tuma* in this way, perhaps we can now account for the types of *tuma* that relate to illness and blood loss (which comprise a direct physical loss of *nefesh*/life-force), as well as for the other categories of *tuma* we discussed. Consuming non-kosher animals, engaging in idolatry and sexual impropriety, and the notion of the *Mikdash* becoming *tamei*, are not cases of *machala* (illness, loss of physical energy), but they are examples of *chilul*, the draining of *kedusha*—the breach, loss or degradation of the overall vitality of the individual and the society.

Minus-Charge and Plus-Charge

We can conceptualize *tuma* then as that which induces a *lack* or *minus*. When someone becomes *tamei*, when their life-energy or *kedusha* is considered to be diminished, we might say that a sort of "minus-charge" rests on them. This charge would then need to be counteracted by a "plus-charge" in order to resolve or neutralize it.[15]

---

[12] Ibid., 21:4, relating in this case to the *Kohen Gadol*.

[13] *Tuma* is referred to in the rape of Dina, וְיַעֲקֹב שָׁמַע כִּי טִמֵּא אֶת דִּינָה בִּתּוֹ (*Bereshit* 34:5), and *chilul* in relation to Reuven and Bilha, כִּי עָלִיתָ מִשְׁכְּבֵי אָבִיךָ אָז חִלַּלְתָּ (*Bereshit* 49:4). Both cases imply the diminishment/degradation of vitality in the individual and/or the family.

[14] As in, חסרון בנפש, "In truth, all *tuma* relates to a lack in the *nefesh*" (R. Tzadok HaKohen, *Machshavot Charutz* 7); also היינו הטמא לנפש שהחיות נעדר מאתו, "That is '*tamei lenefesh*', that the *chiyut*/life-force is stripped from him" (R. Tzadok HaKohen, *Pri Tzadik, Devarim, Motza'ei Yom HaKippurim*); ענין טומאת מת חסרון החיות, "the matter of *tumat meit* is the lack of *chiyut*" (*Sefat Emet, Parshat Para*); וממילא כשילך מאדם החיות שלו הוא נקרא טמא, "And certainly when a person's *chiyut* leaves him, he is called *tamei*" (R. Kalonymus Kalman Epstein, *Maor Vashemesh, Parshat Tazria*).

[15] Note that regarding electrical charges, the term "minus charge" (or negative charge) refers to that which carries an *excess* of electrons, and "plus charge" (or positive charge)

If *tuma* is conceptualized as a minus-charge, the state of *tahara* (purity) would be a "zero-charge," neutral. *Tahara* is thus a type of *shalom*, a normal, healthy internal equilibrium, one that is maximally conducive to the flow of life-energy. It is purity in the sense of "conductivity" to *kedusha*. That is *tahara* as a state. *Tahara* as a *process* however would constitute adding "plus-charge" to minus in order to achieve neutralization.

Tahara via Water and Time

Immersion in water is a method of *tahara* prescribed for many types of *tuma*. This is typically understood in the sense of water being an agent for washing off impurities. However, if *tuma* represents a lack of life-energy, a "minus-charge," then we might look at immersion in water more as a method of *restoration*, an act which revitalizes, which adds "plus charge" and neutralizes the feeling of depletion. Indeed, people often feel a sense of renewal and restoration upon immersion in water. Water produces a feeling of newness, being refreshed and *tahor*, purified. This feeling is enhanced with *mayim chaim*, moving/fresh water, or water poured over one's body or hands, moving across the skin. It is the contact between water and skin[16] which enlivens and invigorates.

In addition to water, another element the Torah includes as part of the *tahara* process is *time*. Like water, time can be understood in terms of replenishment, healing and neutralizing the sense of depletion. The more severe categories of *tuma* (e.g., contact with a dead person[17]) require a wait of seven or more days, and for more minor forms of *tuma* the Torah speaks about waiting until evening, after which time the person is *tahor*.[18]

---

refers to that which has a *deficit* of electrons. Here however, the term "minus" is used to refer to a lack, and "plus" to refer to an abundance or excess.

[16] According to Halacha, a person is required to be clean of any dirt or other obstructions on the skin before immersing in water for *tahara* purposes. (See Rambam, *Hilchot Isurei Biya* 11:16; also *Orach Chaim* 161:1.)

[17] Called "*tumat meit*." See p. 212, Note 19, regarding the *para aduma* procedure, whose purpose is to remedy this type of *tuma*.

[18] The time requirement is not a standalone method of *tahara* but rather a factor that is added to the immersion requirement. See Ibn Ezra (on *Vayikra* 11:24) who says regarding יִטְמָא עַד הָעָרֶב (which makes no mention of immersion) that the Torah is using abbreviated language and that in fact the person must also immerse in water. One who has immersed in a *mikveh* but is waiting for evening is called a "*tevul yom*" and has a specific status in Halacha with regard to *tuma*.

In the latter case however, it is clearly not the *duration* of time which does the healing, because in theory a person could become *tamei* one minute before the onset of evening, then immediately immerse in water and right away find him or herself *tahor*. If not duration, perhaps the operative factor is that evening is understood to be the start of the new day,[19] and so like water, evening is thought to impart a feeling of newness, replenishment, a fresh beginning. Also, just as water envelops the person immersing, so too the dark of night might be thought to "envelop" or surround a person.[20]

Nefesh as the Locus of Tuma and Tahara

The Torah uses the expression "*tamei lenefesh*,"[21] meaning that the *nefesh* is understood as that which becomes *tamei* (and likewise *tahor*). The question is, what exactly is the "*nefesh*"? The word is translated a number of different ways—typically "soul," "life" or "person," depending on the context. It can also convey "energy" or "revitalization," as in:

נָתְנוּ מַחֲמַדֵּיהֶם בְּאֹכֶל לְהָשִׁיב נָפֶשׁ

"they traded their precious things for food, to restore [their] nefesh/energy"[22]

וּבַיּוֹם הַשְּׁבִיעִי שָׁבַת וַיִּנָּפַשׁ

"and on the seventh day, He desisted [from creating] and was revitalized"[23]

Food restores *nefesh*. Rest restores *nefesh*. When we eat and rest, we become re-energized, revitalized. As we just discussed, immersion in water also has the capacity to invigorate—it restores *nefesh*. Torah likewise is thought to restore *nefesh*.[24] *Nefesh* refers to the "enlivening" aspect of a living being, that which animates, imparts vital energy. In the previous chapter, we spoke about the various human energy cycles (emotional, sexual, financial, etc.), each having its own metabolism. The *nefesh* is

---

[19] As in, יטמאה עד הערבי על כל פנים הוא נשאר טמא עד שיתחיל יום חדש (R. S. R. Hirsch on *Vayikra* 22:6).

[20] In the sense of, אַךְ חֹשֶׁךְ יְשׁוּפֵנִי, "Surely darkness will envelop/hide me" (*Tehilim* 139:11). See p. 198, for further discussion on the connection between darkness and *mayim*.

[21] See *Vayikra* 24:4; *Bamidbar* 5:2, 9:6–7, 9:10.

[22] *Eicha* 1:11

[23] *Shemot* 31:17

[24] As in, תּוֹרַת ה׳ תְּמִימָה מְשִׁיבַת נָפֶשׁ (*Tehilim* 19:8). Immersion in Torah learning has the capacity to invigorate, and in fact is compared in the Midrash to immersion in a *mikveh*: דברי תורה מקוה טהרה הן לישראל (*Eliyahu Rabbah, Parsha* 18).

the expression of all these combined.[25] It is the sum total of a person's life-energy. In this sense, *nefesh* can connote both "life" and "person."

Blood as Nefesh

In addition, the Torah associates *nefesh* with blood, as the *pasuk* says:

כִּי הַדָּם הוּא הַנָּפֶשׁ

"because the blood is the nefesh"[26]

That is, a person's *nefesh*, his or her energy for living, is very much tied to the blood and blood-flow. When blood is flowing through the body as it should, the person is alive and vibrant. When not, or when blood is lost, the person's *nefesh* is diminished, drained.

We might then make the following *drash* regarding the use of water for *tahara*: Within the body, there is the *basar* (flesh) and the *nefesh* (blood). The flesh is static, and the blood is dynamic, flowing. Within the Earth, soil/rock might be likened to *basar*, and flowing water (*mayim chaim*) to blood, *nefesh*. Thus, water heals the *nefesh* (in the *tahara* process) because it is seen as a kind of "*nefesh*" itself.

Tuma and Gender of a Newborn

Regarding childbirth, the Torah states that a post-partum mother is *tamei* for twice the amount of time following the birth of a girl (two weeks) as she is following the birth of a boy (one week).[27] How are we to understand this? If we define *tuma* as a loss of *nefesh* (life-energy), perhaps we can make the following speculation: In childbirth, not only does the mother lose *nefesh* through the loss of her own blood, but she also loses the *nefesh* associated with her baby. During pregnancy, the *nefesh* of the baby is subsumed within the *nefesh* of the mother. At birth, when the

---

[25] Thus, observance of the *mitzvot* (which address the various human energy cycles—emotional, intellectual, financial, etc.) is associated with the *nefesh*, as in, ומעשה המצוות הוא על ידי הנפש (R. Tzadok HaKohen, *Pri Tzadik, Parshat Masei*). Regarding money being a part of a person's *nefesh*, the Talmud states, כל הגוזל את חברו אפילו שוה פרוטה כאילו נוטל נפשו ממנו, "Anyone who steals from his neighbor, even the amount of a *pruta*, it is as if he is taking [i.e., removing some of] his *nefesh* from him" (*Bava Kama* 119a).

[26] *Devarim* 12:23; see also *Vayikra* 17:11, 17:14.

[27] See *Vayikra* 12:1–5. As the Torah describes, this initial period of *tuma* is then followed by a lesser *tuma*, which for a boy lasts an additional 33 days (for a total of 40 days), and for a girl, an extra 66 days (for a total of 80 days). Again, the total time is double for a girl.

baby separates, this is experienced by the mother as a loss, a sudden re-duction of her total *nefesh*. Therefore, when the Torah says that the birth of a girl imparts twice the *tuma* as that of a boy, this implies *not* that a girl is more "*tamei*." Just the opposite—it implies that a girl possesses twice the *nefesh*, double the life-energy. Thus, her leaving the mother constitutes double the loss of *nefesh* and requires twice the amount of time to be healed, replenished.[28]

Transfer of Tuma

The state of *tuma* can be incurred spontaneously, or it can be contracted one from another. The standard way of understanding how *tuma* is able to transfer follows the model of disease and contagion, wherein the dis-ease agent passes from one to another.[29]

Fig. 21   Transfer of Tuma via contagion

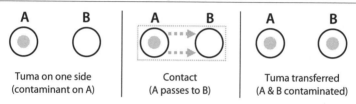

A B	A B	A B
Tuma on one side (contaminant on A)	Contact (A passes to B)	Tuma transferred (A & B contaminated)

But perhaps we can propose an alternative model for transference, relating to the idea of *tuma* as a "minus-charge." As we discussed, the drain of energy, the *chol*, caused by *tuma*, might be expressed conceptu-ally as a minus-charge or vacuum. Like a vacuum that draws substance into it, a minus-charge draws or attracts that which is relatively plus-

---

[28] This explanation accords with an idea brought by R. Shmuel Bornsztain (*Shem Mishmuel, Parshat Tazria*). He quotes his father (the *Avnei Nezer*), who poses the question as to why there should be any *tuma* associated with childbirth and explains according to the Zohar: מפני שכוחות הטומאה משתוקקין לדבוק במקום שהיתה בו קדושה, "because the forces of *tuma* tend to attach to a place where there was *kedusha*." The implication is that the more *tuma* there is in a particular place, the more *kedusha* there must have been—double the *tuma* indicates double the *kedusha*. Thus it supports the idea that a girl is understood to possess twice the *kedusha/chiyut*, accounting for the greater loss at birth and the subsequent longer period of *tuma*. (Thanks to my son Daniel Asher נ"י for pointing out this source.)

[29] In the case of *tuma* however, it also requires that the receiver be "*mekabel tuma*," capa-ble of receiving *tuma*. This depends on a myriad of factors—the receiving object's material, size, whether or not it is considered a *kli* (a vessel/utensil), whether it is wet or dry, etc.

charged.[30] *Tuma* might then be seen as having the action of pulling, drawing inward.[31]

So aside from thinking of the transfer of *tuma* in terms of Person A (with *tuma*) imparting something *to* Person B, we might understand it the opposite way—where Person A has a minus-charge/vacuum which draws *from* Person B, leaving Person B with a minus. However, unlike electrical charges, where plus flowing into minus produces a cancellation of both charges, the transfer of *tuma* does not result in a cancellation. The *nefesh* drawn out of Person B does not get integrated into Person A. The energy is lost, wasted, and so *both* are left with a minus. Both are now *tamei*.[32]

Fig. 22   Transfer of Tuma via minus-charge

A **B**	**A** **B**	**A** **B**
Tuma on one side (minus-charge on A)	Contact (A draws from B)	Tuma transferred (A & B minus-charged)

Sleep as a Partial Death

In all our discussion of *tuma* thus far, we have not mentioned sleep. We have however talked about "rest" as something which restores and revitalizes the *nefesh*. So why would we be considered *"tamei"* then when we wake up from sleep? If anything, we might suppose the opposite—that one could go to sleep *tamei* and wake up *tahor*.

Chazal liken sleep to death. Death is the most drastic loss of *nefesh*, and as such it constitutes the most severe level of *tuma*.[33] According to

---

[30] "Relatively," meaning that something that is neutral (*tahor*) functions as a "plus" relative to that which is minus-charged (*tamei*).

[31] *Tuma* is in fact described this way—that the various *tumot* מושכות את האדם, they "pull at a person" (see e.g., *Shem Mishmuel, Parshat Vayera*). More specifically, the concern is about our energies being drawn מהקדושה אל הטומאה, "from *kedusha* to *tuma*" (see e.g., *Likutei Maharil, Parshat Yitro*). That is, there is a tendency for plus to flow into minus.

[32] Cf., p. 212, Note 19, regarding the *para aduma*, where *tuma* is incurred but where the *nefesh* drawn out is utilized. See also p. 184, about *machloket shelo l'shem shamayim*, for a related concept involving energy that is lost, not *mitkayem*.

[33] As in, המת יותר חסר ומטמא טומאה חמורה (Abarbanel on *Vayikra* 11).

the Talmud, sleep is "one-sixtieth of death."[34] How is sleep like death? The most obvious connection is the loss of consciousness. The *neshama* is thought to "leave us" during sleep, akin to the *neshama* leaving a person upon death. Meaning, the conscious mind is blocked, impaired, temporarily out of commission during sleep, which is analogous to the total and permanent loss of consciousness that occurs at death.[35]

Additionally, despite the fact that sleep functions to revitalize a person, during sleep itself the body's metabolism slows down—heart rate and blood pressure drop, respiration and core body temperature decrease.[36] So perhaps after having one's vital signs/*nefesh* diminished during sleep—again, something analogous to the total cessation of the vital signs at death—the person is seen as having incurred a state of slight *tuma*, requiring *netilat yadayim* as a restorative measure.

Still, *tuma* is just one of the reasons given for *netilat yadayim*, and notably it does not account for the term "*netilat yadayim*" itself.

Netilat Yadayim and Netilat Lulav

The Torah's rationale for prescribing the washing of the body or hands[37] is to negate the state of *tuma*. However, with *netilat yadayim* as we have it today, clearly other factors are involved. The *bracha* said after washing is not worded "*al taharat yadayim*" (on purifying the hands) or even "*al rechitzat yadayim*" (on washing the hands), but rather "*al netilat yadayim*." The word *netila* means "taking" or "lifting" and implies preparing the hands for use. This speaks more to the reasons of *avoda* (preparation

---

[34] See *Brachot* 57b. The idea of "one-sixtieth" (which the *gemara* also applies to other topics, e.g., "Shabbat is one-sixtieth of *Olam Haba*," "dreams are one-sixtieth of prophecy," etc.) is explained by the Maharsha. He says that either the number sixty is symbolic of a maximally high number, meaning in our case that sleep is nothing compared to death, or that the number sixty stems from the *halachic* principle of "*bitul b'shishim*." This principle stipulates that one needs sixty parts kosher food to nullify one part non-kosher food that fell into it. Meaning, the non-kosher portion must comprise no more than 1/61 of the total in order to be nullified—any more than that and the taste of the non-kosher food is considered to be discernible. So if we say that sleep is 1/60 of death, that is slightly more than 1/61, meaning that sleep gives us just the slightest taste of what death is like.

[35] See p. 119, regarding the *neshama* and loss of consciousness.

[36] This is the case during the vast majority of sleep, although these factors rise during REM sleep.

[37] The Talmud suggests that in fact washing the hands has the status of immersing the entire body (see *Brachot* 15a, and Rashi ד"ה דכתיב ארחץ בנקיון).

for service) and *briya chadasha* (renewal of life) brought at the beginning of the chapter.

There is another *bracha* that invokes *netila*, and that is "*Al Netilat Lulav*," said on Sukkot before waving the four species. Of the four, the *lulav* is seen in Kabbalah as corresponding to *yesod*.[38] A *yesod* is a structure, a *kli* primed for use, for transmitting life. Likewise, the hands are *kelim* (tools) for acting and for giving, transmitting,[39] and in this sense can be likened to *yesod*, in the sense of:

אַף יָדִי יָסְדָה אֶרֶץ
"My hand has even laid the foundation of the earth"[40]

In sum, with *netilat yadayim*, not only do we restore *tahara* to the hands, but we lift them up, say the *bracha*, and in so doing prepare to utilize them in our daily activities as instruments of Life.

---

[38] Additionally, the *etrog* corresponds to *malchut*, the three *hadasim* to *chesed-gevura-tiferet*, and the two *aravot* to *netzach-hod*.

[39] When the hands are viewed as *kelim*, the idea of *briya chadasha* is particularly apt. Having been "newly created," the hands are prepared for first use through contact with water, similar to doing *tevilat kelim*, immersing new vessels in the *mikveh* before using them for the first time.

[40] *Yeshayahu* 48:13

Asher Yatzar
אשר יצר

בָּרוּךְ אַתָּה ה' אֱ-לֹהֵינוּ מֶלֶךְ הָעוֹלָם, אֲשֶׁר יָצַר אֶת הָאָדָם בְּחָכְמָה, וּבָרָא בוֹ נְקָבִים נְקָבִים חֲלוּלִים חֲלוּלִים, גָּלוּי וְיָדוּעַ לִפְנֵי כִסֵּא כְבוֹדֶךָ, שֶׁאִם יִפָּתֵחַ אֶחָד מֵהֶם אוֹ יִסָּתֵם אֶחָד מֵהֶם, אִי אֶפְשָׁר לְהִתְקַיֵּם וְלַעֲמוֹד לְפָנֶיךָ, בָּרוּךְ אַתָּה ה' רוֹפֵא כָל בָּשָׂר וּמַפְלִיא לַעֲשׂוֹת.

The *bracha* of *Asher Yatzar*, said after relieving oneself, focuses on the wondrous functions of the body that make our continued day-to-day existence possible.

אֲשֶׁר יָצַר אֶת הָאָדָם בְּחָכְמָה
Who formed the human with thought

Yetzira and Compression

The word *yatzar* (יצר) means to impart form or shape. It is related linguistically to the word *tzar* (צר), which as an adjective means "narrow," and as a noun means "distress" or "enemy." The distress and narrowness of *tzar* connote being squeezed, having pressure applied. A *tzar*/enemy is one who oppresses, in the sense of "pressing" upon us. *Yetzira* (יצירה, formation) is a creative act that confers shape by pressing, as a potter does with a piece of clay. In fact the word *yotzer* (יוצר) is used in Tanach to mean "potter."[1] And indeed the Torah describes human beings as being molded out of the soil:

וַיִּיצֶר ה' אֱ-לֹהִים אֶת הָאָדָם עָפָר מִן הָאֲדָמָה
"And Hashem-Elokim formed the earthling [out of] soil from the earth"[2]

---

[1] As in, אֲנַחְנוּ הַחֹמֶר וְאַתָּה יֹצְרֵנוּ, "We are the material/clay, and You are our potter" (*Yeshayahu* 64:7).

[2] *Bereshit* 2:7. (This is wet soil, clay; see 2:6.) See Abudraham on *Birchot HaShachar*, who says that the first part of *Asher Yatzar* is based on this *pasuk*.

So when *yetzira* is invoked in the concept of Creation, it implies compressing and organizing matter, thereby imparting shape, form.

Formations of Chochma

The *bracha* states that we are formed with *chochma*, "wisdom." It is *chochma* as distinct from *bina*, "discernment." Earlier, we discussed the "right" and "left" distinctions in the *sephirot* model.[3] The right-set of *sephirot* relates to energy and power, and the left-set to organization and delineation. The right is channeled by the left, power honed by delineating limits and bounds. *Chochma* is a right-side function, meaning where it comes to the mental domain it could be liked to pre-articulated thought, a stream of consciousness or abstract idea. *Chochma* has energy and power but as yet no concrete expression.[4] The left-side counterpart of *chochma* is *bina*, the discernment function. *Bina* (בינה) distinguishes *bein* (בין, between) one thing and another[5]—true and false, yes and no, one and zero, innocent and liable, *tov* and *ra*. The job of *bina* is to package and filter *chochma* into meaningful, articulable thoughts. The resulting thought-product is *da'at*, awareness or knowledge. In sum, *chochma* is the dynamic, energetic, "*chaim*" component. *Bina* is the judgment-oriented, analytical, "*din*" component. *Da'at* is *chochma* channeled and "formed" by *bina*, producing a focused, coherent, articulated flow of thought.

The phrase "formed the human with *chochma*" is generally taken to mean that human beings were formed with wisdom, meaning "wisely." But perhaps we can offer another interpretation. As we said above, *chochma* is conceptualized as pre-articulated thought, a sort of "raw material" of the mind. In fact, there is an idea in the tradition that *chochma* is really the raw material of Creation itself, the "substance" out of which

---

[3] See p. 73.

[4] E.g., כידוע חכמה היא אותיות כח מה, שהוא דבר שהיא בכח לגמרי ואין בו שום יציאה לפועל (R. Tzadok HaKohen, *Yisrael Kedoshim* 5).

[5] The Talmud says about the word נבון (from בינה) that it describes a person שמבין דבר מתוך דבר, "who understands one thing from another thing" (*Sanhedrin* 93b). That is to say, *bina* is the capacity for comparative reasoning and logic.

the world is formed.[6] Indeed, similar to the phrasing of our *bracha*, the *pasuk* says about the formation of the world:

ה׳ בְּחָכְמָה יָסַד אָרֶץ

"*Hashem, with chochma, laid the foundation of the earth*"[7]

Again, the standard interpretation of "with *chochma*" is that the earth was created "wisely." But if we think of *chochma* as the base material of Creation, then to say that the world is formed "*bechochma*" can also carry the connotation that it is made "out of *chochma*." Meaning, the world is understood essentially to be a construction of *thought*. Likewise, to say that human beings are formed "with *chochma*" can mean that *chochma* is the base material (the "clay") out of which we are fashioned. That is to say, we too are formations of thought.

This relates to something we spoke of earlier—the concept that the Creation is built within the mind of the Creator.[8] According to this idea, everything is "thought-stuff." What we perceive around us has no real "*mah*" (lit., "what") to it, no actual material substance, in the sense of:

תֹּלֶה אֶרֶץ עַל בְּלִי מָה

"*He hangs the earth over nothing*"[9]

In this model, the whole of Creation, ourselves included, hangs on nothing—it is all thought, consciousness, a manifestation of sheer will.

וּבָרָא בוֹ נְקָבִים נְקָבִים חֲלוּלִים חֲלוּלִים
and carved out within him numerous openings and hollows

Briya as Carving Out a Space

Unlike *yetzira*, which applies pressure to impart shape, *briya* (בריאה, creation) comes from the root *bara* (ברא), to create and give shape by carving out, paring, cutting away or clearing a space, as in:

---

[6] As in, החכמה הוא חומר הראשון והוא נקרא בלשון חכמים 'חומר היולי', "*Chochma* is the first material, and it is referred to by scholars as 'prime matter'" (R. Menachem Nachum of Chernobyl, *Me'or Einayim, Parshat Bereshit*).

[7] *Mishlei* 3:19. See Abudraham on *Birchot HaShachar*, who cites this *pasuk*.

[8] See p. 76.

[9] *Iyov* 26:7.

עֲלֵה לְךָ הַיַּעְרָה וּבֵרֵאתָ לְךָ שָׁם

"ascend toward the forest and clear for yourself [a space] there"[10]

The *bracha* of *Asher Yatzar* therefore speaks about the creation of *nekavim* and *chalulim* (body cavities and spaces) in terms of *briya*, meaning they are carved out, cleared, to allow for materials to circulate, pass through or be stored by the body. A *nekev* is an opening or hole, a two-dimensional space, and a *chalul* is from *chalal*, a hollowed out, empty, three-dimensional space.[11] In this case, *chalul* refers to an artery or hollow organ.

Fig. 23   Openings and Arteries – 2-D and 3-D space

Nekev
(2-D space, hole)

Chalul
(3-D space, hollow)

In terms of how the *bracha* is structured, the first action is *yetzira,* producing the basic "form" of a human out of *chochma*. After that comes *briya,* creating arteries and vessels within that form.[12]

Fig. 24   Actions of Yetzira and Briya

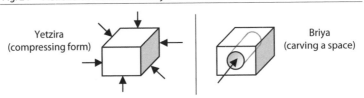

Yetzira
(compressing form)

Briya
(carving a space)

This idea of *yetzira* and *briya* also comports with the verse:

יוֹצֵר אוֹר וּבוֹרֵא חֹשֶׁךְ

"Who forms light and creates darkness"[13]

---

[10] *Yehoshua* 17:15. See the entry for בָּרָא in the *Brown, Driver, Briggs Lexicon*, as well as in the *Gesenius Hebrew and Chaldee Lexicon*.

[11] See p. 56, regarding the word *chalal*.

[12] This is *briya* in terms of a space or hollow being carved out *within* something. But the verb *bara* meaning "carve" or "whittle" also connotes carving a shape *on the surface*—like chiseling a sculpture. As such, the word *briya* is used more generally to imply a "creation."

[13] *Yeshayahu* 45:7, said in the *brachot* of *Kriyat Shema* of *Shacharit*.

Why not *"borei ohr veyotzer choshech"*? Why is *yetzira* associated with light and *briya* with darkness? We might understand it as follows: In Kabbalah, Creation is conceptualized as a *tzimtzum*, wherein uniformly distributed *ohr* (light/energy) is compressed, simultaneously creating an adjacent space where there is no *ohr*.[14] So we have pressure applied to light—*"yotzer ohr,"* accompanied by creating/carving out a space of darkness, absence of light—*"borei choshech."*[15] Thus, *yetzira* and *briya* in this context comprise two sides of the same action.

Fig. 25   Yotzer Ohr and Borei Choshech

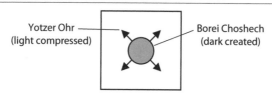

Yotzer Ohr
(light compressed)

Borei Choshech
(dark created)

How "Nothing" Becomes Something

If it is *choshech* which is created, and in fact *ohr* is already present at the beginning of Creation, how do we account for the Creation narrative saying *"vayehi ohr"* ("and there was light")? Also, if *ohr* is understood to pre-exist Creation, what do we do with the philosophical notion within the tradition of creation *"yesh me'ayin,"* *ex-nihilo*, whereby existence is created out of nothingness?

Perhaps the answer to both is as follows: If the only thing that exists is an utterly uniform "something," without any form or distinction whatsoever, then that something is effectively a "zero." It is nothing. For instance, if all one ever saw was the color red, it would cease to be red. Red is only red when there is a spectrum to offset it, to distinguish it. Likewise, if the entirety of one's experience is 100% light without darkness, without shadows or defining contours, then it would not be recognizable as "light" per se. That is to say, even though there is

---

[14] See p. 57, for more discussion on the *tzimtzum* model of Creation.

[15] The notion of carving out a space of darkness may also help to explain *Bamidbar* 16:30, wherein Korach's demise is described as a "בריאה." The text speaks of the earth "opening up its mouth" and swallowing Korach and his assembly, who fall into the dark abyss. Opening up to create a vacant space is precisely how we have described *briya*. (See p. 184, for further discussion of Korach.)

light "before" the beginning, that light is a "zero" until such time as darkness is created to offset it, to give it a space in which to radiate and be perceived.[16]

Thus we have *yesh me'ayin*—first there is a "zero," nothingness, and yet we find that something arises from nothing. *Ohr* per se comes into existence once the first distinction is made, via *tzimtzum*. Before that, the *ohr* is effectively non-*ohr*. What we are really talking about then is "relational" *yesh me'ayin*, meaning that in the pre-*tzimtzum* state there is indeed something (*yesh*), however functionally speaking it is nothing (*ayin*) relative to the post-*tzimtzum* state. And so the relational *yesh me'ayin* picture presented in Kabbalah allows us to simply bypass the philosophical conundrum (pseudo-question) about how something could possibly emerge from nothing.

גָּלוּי וְיָדוּעַ לִפְנֵי כִסֵּא כְבוֹדֶךָ
It is exposed and known before the seat of Your Kavod

Kavod and Kevod Hashem

The word *kavod* (כבוד) is typically translated as "honor" or "glory." More precisely though, it connotes "weightiness," as in the adjective *kaveid* (כָּבֵד), "heavy," referring to physical weight, mass. For instance, the liver is called the *kaveid*, some suggest because it the heaviest internal organ.[17] The word *kavod* is often used to refer to riches, treasure,[18] suggesting both the sheer weight/mass of wealth, being "loaded down" with riches, and the weighty stature of the one in possession of those riches. One who has *kavod* is thus seen as having "amassed" physical possessions, power, and/or a following, the respect and awe of others. Someone with *kavod* exudes an aura of gravitas, exerts a kind of "gravitational pull" on others. In short, *kavod* is a manifestation of one's level of "influence," in the literal sense of all that "flows in" to them, and which in

---

[16] As in, לית נהורא אלא בחשוכא ולית חשוכא אלא בנהורא, "There is no light except with darkness, and there is no darkness except with light" (*Zohar* 1:32a).

[17] See e.g., *Encyclopedia of Jewish Medical Ethics* by Steinberg & Rosner, p. 610; also see the entry for כָּבֵד in the *Brown-Driver-Briggs Lexicon*.

[18] See *psukim* such as, בֹּזּוּ כֶסֶף בֹּזּוּ זָהָב וְאֵין קֵצֶה לַתְּכוּנָה כָּבֹד מִכֹּל כְּלִי חֶמְדָּה (*Nachum* 2:10), referring to abundant treasures, and וּמֵאֲשֶׁר לְאָבִינוּ עָשָׂה אֵת כָּל הַכָּבֹד הַזֶּה (*Bereshit* 31:1), where Lavan's sons accuse Ya'akov of taking all their father's wealth.

turn expresses itself outwardly as an aura, a glow, a sense of glory and majesty.

The Torah also speaks of something called the *"kevod Hashem,"* usually translated as the *"glory of Hashem."* The *kevod Hashem,* together with the *Anan Hashem* (the "cloud," otherwise known as the *Ananei HaKavod*), make up the *Shechina* as depicted in the Torah. Throughout *Tanach,* the *kevod Hashem* is described as something which is seen,[19] which travels and rests in a given location,[20] and which fills a space.[21] It is associated with light and brightness,[22] is described as having the appearance of a consuming fire,[23] a glow,[24] a rainbow in a cloud.[25] It causes the ground to light up,[26] the *Mishkan/Mikdash* to light up,[27] and is presumably the reason Moshe's face radiates.[28]

That is to say, the main expression of the *kevod Hashem,* of *Hashem's* "influence" in the world, is *ohr* (light/energy). And since *Hashem* is the will for Life, that *ohr* (the manifestation of that will) is the *ohr hachaim,* the aura of life. This influence/aura is understood to permeate all matter, as the *pasuk* says:

קָדוֹשׁ קָדוֹשׁ קָדוֹשׁ ה׳ צְבָא-וֹת מְלֹא כָל הָאָרֶץ כְּבוֹדוֹ

"Kadosh, kadosh, kadosh is Hashem [commander] of legions,
all the earth is filled with His kavod"[29]

---

[19] As in, וּבֹקֶר וּרְאִיתֶם אֶת כְּבוֹד ה׳ (*Shemot* 16:7). Also see *Shemot* 16:10; *Vayikra* 9:6, 9:23; *Bamidbar* 14:10, 16:19, 17:7, 20:6.

[20] As in, וַיִּשְׁכֹּן כְּבוֹד ה׳ עַל הַר סִינַי (*Shemot* 24:16), and וַיַּעַל כְּבוֹד ה׳ מֵעַל תּוֹךְ הָעִיר (*Yechezkel* 11:23). Also see *Yechezkel* 10:4, 10:18, 11:22, 43:2, 43:4, as well as the movements of the עמוד הענן in the desert (*Shemot* 14:19, *Bamidbar* 9:15–23), where it is implied that the *kevod Hashem* accompanies the cloud (see *Shemot* 16:10).

[21] As in, וּכְבוֹד ה׳ מָלֵא אֶת הַמִּשְׁכָּן (*Shemot* 40:34). Also see *Bamidbar* 14:21; *I Melachim* 8:11; *Yeshayahu* 6:3; *Yechezkel* 10:4, 43:5, 44:4; *Tehilim* 72:19.

[22] As in, קוּמִי אוֹרִי כִּי בָא אוֹרֵךְ וּכְבוֹד ה׳ עָלַיִךְ זָרָח (*Yeshayahu* 60:1).

[23] As in, וּמַרְאֵה כְּבוֹד ה׳ כְּאֵשׁ אֹכֶלֶת בְּרֹאשׁ הָהָר (*Shemot* 24:17).

[24] See below, *Yechezkel* 1:28 (Note 25) and 10:4 (Note 27).

[25] See: כְּמַרְאֵה הַקֶּשֶׁת אֲשֶׁר יִהְיֶה בֶעָנָן בְּיוֹם הַגֶּשֶׁם כֵּן מַרְאֵה הַנֹּגַהּ סָבִיב הוּא מַרְאֵה דְּמוּת כְּבוֹד ה׳ (*Yechezkel* 1:28). It is unclear whether the term קשת is used here to indicate color (see Malbim on *Shemot* 24) or perhaps the arc of the glow, with an emphasis on the word סביב.

[26] As in, וְהָאָרֶץ הֵאִירָה מִכְּבֹדוֹ (*Yechezkel* 43:2).

[27] As in, וְהֶחָצֵר מָלְאָה אֶת נֹגַהּ כְּבוֹד ה׳ (*Yechezkel* 10:4).

[28] Implied from Moshe's request, הַרְאֵנִי נָא אֶת כְּבֹדֶךָ (*Shemot* 33:18; see *Kad Hakemach,* Rabbeinu Bachye, essay on *Tzedaka*).

[29] *Yeshayahu* 6:3

The words *kadosh* and *kavod* are mentioned here in the same breath, because *kavod* is the property which makes something *kadosh*, as it says:

וְנֹעַדְתִּי שָׁמָּה לִבְנֵי יִשְׂרָאֵל, וְנִקְדַּשׁ בִּכְבֹדִי.

*"And I will present Myself [in the Mishkan] to the Children of Israel,
and it will become kadosh with My kavod."*[30]

Meaning, *kedusha* occurs where life-energy is "amassed," concentrated, focused and restricted to a given space.

Shem and Kavod

Apart from *kavod*, there is another term used in the Torah in relation to the *Shechina*, and that is "*shem*," as it says:

בַּמָּקוֹם אֲשֶׁר יִבְחַר ה' לְשַׁכֵּן שְׁמוֹ שָׁם

"in the place that Hashem will choose to localize His name there"[31]

A *shem* is a name, but it also denotes a reputation or legacy.[32] To say that the *shem Hashem* resides in a given location means that the "legacy of Life" is localized there—in the form of Torah,[33] and in the form of *Am Yisrael*.[34] But the *shem Hashem* is simply the theoretical Life principle. It is only when that principle is put into practice that life itself actually becomes manifest in the world. Just as there is the "idea" of *ohr*, and then there is "*vayehi ohr*," actual *ohr*, so too there is the *shem Hashem*, and there is *kevod Hashem*—life as a concept/legacy versus life in concrete manifestation. The more this life-legacy is spread, disseminated, known, the more the influence of life becomes manifest, as it says:

וּבָרוּךְ שֵׁם כְּבוֹדוֹ לְעוֹלָם וְיִמָּלֵא כְבוֹדוֹ אֶת כָּל הָאָרֶץ

*"And may the legacy of His life-influence be propagated to the unseen-farthest-reaches,
[so that] His life-influence fills all the earth"*[35]

---

[30] *Shemot* 29:43

[31] *Devarim* 16:2; also see numerous mentions in *Devarim* 12, 14, 16, plus *I Melachim* 14:21.

[32] As in, וְנַעֲשֶׂה לָּנוּ שֵׁם (*Bereshit* 11:4). See also *Devarim* 25:6, regarding the *mitzva* of *yibum*, where *shem* implies "legacy" in the sense of actual progeny.

[33] As in Torah being localized in the *Aron/Luchot*, and as coming out from *Tzion*.

[34] *Am Yisrael* is considered as having the *shem Hashem* invoked upon it, as the *pasuk* says: וְרָאוּ כָּל עַמֵּי הָאָרֶץ כִּי שֵׁם ה' נִקְרָא עָלֶיךָ (*Devarim* 28:10). (See also p. 142, regarding the connection between *Hashem, Torah* and *Am Yisrael*.)

[35] *Tehilim* 72:19

The Kisei HaKavod

The *bracha* speaks about the *Kisei HaKavod*, generally translated as the "Throne of Glory." *Hashem* is depicted in Tanach as sitting on a throne, surrounded by the heavenly host.[36] But in the same way that the notion of *Hashem* as "king" can be taken as a metaphor for that which exerts influence,[37] so too the "throne" can be understood metaphorically,[38] whereby the *Kisei HaKavod* is the "seat of influence." That is, the idea of a king sitting on the throne is a way of speaking about a system which is active, online, able to impart influence. The influence in this case is the *retzon hachaim*, the will for Life.

The *Kisei* is the theoretical place from which the *kavod*/influence of *Hashem* is transmitted, the theoretical source of *ohr*. It is "theoretical" because in the *Kedusha tefila*, the following question is asked:

אַיֵּה מְקוֹם כְּבוֹדוֹ

"Where is the place of His kavod?"[39]

In other words, those who seek out the location of this *Kisei* are inevitably befuddled, cannot identify any specific "place." *Hashem*'s *kavod* appears everywhere, life and energy being transmitted in every corner of the world, and yet there seems to be no place where that transmission is sourced. All the majesty of Creation, all energy, movement and life, simply *is*.

Perhaps this inability to locate a source can be related back to the idea of *chochma* as the "material" out of which Creation is built.[40] Meaning, if one were theoretically to exist as a "thought" in consciousness, a construct within the mind, there would be no "place" per se where one could see things enter into the mind. Rather, thoughts just materialize. There is a declaration of *"yehi ohr,"* and *ohr* simply appears.[41]

---

[36] See e.g., *I Melachim* 22:19.

[37] Indeed according to the Rambam, the idea of *Hashem* as king, like all such human-oriented descriptions, *must* be taken as a metaphor. (See *Moreh Nevuchim* 46.)

[38] See Radak, *I Melachim* 22:19, דרך משל כמו המלך יושב על כסאו ועבדיו עומדים לפניו; also Rambam, *Moreh Nevuchim* 9.

[39] From the *Musaf Kedusha* for Shabbat and Yom Tov.

[40] See p. 100.

[41] Thus giving the impression of *"yesh me'ayin."*

And yet despite the "where is the *kavod*" quandary, we go on to say in *Kedusha*:

בָּרוּךְ כְּבוֹד ה' מִמְּקוֹמוֹ

"May kevod Hashem be propagated from its place"[42]

As if to say: Whatever "place" the *kevod Hashem* is coming from, may there be more of it!

The Mikdash as the Kisei HaKavod

There is however a *Kisei HaKavod* whose location is specified. The *pasuk* states:

כִּסֵּא כָבוֹד מָרוֹם מֵרִאשׁוֹן מְקוֹם מִקְדָּשֵׁנוּ.

"Your Kisei Kavod, elevated from the beginning, the place of our Mikdash."[43]

The *Mikdash* is understood to serve as a "seat" of sorts for the *Anan HaKavod* ("Cloud of Glory") to rest, and from where the *kevod Hashem* emanates.[44] Specifically, it is the space above the Ark, on top of the *keruvim*, which is described as having the appearance of a *kisei*,[45] and where *Hashem* is described as "sitting."[46] The Midrash as well speaks about the Ark as corresponding to the *Kisei*.[47] Additionally, the *Kisei HaKavod* is described in the first chapter of *Yechezkel*, in what is known in the tradition as the "*ma'aseh merkava*," the "workings of the chariot." Much of this description is repeated in the tenth chapter, this time in a vision regard-

---

[42] *Yechezkel* 3:12; also in the *Musaf Kedusha*. Note that the phrases ברוך כבוד and ברוך שם כבוד have a subtle difference—the first relates to spreading *life itself* and the second to spreading the *will for life*. The phrase ברוך כבוד conveys the desire that the *kevod Hashem*, the very aura of life, be propagated. The phrase ברוך שם כבוד however connotes propagating the *shem Hashem*, the legacy or will for life, which holds the *potential* to manifest as *kavod*. *Baruch shem* thus reflects the desire to disseminate a certain *seed* within consciousness, that the idea of the Life principle should spread to as much of humanity as possible. However, the extent to which that seed germinates, brings forth life in tangible form, depends on whether the Life principle remains simply an idea, or whether we nurture it, act on it, bring *chaim*, *simcha*, and *shalom* into concrete manifestation.

[43] *Yirmiyahu* 17:12

[44] As in, והיכל המקדש הוא הנקרא כסא הכבוד, וסודו עמוק (Radak on *Tehilim* 132:2).

[45] As in, וְהִנֵּה אֶל הָרָקִיעַ אֲשֶׁר עַל רֹאשׁ הַכְּרֻבִים, כְּאֶבֶן סַפִּיר כְּמַרְאֵה דְמוּת כִּסֵּא (*Yechezkel* 10:1).

[46] As in, ה' מָלָךְ יִרְגְּזוּ עַמִּים יֹשֵׁב כְּרוּבִים (*Tehilim* 99:1).

[47] As it says, והארון כנגד הכסה (*Bamidbar Rabbah* 4:13). The idea is that the *Kisei* in the *Mikdash* corresponds to a "higher" *Kisei*. This is also how some understand the above *pasuk*, *Yirmiyahu* 17:12 (see *Metzudat David*).

ing the *Mikdash*. All this constitutes further evidence of the parallel between the Creation and the *Mikdash*, as we discussed earlier.[48]

However, in sharp contrast to the *Kisei HaKavod* of Creation, which has no *makom* (place)—i.e., no *kiyum* (fixed existence), the *Kisei HaKavod* of the *Mikdash* is referred to specifically and often as the "*makom*," the "place."[49] So the above verse "*baruch kevod Hashem mimkomo*" might also be understood in the more specific sense of *kevod Hashem* being projected outward from the *mekom haMikdash*.

Human Consciousness as the Kisei HaKavod

In addition, there is one other location of the *Kisei HaKavod* that perhaps can be identified. That is the "seat" of human consciousness.[50] The *Kisei HaKavod* is the place where the *shem Hashem* resides, where the will for Life localizes, and from where the aura of life (*kavod*) becomes manifest. When we act as agents of that will, when we radiate a desire for life, embrace *chaim* in thought and action, we in effect replicate the *Kisei*. It is from each individual that the will for Life is made manifest in the world. This concept is expressed in the famous *piyut*:

בְּלִבָּבִי מִשְׁכַּן אֶבְנֶה לְהַדַר כְּבוֹדוֹ

"In my heart I will build a Mishkan, for the splendor of His kavod"[51]

In fact, let us say further: *All* the above esoteric descriptions of the "*Kisei*," and of *ohr* and *kavod* being projected, might be taken as a *mashal*, an allegory. The *nimshal*, the concrete, real-life actualization of all this, is precisely where it localizes in the human experience, where *ohr* and *kavod* describe our experience of great vitality and enlightenment. And not only do we reflect on the experience of such *ohr* and *kavod* when we perceive it around us, but we are also called upon to be beacons of it ourselves.

---

[48] See p. 47. Regarding Yechezkel, see Note 39, p. 48.

[49] See the *pasuk* quoted above, *Yirmiyahu* 17:12. The Torah itself uses the word "*makom*" extensively to describe the future *Mikdash*: וְקַמְתָּ וְעָלִיתָ אֶל הַמָּקוֹם אֲשֶׁר יִבְחַר ה' אֱ-לֹהֶיךָ בּוֹ (*Devarim* 17:8, with sixteen similar mentions throughout *Devarim*). Also see *Bereshit* 22:4 and 28:11, where "*makom*" according to the Midrash refers to the *mekom haMikdash*.

[50] As in, והנשמה כסא לאור שכינה (*Mekor Mayim Chaim, Ba'al Shem Tov Al HaTorah, Parshat Noach*); also חכמה ושכל ומשכנה במוח והיא הנקראת נשמה (Rabbeinu Bachye, *Bereshit* 2:7). (See p. 119, regarding the connection between the *neshama* and consciousness.)

[51] Composed by R. Elazar Azikri and found in his work *Sefer Charedim*.

שֶׁאִם יִפָּתֵחַ אֶחָד מֵהֶם אוֹ יִסָּתֵם אֶחָד מֵהֶם
that if one of them were to rupture, or one of them were to close up

---

The *bracha* of *Asher Yatzar* is speaking about the body, particularly those arteries and passageways responsible for moving materials through the body and out of the body. To do their job effectively, it is critical that such structures be in good working order. The above statement mentions two possible structural problems that would hinder the flow through vessels: rupture and blockage. We spoke earlier about *netzach* and *hod* in relation to modulating flow.[52] Now we will discuss *chesed* and *gevura*, which can be understood as pertaining to the structural integrity that allows for an effective, usable flow.

Chesed and Outpouring

If an artery is too delicate or flimsy, it will rupture (יִפָּתֵחַ), spring a leak. Using *sephirot* terminology, this would be an overdominance of *"chesed,"* where there is a lack of sufficient structure or boundaries, and energy is released, diffused chaotically. The word *chesed* is usually translated "kindness." That is, *chesed* refers to the outpouring or giving of one's energy freely. As an abstract concept, *chesed* is energy without any bounds placed on it.[53] It is giving which lacks direction, meaning that it goes in *all* directions, diffusing anywhere and everywhere it can.[54] In real life however, *chesed* must have bounds. When it does not, the same word *chesed* can mean "disgrace," meaning a degree of openness to the point where the person is exposed, shamed. This sense of *chesed* is used in Tanach regarding a person being exposed/disgraced for issuing slander,[55] as well as regarding uncontrolled sexuality as expressed between siblings.[56] Certainly, too much *chesed* even in the sense of "kindness" can be counterproductive if what is needed are boundaries and discipline.

---

[52] See p. 31.

[53] See Arizal's *Etz Chaim* 18:5, which refers to *chesed* as spreading out יותר מן השיעור, beyond any boundary. Also see *Inner Space*, R. Aryeh Kaplan, p. 61, which describes *chesed* as "being unrestrained, being unbounded, and perhaps even undisciplined."

[54] As such, *chesed* is likened to *mayim*/water (see e.g., Rabbeinu Bachye on *Shemot* 15:8; Shelah on *Mesechet Pesachim, Perek Torah Ohr*).

[55] As in, פֶּן יְחַסֶּדְךָ שֹׁמֵעַ וְדִבָּתְךָ לֹא תָשׁוּב (*Mishlei* 25:10).

[56] As in, וְאִישׁ אֲשֶׁר יִקַּח אֶת אֲחֹתוֹ בַּת אָבִיו אוֹ בַת אִמּוֹ...חֶסֶד הוּא (*Vayikra* 20:17).

We alluded to this earlier as an overdominance of the *Hashem/chaim* attribute, where lack of structure can lead to wild or chaotic behavior.[57] Such is the case with unbridled *chesed*.[58] In *Asher Yatzar*, the lack of structure under discussion pertains to the body, whereby that lack leads to the rupture of vessels and subsequent loss of life-energy.

Gevura and Restraint

On the other hand, if a vessel becomes too thick or hardened it can close up (יִסָּתֵם), impeding flow. Where there is such a predominance of structure that flow is actually obstructed, that state would be termed an overdominance of "*gevura*," restriction. The word *gevura* is usually understood to mean "strength." But this is not to be confused with strength of force, as in energy directed outward (which if anything is closer to *chesed*, not *gevura*). Rather, the strength of *gevura* is that of "restraint."[59] There is a natural tendency for entropy and diffusion, for allowing nature to take its course and for instinct to rule. One must consciously intervene in order to create and preserve order, to restrict a flow of energy to one place or one direction,[60] and to harness one's energies and instincts effectively. This intervention requires strength, the strength of *gevura*.[61] *Gevura* relates to withholding, channeling and compressing, restricting flow in order to impart direction and form. However, *gevura* also must be applied in judicious measure. When restriction is piled on top of restriction to the point where healthy flow is obstructed, this hurts the system as much as if there were too little structure, since the end result is less life in the system, and potentially a breakdown of the system.

---

[57] See p. 76.

[58] This is in the sense of Yishmael being likened to the חסד דסיטרא אחרא, the dark side of *chesed* (see R. Tzadok HaKohen, *Yisrael Kedoshim* 6). He is called a פרא אדם (*Bereshit* 16:12), a wild person whose energy lacks proper boundaries.

[59] The Arizal describes *gevura* as that which does not allow *ohr*/energy to spread continuously, but rather נותנת לו קצבה ומדה, "gives it an allowance and measure," שעד שם יתפשט האור ולא יותר, "so that the *ohr* spreads out to there and not beyond" (*Etz Chaim* 18:5).

[60] Strictly speaking, energy is not a "thing" that moves from place to place. Energy is movement itself, as in "kinetic energy." The term "energy" is used here (and throughout the book) colloquially to describe things that relationally speaking are dynamic and flowing, as opposed to static, as well as to describe the "experience" of energy, vitality.

[61] As it says, איזהו גיבור, הכובש את יצרו, "Who is a *gibor*? One who overcomes his inclinations" (*Avot* 4:1).

Discipline, rules and borders, without sufficient "give," can be destructive. This relates to what we spoke of as an overdominance of the *Elokim/din* attribute,[62] where the obsession with putting up boundaries results in boxing oneself (or others) in, stifling vitality and expression. Too much *gevura* closes up vessels and blocks flow.

Tiferet and Vibrant Flow

In order to create a balanced, working system, a robust and healthy flow, it is necessary to apply both *chesed* and *gevura*. To be precise, *gevura* is required in order to *channel* the flow of *chesed*, to give it direction, in the sense of:

כִּי גָבַר עָלֵינוּ חַסְדּוֹ

"For He has strongly-constrained His chesed upon us"[63]

The proper application of *chesed* and *gevura*, expressed by the fine-tuning of flow and restriction, will produce *tiferet*, a focused flow.

Fig. 26   Properties of Chesed, Gevura and Tiferet

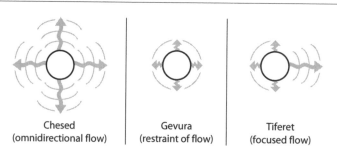

| Chesed | Gevura | Tiferet |
| (omnidirectional flow) | (restraint of flow) | (focused flow) |

The word *tiferet* connotes beauty, splendor or glory. It is considered to be a synonym of *kavod*[64] and is therefore related to *kedusha*.[65] *Kedusha*, as we

---

[62] *Gevura* is also associated with *din*, judgment, as is the name *Elokim*.

[63] *Tehilim* 117:2

[64] The two words often go together, as in וְעָשִׂיתָ בִגְדֵי קֹדֶשׁ לְאַהֲרֹן אָחִיךָ לְכָבוֹד וּלְתִפְאָרֶת (*Shemot* 28:2) and פְּאֵר וְכָבוֹד נוֹתְנִים לִשְׁמוֹ (*Shacharit* of Shabbat). *Kavod* and *tiferet* both have the connotation of "glory," but *kavod* emphasizes the aspect of weightiness and influence, while *tiferet* emphasizes the aspect of beauty and radiance.

[65] As in, מדת תפארת נקרא קדוש (R. Tzvi Elimelech Shapiro, *Bnei Yissachar, Ma'amarei Kislev-Tevet* 4, *Hallel v'Hoda'ah*); also מדת התפארת שרשה בקדושה (*Shem Mishmuel, Parshat Vayera*). Another hint to the *tiferet-kedusha* connection is in the first three *brachot* of

have discussed, is a combination of restriction and intensification, a type of focus. *Tiferet* is also about focus, with an emphasis on the resultant beautiful and vibrant life-energy flowing within and around systems that are in a state of balance and health.

In terms of the body's vessels functioning effectively, an overdominance of *chesed* (not enough structure) results in rupture, and an overdominance of *gevura* (too much structure) results in blockage. *Tiferet* is a state of optimal flow, the sign of a thriving system.

Fig. 27　Chesed, Gevura and Tiferet and flow-dynamics

Chesed-dominant	Gevura-dominant	Tiferet
(chaotic flow)	(obstructed flow)	(optimal flow)

אִי אֶפְשַׁר לְהִתְקַיֵּם וְלַעֲמוֹד לְפָנֶיךָ

it would not be possible to maintain self-existence and stand before You

Finely-tuned Body and Creation

If our bodies did not continually maintain each and every one of the vessels/passageways required to transport nutrients, waste, hormones, electrical impulses and everything else needed to sustain life at each and every moment, we would not be able to survive, let alone stand and make this very *bracha*.

The question is, why is the idea that our existence depends on the proper workings of the body preceded by the phrase, "It is revealed and known before the seat of Your *kavod*"? Isn't this fact obvious to everyone? It hardly seems like an esoteric mystery that would need to be "revealed" before the *Kisei HaKavod*.[66] There must therefore be something

---

the *Shemona Esrei*—*Avot, Gevurot* and *Kedushat Hashem*—which appear to correspond to *chesed* (as in "*chasdei avot*"), *gevura* and *tiferet* respectively.

[66] The idea of "mystery" is echoed in *Sefer Abudraham, Birchot HaShachar*, which explains the phrase, גְּלוּי וְיָדוּעַ לִפְנֵי כִסֵּא כְבוֹדֶךָ as a reference to the *pasuk*, הוּא גָּלֵא עַמִיקָתָא וּמְסַתְּרָתָא, "He reveals deep and hidden things" (*Daniel 2:22*).

about the *Kisei HaKavod* which is especially relevant here. Perhaps it is as follows: The *Kisei*, like a *chalul*/artery, can be understood as a "vessel" for transmitting life. It is known that if this *Kisei* were to theoretically break down, the world would not be *mitkayem*—it would cease to stand/exist. Meaning, the world requires certain structures, physical laws, to be in place. These are so finely tuned for our existence, that if one of them were to change in the slightest, it would throw off the entire Creation. So too, if one of the structures essential for human life were to break down, we would not be *mitkayem*, not be able to stand.

רוֹפֵא כָל בָּשָׂר וּמַפְלִיא לַעֲשׂוֹת
Who heals all flesh and makes wonders – to produce

It is not only the fact that vessels continue functioning which is wondrous. It is equally if not more miraculous that the body heals them when they break down. When speaking about *Hashem* as a *rofeh*, a healer, we are saying that built into the most basic components of our physical being is the will for Life. When our internal structures are damaged, natural mechanisms kick in to repair the damage and keep us going.

The Underlying Intent to Produce

The closing phrase *mafli la'asot* is usually translated "acts wondrously" or "performs wonders." Literally however, the phrase means "causes wonders to do," which is a somewhat obscure and awkward expression.[67] The question is, why not use the more straightforward phrase, *oseh peleh*, "does wonders,"[68] rather than *mafli la'asot*?

Perhaps we can learn something from the distinction between these two formulations. That is, while *oseh peleh*, "does wonders," focuses on the wondrous act (*peleh*) itself, *mafli la'asot* sees making wonders as a means to an end, causing wonders in order "to do," to make or produce. This is suggestive of the final verse in the Creation narrative:

---

[67] The expression מַפְלִיא לַעֲשׂוֹת occurs once in Tanach, in *Shoftim* 13:19. There are however similar constructions, e.g., הִגְדִּיל לַעֲשׂוֹת (*Yoel* 2:20).

[68] See e.g., *Shemot* 15:11 (Song of the Sea); *Tehilim* 77:15, 78:12.

כִּי בוֹ שָׁבַת מִכָּל מְלַאכְתּוֹ אֲשֶׁר בָּרָא אֱ-לֹהִים לַעֲשׂוֹת
"for on [the seventh day] He desisted
from all the work that Elokim created—to produce"[69]

The Torah says that *Elokim* created in order "to do," "to produce." The *bracha* says that *Hashem* makes wonders in order "to do." But to do or produce *what* exactly? What is the goal, the intent of all the creating and wondrous works?

As we continue to reiterate, the intent/will of *Hashem* is the will for Life. Behind the unfathomably vast works of Creation, including all the wonders of the body, is the great drive to produce, sustain and foster *life*. At the root of Creation is the notion that life is better than non-life, existence better than non-existence. Thus, when we say *"mafli la'asot,"* yes, it is certainly to acknowledge the great wonders and healing we experience daily and too often take for granted. But even more so it is to recognize that all the wonders found in our world, and in our very own bodies, serve the specific intent "to do," to achieve the *"tachlis"* (practical result) of advancing the agenda of Life and thereby bringing the will of Creation to fruition. What's more, *we* were created in order "to do"—to make that will for Life a concrete reality in the world.

---

[69] *Bereshit* 2:3. If not for the intervening word אֱ-לֹהִים, the *pasuk* would end בָּרָא לַעֲשׂוֹת, a construction similar to מַפְלִיא לַעֲשׂוֹת. And so if one were take the common figurative translation "does wondrously" and apply it to the Creation story, this would conceivably yield the rather novel translation, "which *Elokim* did creatively." In any case, we are applying the literal translation "to do" (or "to produce") in both instances.

Elokai Neshama
א-להי נשמה

אֱ-לֹהַי נְשָׁמָה שֶׁנָּתַתָּ בִּי טְהוֹרָה הִיא, אַתָּה בְרָאתָהּ, אַתָּה יְצַרְתָּהּ, אַתָּה נְפַחְתָּהּ בִּי, וְאַתָּה מְשַׁמְּרָהּ בְּקִרְבִּי, וְאַתָּה עָתִיד לִטְּלָהּ מִמֶּנִּי וּלְהַחֲזִירָהּ בִּי לֶעָתִיד לָבוֹא, כָּל זְמַן שֶׁהַנְּשָׁמָה בְקִרְבִּי, מוֹדֶה אֲנִי לְפָנֶיךָ ה' אֱ-לֹהַי וֵא-לֹהֵי אֲבוֹתַי, רִבּוֹן כָּל הַמַּעֲשִׂים אֲדוֹן כָּל הַנְּשָׁמוֹת, בָּרוּךְ אַתָּה ה' הַמַּחֲזִיר נְשָׁמוֹת לִפְגָרִים מֵתִים.

After acknowledging the wondrous workings of the body, the focus moves to the *neshama,* appreciating our unique consciousness.

אֱ-לֹהַי נְשָׁמָה שֶׁנָּתַתָּ בִּי
My Conscious Guide, [the] conscious-identity that You placed in me

Nefesh, Ruach and Neshama

Like *nefesh,* the word *neshama* is often translated "soul." *Neshama* (נשמה) however literally means "breath," as in the word *neshima* (נשימה).[1] *Nefesh* refers to the life-blood[2] and *neshama* to the breath of life[3]—blood-flow and breathing being the two functions/movements most recognizably associated with life.

Another word used in Tanach to connote breath is *ruach.*[4] But *neshama* and *ruach* are two different aspects of breath. *Neshama* connotes "a breath," as in an inhalation, an act of breathing,[5] and *ruach* refers to the air itself moving in and out.[6] As such, *ruach* also connotes "wind,"

---

[1] Note that there is no word "*neshima*" in Tanach, only *neshama*—referring to breath. The distinction between *neshama* as "soul" and *neshima* as "breath" first appears in Chazal.

[2] See e.g., *Devarim* 12:23, כִּי הַדָּם הוּא הַנָּפֶשׁ.

[3] As in, וַיִּפַּח בְּאַפָּיו נִשְׁמַת חַיִּים (*Bereshit* 2:7).

[4] As in the phrase רוּחַ פִּיו (see *Iyov* 15:30).

[5] As in the verb נשם, which can connote gasping or panting (see e.g., *Yeshayahu* 42:14). In this sense, the *pasuk* וַיִּפַּח בְּאַפָּיו נִשְׁמַת חַיִּים means imparting a first inhalation.

[6] As in, כֹּל אֲשֶׁר נִשְׁמַת רוּחַ חַיִּים בְּאַפָּיו, "Everything that [has] a breath of life-imbuing air in its nostrils" (*Bereshit* 7:22).

i.e., any movement of air. *Ruach* also means "spirit," as in that which "moves" a person—emotionally, intellectually or creatively.[7] In addition to being related to *neshama*, *ruach* is also linked to *nefesh* by virtue of its textual connection to *basar*, flesh.[8] The *ruach* of *basar* may refer to the movement/life-energy associated with living beings, or to the movement of blood itself.[9]

However, *ruach* and *neshama* have come to be understood as having a more "spiritual" character,[10] as opposed to the more body-oriented *nefesh*.[11] What do we mean by the term "spiritual"? The tradition understands spirituality as pertaining to the domain of the conscious mind, whereby the term *ruchani* ("spiritual," as in *ruach*) is equated with the term *sichli* ("mental," as in *sechel*).[12]

A further distinction is then made between *ruach* and *neshama*. *Ruach* is associated with the *lev* (the heart)[13] and encompasses everyday mental processes, which are necessarily colored by a person's physi-

---

[7] See e.g., *Shemot* 31:3 (creative), *Devarim* 34:9 (intellectual), *Shoftim* 9:23 (emotional). Note that the association between breath and spirit is not unique to the Hebrew language. The English word "spirit" itself derives from the Latin *spiritus*, meaning "breath." The word "inspiration" (also from *spiritus*) carries this dual-meaning, connoting "breathing in" as well as being emotionally/intellectually moved or stimulated.

[8] As in, כָּל בָּשָׂר אֲשֶׁר בּוֹ רוּחַ חַיִּים (*Bereshit* 6:17).

[9] As in, כי נפש כל בשר ורוח החיוני שבאדם בדם שבלבו הוא שמתנועע תמיד (*Haktav v'Hakabbalah*, *Vayikra* 20:9), wherein *nefesh* and *ruach* are tied to the movement of the blood.

[10] Indeed the word *"ruchaniut"* (spirituality) comes from *ruach*.

[11] In the sense of הנפש המלובשת בגוף (R. Tzadok HaKohen, *Pri Tzadik*, *Vayikra*). One likely reason for the distinction between *ruach/neshama* and *nefesh* is the simple fact that air/breath is less visible and physically substantial than blood. Air is not seen directly, yet its movement can be observed, felt—hence the notion of air/wind/breath being less physical and more spiritual.

[12] As in, העולם השכלי והרוחני והעולם הגשמי (Abarbanel, *Bereshit* 1); האור הרוחני השכלי (Malbim, *Bereshit* 1); וברוחני ושכלי שהוא כח הנשמה (R. Tzadok HaKohen, *Takanat HaShavin*), to cite just a few examples.

[13] As in, הלב משכן הרוח (Ibn Ezra, *Kohelet* 1:16); הרוח הוא בלב (R. Tzadok HaKohen, *Dover Tzedek*; also *Likutei Moharan* 8:2). See also *psukim* wherein *ruach* is associated with the *lev*, e.g., *Yeshayahu* 65:14, *Yechezkel* 11:19, *Tehilim* 51:19. Cf., *Tikunei Zohar*, 21:49a, where *ruach* is associated with the lungs, which are thought to "cool" the heart, i.e., control the passions. Note that the *nefesh* is also associated with the heart, due to its connection with the blood (see R. Tzadok HaKohen, *Pri Tzadik*, *Kedushat Shabbat* 3), or in the sense of the heart being commander over the *nefesh*, likened to a king amidst a war (see R. Moshe Cordovero, *Pardes Rimonim* 21:8).

cal/emotional state. The *neshama*, by contrast, is understood as relating more directly to the mind per se, to human consciousness itself.[14]

Neshama, Brain and Consciousness

While every breath of life is a tremendous gift, clearly the *bracha* is referring to the *neshama* as more than just breath. As we discussed briefly in *Modeh Ani*, the concept of *neshama* is related to consciousness, the mind.[15] The tradition in fact identifies the brain as the seat or location of the *neshama*, as it says:

וְעַל הָרֹאשׁ נֶגֶד הַמֹּחַ, שֶׁהַנְּשָׁמָה
שֶׁבְּמֹחִי עִם שְׁאָר חוּשַׁי וְכֹחוֹתַי
כֻּלָּם יִהְיוּ מְשֻׁעְבָּדִים לַעֲבוֹדָתוֹ

"And on the head, by the brain, so that the neshama
—which is in my brain—along with my other senses and abilities,
should all be subjugated to His service"[16]

Granted, identification of the *neshama* with the brain can be made even if *neshama* is related to *neshima*, breath. When a person breathes air, particularly through the nose, the breath (i.e., "spirit") looks as if it is being drawn up the nostrils toward the brain.[17] However, as we spoke about in *Modeh Ani*, the *neshama* is said to be "restored" upon awakening. This cannot refer to breath, since it is plainly obvious to any observer that breathing does not cease during sleep. Rather, it is one's *consciousness* which slips away when falling asleep and returns when waking up. And of course it is consciousness that is most closely associated

---

[14] To be clear, there is no such thing as human consciousness and thought in a vacuum, devoid of any emotional/physical component. The mind and body are always interconnected. Rather, when we speak about the *neshama*, it is to evoke the *faculty* of the mind—the very capacity for abstract thought, self-awareness, will and choice, etc.

[15] See p. 32.

[16] From the *tefila* said before putting on *tefilin*. See also, הנשמה שהיא במוח (*Orach Chaim* 25:5); עיקר האדם דזהו החכמה שבמוח שהוא נשמה שנתת בי טהורה (R. Tzadok HaKohen, *Machshavot Charutz* 1); הנפש החכמה...ומשכנה במוח והיא הנקראת נשמה (Rabbeinu Bachye on *Bereshit* 2:7).

[17] Some describe the *neshama* as entering and exiting the body through the nose (see Rabbeinu Bachye on *Bereshit* 2:7). In a similar vein, the Midrash speaks about Ya'akov as dying by way of a sneeze, whereby all his spirit is blown out through his nostrils (see *Pirkei d'Rabi Eliezer* 52). Sneezing is also described as having the capacity to revive a person, by purging a destructive spirit from the body (see *II Melachim* 4:32–35).

with the brain. The *neshama* refers to the faculty of *sechel*, conscious thought.[18] That is what returns to us when we awaken.

Neshama and Identity

The *nefesh* is associated with blood and blood-flow, and in the larger sense with a person's "energy," one's overall state of *shalom* or well-being (physical, emotional, intellectual, etc.) at a given time. And while the *nefesh* tells us a great deal about a person, it is not the aspect of a human being linked to unique individuality. That, according to the tradition, is the domain of the *neshama*.

The way the Midrash puts it, a specific *neshama* is assigned to a particular fetus.[19] To put it in our terms, every individual is imbued with a distinct consciousness. So yes, as human beings we *all* possess conscious awareness—we perceive the world through the various senses and faculties, ponder life and are aware of our own existence. However, every mind is utterly unique. No two people share the same perspective, the same experience. Each of us is alone in our inner world, looks out with our own set of eyes. Such is the uniqueness which the concept of the *neshama* conveys.

One might ask: Why does this *bracha* begin "*Elokai neshama*" (from *Elokim*) and not "*Hashem neshama*"? One possibility is the fact that *Elokim*, like *neshama*, is related to consciousness. *Elokim* is associated with the cognitive domain, analytical thinking. It corresponds to the *midat hadin*, the attribute of judgment, that which differentiates between one thing and the next. Likewise, the *neshama* is associated with the mind. It constitutes the root distinction between two individuals, that which gives each of us our separate identities. Thus the *bracha* begins by invoking *Elokim*.

The Midrash also speaks about the *neshama* as being carried within the "seed" inside the mother's womb, and that one's characteristics (e.g., whether the person will be male or female, strong or weak, short or tall, nice looking or unsightly, etc.) are "decreed" upon that seed.[20] Again, this speaks to individuality—and it is also rather analogous to DNA. Our genetic material is likewise carried in the "seed" and is what differ-

---

[18] As in the phrase, נשמת חיים המשכלת (*Kli Yakar, Parshat Bereshit* 2:7).

[19] The *neshama* is told, היכנסי בטיפה זו שביד פלוני (*Tanchuma, Parshat Pekudei* 3).

[20] As it says, הקב"ה גוזר על הטיפה מה יהא בסופה, אם זכר אם נקבה, וגו' (Ibid.).

entiates us, imparts our individual characteristics. DNA delineates not only our physical attributes but also aspects of our personality, how we are inclined to think and behave. The Midrash however singles out one specific attribute that is *not* decreed. That is a person's ability to choose between *tov* and *ra*, constructive action and destructive action.[21] So as predefined as the *neshama* is in many ways, it is not something that is "fixed" in any absolute sense. Rather, the *neshama*, individual human consciousness, is something that is continuously evolving based on our choices and experiences.

Neshama and Shem

There is an understanding in the tradition that sees the term *neshama* (נשמה) as rooted in the word *shem* (שם), "name."[22] This is sometimes described in terms of a name representing the "essence" of a thing. For instance, regarding the Eden narrative wherein Adam names the animals,[23] some describe Adam as looking to the animals' essential characteristics and on that basis formulating their names. One example is Rabbeinu Bachye,[24] who states:

האותיות שצרף בשמותיהן
הכל לפי טבעיהן ומדותיהן

"The letters that he arranged in their names,
all was according to their nature and their characteristics."[25]

This interpretation is based on the idea that each of the Hebrew letters carries a specific meaning (*aleph* as "ox" or "power," *bet* as "house" or "distinction," etc.), whereby putting a string of letters together communicates a more complex idea or set of characteristics. However, what is attributed to the Hebrew letters is more than just the ability to describe something already in existence—they are also thought to

---

[21] As it says, הדבר ההוא נותנו בידו של אדם בלבד (Ibid.).

[22] As in, נשמה הוא שם מיוחד לנשמת אדם (Radak on *Bereshit* 2), and השמות הם השורש לנשמות (*Kedushat Levi, Parshat Toldot*). See also *Tanchuma, Pekudei* 3, which implies that each *neshama* has a distinct *shem*.

[23] See *Bereshit* 2:19–20.

[24] R. Bachye ben Asher (mid-13th century–1340), prominent Torah commentator.

[25] Rabbeinu Bachye on *Bereshit* 2:19. Also see *Bereshit Rabbah* 17:4, where Adam is depicted as naming all the animals, as well as himself, and even *Hashem* ("אד-ני"), according to their characteristics.

have the capacity to bring the things themselves into existence, as the Talmud says:

יודע היה בצלאל לצרף אותיות
שנבראו בהן שמים וארץ.

"Betzalel knew how to arrange the letters
through which the heavens and earth were created."[26]

How are letters seen as bringing forth existence? Through an act of speech, as the Torah says:

וַיֹּאמֶר אֱ-לֹהִים יְהִי אוֹר וַיְהִי אוֹר.

"And Elokim said, 'Let there be light,' and there was light."[27]

The question is, why does the Torah not simply say, "*Elokim* created light"? Why do we need the statement "Let there be light" before actual light gets created? Clearly, the assumption operating in the Torah is that the way the Creator creates *ohr* is by invoking the phrase "*yehi ohr.*" In this way, the "word" *ohr* becomes the "thing" *ohr*.

Likewise, there is a *drash* commonly made about the word "*davar*" that since it means both "word" and "thing," this indicates that "words create things," that our speech generates (or affects) material existence. However, the idea of "speaking and creating" also brings to mind notions of magic, like the magic word "*abracadabra.*"[28] One way to preempt interpretations that unwittingly back into a magical orientation is to instead look at the idea in terms of consciousness. When we say a word, a thought or image of that word will often appear in the mind. The word invokes the "thing." If we look at the Creation as a process that takes place in consciousness, we can simply say the same thing—that *ohr* appears in the Creator's mind upon invoking *ohr*, i.e., with the phrase "*yehi ohr.*" Thus, the Torah's use of the *yehi ohr/vayehi ohr* formulation, far from being a type of word magic, speaks to creativity and imagination, the

---

[26] *Brachot* 55a. See also *Sefer Yetzira* 2:2: "Twenty-two foundation letters… with them He formed all that was formed, and all that would be formed in the future."

[27] *Bereshit* 1:3

[28] Incidentally, part of the folklore regarding the origin of the word *abracadabra* is that it stems from the Aramaic phrase *avra kedabra*, "I create as I speak." Though also suggested as a possible origin is the Latin *abre cadaver*, "open a corpse," relating to necromancy.

experience of "conjuring" things in the mind with words, wherein they seem to appear from nothing.[29]

In addition, there is a technology-related metaphor that may help make meaning out of the idea of words (*otiyot* and *shemot*) creating "things."[30]

Shemot and Computing

Consider the everyday computer. Each of the objects we view on the screen is ultimately sourced in a string of binary digits, a sequence of instructions. When input is received and certain instructions are "called," "invoked" or "run," we get the output that displays on the screen. To type the letter "W" is analogous to saying, "*Yehi W,*" and to see it immediately appear on the screen (seemingly "out of nowhere") is analogous to "*Vayehi W.*" Yet there is certainly no magic involved in computing. So perhaps we can think of a *shem* (name) or *davar* (word) as being analogous to a "program," each being a string of *otiyot* (letters) that conveys a "function" of sorts. Run the program, and you get the *thing*.

The computing metaphor might also infuse new meaning into two well-known and related statements in the Midrash:

האומן אינו בונה מדעת עצמו אלה אלה דיפתראות ופינקסאות...
כך היה הקב"ה מביט בתורה ובורא את העולם.

"The craftsman does not build on his own, but [uses] plans and descriptions... similarly Hashem looked into Torah and created the world."[31]

וכשברא הקב"ה את עולמו נתיעץ בתורה

"and when Hashem created His world, He consulted with the Torah"[32]

The Midrash analogizes Torah to a blueprint, a set of instructions that predated the world and was referred to in order to create the world. If we were to rewrite this *midrash* today, we might instead liken Torah to a

---

[29] We can also say as follows: The language of "*yehi*" is *declarative*, not causal. Just as the words "Let the games begin" declare the start of a sporting event but do not physically "cause" it, so too "Let there be light" proclaims that *ohr* should exist but does not "cause" *ohr*.

[30] I say "make meaning," as opposed to "explain," to preclude any possible insinuation that the original Torah concept was somehow informed by modern technology.

[31] *Bereshit Rabbah* 1:1; also *Yalkut Shimoni, Parshat Bereshit.* דיפתראות ופינקסאות refers to plans and descriptions (i.e., blueprints) but literally means "scrolls and tablets" (See *Dictionary of the Talmud*, M. Jastrow, entry for פינקס).

[32] *Tanchuma, Parshat Bereshit* 1

"program" (one long string of *shemot*) that, when run/invoked, creates the world. This is in fact a much more *intimate* conceptualization of Torah. Whereas a blueprint is something that sits off to the side and is merely "consulted" with, a computer program actually generates what we see on the user interface. What's more, unlike a blueprint, which can be filed away after the construction is completed, a computer program must be continually running in order to keep the application going. Also, a computer program is interactive and dynamic, as compared to a static blueprint. The computer programming metaphor thus fits the traditional concept of Torah arguably better than the blueprint.

Names of the Five Books of the Torah

The programming metaphor can also be nicely encapsulated in the five books of the Torah:

- **Bereshit (Elements)**
  Bereshit bara Elokim "et" (א-ת, *alef* through *tav*)[33]—the *otiyot* (letters) are created, the basic elements and functions of the language formed, to be used in…

- **Shemot (Programs)**
  The programs are written—Torah in all its *shemot* is given,[34] basic elements combined to form usable programs and subroutines, called/invoked in…

- **Vayikra (Call/Invocation)**
  The *shemot* are invoked—subroutines are called, programs run, instructions carried out, input/output commands executed. The invocation is done with…

- **Bamidbar (Speech Input)**
  Midbar = medaber, "speaking"[35]—*shemot*/programs are triggered, invoked, via the input event of speech, the end result being…

- **Devarim (Output)**
  "Things" are output to the user interface—practical, interactive applications come online. Concrete realization of the Torah/instruction is achieved. Concept becomes reality.

---

[33] See *Zohar* 1:29b, א״ת לעילא והוא חילא דכללא דעשרין ותרין אתוון, "[The word] *'et'* above, this is the power that includes the twenty-two letters."

[34] See Ramban, *Introduction to Sefer Bereshit*, כל התורה כולה שמותיו של הקב״ה, "The entire Torah consists of names of HaKadosh Baruch Hu."

[35] See e.g., *Shemot Rabbah* 2:4, אין מִדְבָּר אלא דיבור, "There is no reference to *'midbar'* (desert) that does not imply *dibur* (speech)." Linguistically however it may be that the word *midbar* (meaning a "desolate place") is not derived from *dibur* but rather from *dever* (plague, in the sense of "desolation").

To clarify, the idea here is not to assert that the Torah "is" a program in actuality. Rather, it is to look at the Midrashic concept of Torah as being ultimately about creation and creativity. And it is choosing to look at current and emerging technologies in this creative light, so as to infuse a greater sense of purpose and meaning into our work, and also to reinforce and support the creative work we do by connecting it back to Torah.[36]

טְהוֹרָה הִיא
is pure

Clear Consciousness and Self-access

Tehora (fem., of *tahor*) means pure and unadulterated, unsullied, clean, clear and lustrous. The *bracha* says that the *neshama* we were given is pure. Our consciousness is clear, untarnished. But is this really so? Maybe in those primordial days of early childhood, when we looked at the world through fresh eyes, we might think of ourselves as having been "pure." But now—after years of experiences that have made us more biased and rigid in our thinking, and possibly jaded from all the heartaches and disappointments that are inevitably a part of life—how could that *neshama* possibly be considered "pure"?

Perhaps the *bracha* implies that underneath whatever "dross" may have accumulated on the *neshama* along the way, that pure inner core of our individual consciousness is still there, still accessible. Despite all our accrued biases, we still have the capacity to think clearly, with an open mind. Despite often feeling anxious and weighed down by life, we still have the ability to unburden ourselves and regain that sense of joy and playfulness. Despite being focused on all the petty issues that come up in everyday life, we can still open our eyes to the bigger picture, to the things and people that truly matter to us. Despite our hope and idealism being squelched all too often by what we hear and observe around us, we can still access that spirit of positive creativity, the drive to utilize this day to make a real difference. There is a pure *neshama* within, and we can always connect to it if we so choose.

---

[36] This is what is called an *asmachta*, using a Torah source as a "support" for an idea, as in, להסמיך כל דבר המקובל...באיזה לשון מלשנות התורה (*Torah Temima, Devarim* 28:47).

Or perhaps the *bracha* wants to make the point that there *is no* "dross." The darker shades of life are just as much part and parcel to the human experience as the rest, and in no way does that make a person "impure." Yes, we may sustain a few bruises in life, but our very being and existence by definition cannot be "tainted."

Another way to understand the idea of the *neshama* being pure might be found in the expression "*tahar yoma*" used in the Talmud.[37] *Tahar yoma* means the day has ended. More literally, it suggests that the day has been "purified," cleared, to make way for a new day. So we might think of waking up to a new day as obtaining a kind of *tabula rasa*, a "clear slate," where the previous day washes off of us, the mind is cleared, and we are given the opportunity for a pure, fresh start.

אַתָּה בְרָאתָהּ, אַתָּה יְצַרְתָּהּ
You created it, You formed it

Briya and Yetzira in Consciousness

In *Asher Yatzar*, the order is *yetzira* (אשר יצר) followed by *briya* (וברא בו). But in *Elokai Neshama*, the order is reversed—first is *briya* (אתה בראתה) and afterwards *yetzira* (אתה יצרתה). What is the reason for the change in order? One possibility is that since this *bracha* discusses the creation of conscious human beings, the order specifically reflects the sequence in which these concepts appear in the Creation story—namely, *briya* followed by *yetzira*.[38]

Alternatively, we might say as follows: In *Asher Yatzar*, the body is conceptualized as being formed using *yetzira*, after which the various spaces and arteries are created within the body, using *briya*.[39] In *Elokai Neshama* however, first a new conscious space is opened, carved out, using *briya*. Now that a space exists, the variables shaping a person's characteristics are arranged, formed within this space, using *yetzira*. To use another computer-related analogy, it would be something akin to opening a blank document and then adding content to that document.

---

[37] See *Brachot* 2a–b.

[38] The concept of *briya* is brought in וַיִּבְרָא אֱ-לֹהִים אֶת הָאָדָם (*Bereshit* 1:27), with *yetzira* following later in וַיִּיצֶר ה' אֱ-לֹהִים אֶת הָאָדָם (2:7). (See *Sefer Abudraham, Birchot HaShachar*.)

[39] See p. 99, for a discussion on the definitions of *yetzira* and *briya*.

Fig. 28   Briya and Yetzira in the Neshama – 1

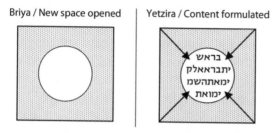

Briya / New space opened | Yetzira / Content formulated

Another way to express this would be to understand *briya* as the "carving out" of various *chukim* (laws, definitions, lit., "etchings") for a given *neshama*, and *yetzira* as the assembly of those definitions and variables into a coherent form.

Fig. 29   Briya and Yetzira in the Neshama – 2

Briya
(Chukim carved out)

Yetzira
(Chukim assembled)

אַתָּה נְפַחְתָּהּ בִּי
You blew it into me

Imparting Consciousness

The *bracha* continues in the order described in the Creation story, where the *nishmat chaim* ("breath of life") is blown into the human:

וַיִּפַּח בְּאַפָּיו נִשְׁמַת חַיִּים וַיְהִי הָאָדָם לְנֶפֶשׁ חַיָּה
"and He blew into his nostrils a breath of life,
and the human became a living creature"[40]

The image is not simply one of Adam taking his first breath, but of being breathed *into*. One *neshama* (breath) is used to initiate another *neshama*,

---

[40] *Bereshit* 2:7; see *Sefer Abudraham, Birchot HaShachar,* which cites this *pasuk* as a source for the phrasing of our *bracha*.

consciousness being imparted to the human being from an already exist-ing consciousness. As such, it is this act which some view as the moment when the *tzelem Elokim* is transmitted to humans.[41] It is the point when humans are imbued with the aspect of *Elokim*—the capacity for *din* and *da'at*, the ability to differentiate between *tov* and *ra*, and between the self and the other.

The name used in the Eden narrative is *Hashem-Elokim* (as opposed to *Elokim* alone, in the initial Creation story). It is therefore both the *Hashem* aspect and the *Elokim* aspect that are "blown into" the human being. Meaning, the consciousness of every person carries both *Hashem* and *Elokim* components—an inclination toward *rachamim, chaim, chesed*, giving, flowing, being and experiencing, as well as an inclination toward *din, da'at, gevura*, creating structure, channeling, analyzing, differentiat-ing and reflecting on oneself and one's experiences.

וְאַתָּה מְשַׁמְּרָהּ בְּקִרְבִּי וְאַתָּה עָתִיד לִטְּלָהּ מִמֶּנִּי
You safeguard it within me, and in the future You are to take it from me

Mortality and the Loss of Consciousness

The consciousness through which we perceive being alive is "on loan" as it were. We experience the world—the outer world and our inner world—for an all too brief period of time, after which it is taken from us. "You safeguard it within me" and "You are to take it from me" both arise from the same internal programming. The same genetic code that compels us to survive and reproduce, that tells the body to heal itself, also stipulates that we die. The structures that enable and safeguard our consciousness are programmed to break down, self-destruct. This is the nature of human life as it has been since Adam and Chava were con-demned to a limited lifespan[42]—that is to say, from humanity's very in-ception. We live and then we die, like all creatures—at least for now.

---

[41] See e.g., Sforno on *Bereshit* 2:7.

[42] As in, בעת שתאכל ממנו תהיה בן מות (Ramban, *Bereshit* 2:17). See also *Bereshit* 6:3.

וּלְהַחֲזִירָהּ בִּי לֶעָתִיד לָבוֹא
and to return it within me in the future to come

Resurrection and the Return of Consciousness

The *bracha* refers to three stages: life, death, and *techiyat hametim* (resurrection, lit., "enlivening of the dead"). There are those who view the idea of resurrection metaphorically, as a way of referring to redemption, such that the transition from exile to redemption is likened to returning life to the dead.[43] However, the predominant approach in the tradition to *techiyat hametim* is a literal one, envisioning a future era when the bodies of the deceased will be reconstructed and *neshamot* will return to them. The Midrash offers some detail as to how this is envisioned to happen:

אדריאנוס... שאיל את ר׳ יהושע בן חנניה,
אמר ליה, מהיכן אדם מניץ לעתיד לבא?
אמר ליה, מלוז של שדרה.

"Hadrian... asked Rabbi Yehoshua ben Chananya,
'From where will a human sprout in the future to come?'
He said to him, 'From the luz bone of the spine'."[44]

According to this *midrash*, *techiyat hametim* is carried out using the *luz* bone.[45] We might take a moment to consider that at the time this state-

---

[43] See e.g., Radak on *Yechezkel* 37:1, and *Sanhedrin* 92b regarding the "Valley of Dry Bones." Also see Ibn Ezra on *Daniel* 12:2: ישני עפר׳ משל על ישראל בגלות, as well as *Yeshayahu* 26:19, "Your dead will live," whose context is exile and the downfall of our oppressors. Also, dew is seen as a catalyst for resurrection, and we begin to add "*morid hatal*" ("He makes the dew descend") in the *bracha* of *techiyat hametim* during Pesach, the time of redemption and start of springtime. *Morid hatal* and *techiyat hametim* can be thus seen as relating to the hope for redemption, and the restoration of life from the "dead of winter."

[44] *Kohelet Rabbah* 12:5. See also *Bereshit Rabbah* 28:3, *Vayikra Rabbah* 18:1. The *midrash* continues with Hadrian asking for proof of this, and so R. Yehoshua ben Chananya immerses a *luz* bone in water and fire, tries to grind it in a mill, pounds it with a hammer over an anvil, but the bone would not be destroyed.

[45] Opinions vary as to whether the *luz* bone (*luz* literally meaning "nut") referred to is the cervical vertebra C1 (Atlas bone) at the back of the skull, where the *tefilin* knot rests (see Arizal, *Likutei Torah, Parshat Shoftim*), or the coccyx at the base of the spine (see *Sefer Ha'aruch Dictionary*). There are also sources that imply that *any* bones/human remains (even a "scoop of dust," see *Pirkei d'Rabi Eliezer* 33) suffice for purposes of resurrection. In addition to the bones, the tradition speaks of *tal techiya*, "dew of resurrection," whose purpose is to soften/moisten dry bones, turning them into a catalyst for recreating the body (see *Yerushalmi Brachot* 5:2). Beyond the question of the "ingredients" for resurrection, there are debates within the tradition as to the order in which the parts of the body will be

ment was made, the notion of taking one piece of the body and using it to construct a whole new body was simply the stuff of fantasy, miraculous beyond anyone's wildest imagination. Now, nearly two thousand years later, this is something we almost take for granted. We have discovered the DNA molecule and are capable of extracting it from tissue such as bone, transferring it to an egg, and producing another living, breathing being with the identical DNA. So not only is the idea no longer relegated to the domain of wild fantasy, but it is so real that the question of reproductive human cloning is now the topic of intense legal and ethical debate.

Techiyat Hametim and Technology

Some have speculated that perhaps emerging technologies point to a future DNA-based *techiyat hametim*.[46] As suggestive as this may sound, the idea also brings up many questions. For one, what about deceased persons for whom no harvestable genetic material remains? Furthermore, to rebuild a person via DNA might comprise a return of the *body*, but how do we understand it as a return of the *neshama*, as the *bracha* under discussion implies? Even if we define *neshama* as "consciousness," whereby consciousness would presumably return to the "new you" in the cloning process, would it really be *you*? How would it be any different from a clone or identical twin? And even if we assume that the person looking out through those new set of eyes *is* you in some existential sense, what difference would it make if you had to begin again with a total blank slate, with no memory whatsoever of your previous life? Isn't it our memories (conscious and subconscious) that make us who we are, at least in any meaningful sense? Short of a miraculous event, or the discovery of a means of retrieving memories out of thin air, or we simply do not concern ourselves with prior memory, it is hard to understand how such a DNA-based *techiyat hametim* would work.[47]

---

rebuilt, when such a resurrection will take place, who will be brought back, and whether or not the resurrected state will be permanent or merely a transitional phase.

[46] See e.g., R. Aryeh Kaplan, *Immortality, Resurrection, and the Age of the Universe: A Kabbalistic View*, pp. 41–42.

[47] R. Kaplan (Ibid.) discusses these questions about a technology-aided *techiyat hametim*. He suggests that to retrieve memories, as well as to recover genetic information where there are no material remains (and also to locate undiscovered remains), will require

It is however conceivable that technologies will emerge for future generations that will solve some of these problems. For instance, discussion is underway about technologies that will allow people to "back up" their memories, so that in the event of a death, not only would we be able to regenerate the body using genetic information, but we would have the capacity to reconstruct the memory as well.[48] And that is not nearly the end of it. Futurists suggest that if and when such an advanced level of technology is attained, it would be accompanied by many more profound technologically-driven changes, such as brains with greatly enhanced processing/thinking speeds, and bodies capable of regrowing missing or damaged tissue—with the capacity to reverse cancer and other diseases, correct blindness and deafness, and so on.[49]

In truth, we probably cannot even conceive of what such a future would look like, since the minds we are using today to think about it are magnitudes less advanced than those which will actually shape that future.[50] But suffice it to say, it would comprise nothing short of a "rebirth" for humankind. Indeed, the Talmud likens resurrection to birth:

---

prophecy. This, he proposes, could explain why in the "Valley of Dry Bones" vision, Yechezkel is told, לָכֵן הִנָּבֵא וְאָמַרְתָּ אֲלֵיהֶם, "Therefore, prophesy and say to [the house of Israel]" (*Yechezkel* 37:12).

[48] This is referred to as "whole brain emulation" or more colloquially as "mind upload/download." Current speculations suggest that this process will involve taking a high-resolution scan of the brain to create a map of all neural connections, which would then be exactingly replicated in the new/target brain, theoretically restoring the person's memories. (See Sandberg A. and Bostrom N., *Whole Brain Emulation: A Roadmap*, 2008, Technical Report #2008-3, Future of Humanity Institute, Oxford University.) Of course, assuming it works, this technology presents its own dilemmas as far as identity, such as it being possible in theory to construct more than one copy of the same person, using DNA plus brain emulation. Which one would be *you*? Both? Neither?

[49] According to inventor/futurist Ray Kurzweil, the future will see "the merger of the vast knowledge embedded in our own brains with the vastly greater capacity, speed, and knowledge-sharing ability of our technology." (*The Singularity Is Near*, Penguin Books, 2006, p. 20.) He says further: "A hybrid scenario involving both bio- and nanotechnology contemplates turning biological cells into computers. These 'enhanced intelligence' cells can then detect and destroy cancer cells and pathogens or even regrow human body parts" (Ibid., p. 221).

[50] To quote Kurzweil (Ibid., p. 29): "Some would say that we cannot comprehend [the future], at least with our current level of understanding. For that reason, we cannot look past its event horizon and make complete sense of what lies beyond." In the words of Arthur C. Clark: "If [a person's] predictions sound at all reasonable, you can be quite sure that in twenty, or at most fifty years, the progress of science and technology has made him seem ridicu-

מַה רֶחֶם מַכְנִיס וּמוֹצִיא

אַף שְׁאוֹל מַכְנִיס וּמוֹצִיא

"Just as a womb takes in [seed] and gives out [a newborn],
so too the grave takes in [a dead person] and gives out [a resurrected person]."[51]

Not only does this characterize death as a sort of "gestation period," but it also may suggest the following: Just as what goes into the womb as a mere drop of sperm comes out miraculously transformed into a living, breathing human being, so too the human who goes into the grave is like a sperm compared to the human that will eventually come out from the grave. Meaning, future human beings will be at a stage of development so far advanced from where we are now that it will be hard to imagine that the one emerged from the other.

All this again is in addition to the question of longevity. In such a future scenario, as long as a person wished to stay alive, and his or her memory data remained intact, one could theoretically live forever.[52]

Living Forever – Greatest Nightmare or Greatest Tikun?

The idea of immortality is introduced in the Torah with a sense of great trepidation:

וַיֹּאמֶר ה' אֱ-לֹהִים, הֵן הָאָדָם הָיָה כְּאַחַד מִמֶּנּוּ

לָדַעַת טוֹב וָרָע, וְעַתָּה פֶּן יִשְׁלַח יָדוֹ

וְלָקַח גַּם מֵעֵץ הַחַיִּים וְאָכַל וָחַי לְעֹלָם.

"Hashem-Elokim said: See, the human has become like one of us,
knowing good and bad; and now, lest he send forth his hand
and take also from the Tree of Life and eat, and live forever!"[53]

---

lously conservative … Only if what I tell you appears absolutely unbelievable have we any chance of visualizing the future as it really will happen." (From *Horizon*, broadcast on BBC television in 1964, in which Clark made what was then thought to be an "unbelievable" prediction, describing what we now know as the Internet Age.)

[51] *Brachot* 15b; *Sanhedrin* 92a.

[52] According to Kurzweil: "Our mortality will be in our own hands. We will be able to live as long as we want…We will fully understand human thinking and will vastly extend and expand its reach. By the end of this century, the nonbiological portion of our intelligence will be trillions of trillions of times more powerful than unaided human intelligence… [T]he growth rates will still be finite but so extreme that the changes they bring about will appear to rupture the fabric of human history." (*The Singularity Is Near*, p. 9.)

[53] *Bereshit* 3:22

Adam and Chava are banished from Eden, the path to the *Etz HaChaim* henceforth blocked off to humankind. But shouldn't that strike us as odd? The Torah tradition clearly looks forward to a time when people live perpetually, never to return to the dust, as in:

מה קדוש לעולם קיים
אף הם לעולם קיימין

*"Just as 'Kadosh' [Hashem] endures forever,
so do [those who are resurrected] endure forever."*[54]

Why then should the notion of Adam and Chava living forever be any cause for distress, something that would have to be prevented?

Some suggest that the concern is over immortal humans coming to be seen as "gods."[55] Others say that by taking away death, there would be no more incentive to follow *Hashem*'s decrees.[56] The straightforward reading of the *pasuk* implies that the problem of eating from the *Etz Ha-Chaim* arises only once Adam and Chava eat from the *Etz HaDa'at*. Indeed it is the *Etz HaDa'at* alone from which Adam is originally commanded not to eat. He is permitted (even commanded) to eat from "all" other trees,[57] presumably including the *Etz HaChaim*.[58] However, something changes with the acquisition of *da'at tov vara*, knowledge of good and bad. Adam and Chava, equipped with this knowledge, constitute a danger that has to be stopped before it is too late, before they eat from the *Etz HaChaim* and live forever. But again, what is the danger?

This of course begs another question: What is the problem with eating from the *Etz HaDa'at* in the first place? If indeed eating from the *Etz HaDa'at* makes us "like *Elokim*,"[59] and we are created to be in the *tzelem Elokim*, why command us not to eat it? If eating from the *Etz HaDa'at*

---

[54] *Sanhedrin* 92a. The pronoun "הם" in הם לעולם קיימין is filled in earlier in the *gemara*: צדיקים שעתיד הקב"ה להחיותן אינן חוזרין לעפרן.

[55] See Rashi on *Bereshit* 3:22, ד"ה ועתה פן ישלח ידו.

[56] See Ramban on *Bereshit* 3:22.

[57] As it says, מִכֹּל עֵץ הַגָּן אָכֹל תֹּאכֵל, "From every tree in the garden you will surely eat." (*Bereshit* 2:16).

[58] Although whether Adam actually ate from the *Etz HaChaim* before eating from the *Etz HaDa'at* is unclear. The verse "lest he send forth his hand and take also from the Tree of Life" may imply that he had not yet eaten from it, or that he did eat from it, and now it was a problem for him to continue doing so. (See Chizkuni on *Bereshit* 2:16.)

[59] See *Bereshit* 3:5, 3:22.

opens our eyes,[60] imparts conscious awareness, why is this something that should be prevented?

Some commentators explain that the *Etz HaDa'at* is in fact *not* something intrinsically forbidden, but rather that its fruit was like *orlah*, fruit from a tree still within its first three years of growth, which is forbidden to eat.[61] The Midrash implies as such:

מי יגלה עפר מעיניך אדם הראשון,
שלא יכולת לעמוד בצווי אפילו שעה אחת,
והרי בניך ממתינין לערלה ג' שנים.

"Who will remove the dirt from your eyes, Adam [so that you can see this]?
For you were not able to keep the command for even one hour/moment,
and yet your children wait for orlah three years!"[62]

In fact there is an idea in the tradition that Adam and Chava's eating from the *Etz HaDa'at* occurred on a Friday just before Shabbat, and had they waited just another three hours until Shabbat, the *Etz HaDa'at* would have become permitted to them.[63] Not only that, but in the same way that the fruit of a tree's fourth year is *kodesh*, so too would the fruit of *da'at* have been *kodesh* in the fourth hour, when Shabbat came in.[64]

What does all this mean? It seems to suggest that *da'at tov vara*, the "fruit of the mind," was not yet ripe, not ready to be eaten. The intent was that the human mind be allowed sufficient time to incubate, to develop in the safety of Eden before fully awakening. By gaining awareness of the world too early, we were like children who prematurely lost our innocence. We now possessed the tremendous power of the mind, but well before we were mature enough to handle it, to wield that power responsibly. So in fact it was we human beings who were perceived as posing the danger. Therefore, we had to be stopped before taking from the *Etz HaChaim*, because that would have made us not only dangerous but also *immortal*—a frightening combination.

---

[60] See *Bereshit* 3:7.

[61] As in, כי אדם הראשון חטא באכילת עץ הדעת קודם זמן התירו שהוא בחינת ערלה (*Ohr Ha-Chaim, Vayikra* 19:26).

[62] *Bereshit Rabbah* 21:7; *Vayikra Rabbah* 25:2.

[63] See *Siftei Kohen Al HaTorah, Vayikra* 19:23, ותקח מפריו ולא המתינה ג' שעות. (Also attributed to the Arizal.)

[64] See *Siftei Kohen Al HaTorah* (Ibid.), ואילו היה ממתין ג' שעות היה נכנס שבת והיה כל פריו קדש הלולים.

Fast forward to today. Humankind appears to be standing nearly within reach of the *Etz HaChaim*. In fact, one could argue that we are actively "sending forth our hand" to take from the Tree with the explicit goal of living forever. And despite the fact that conquering death would arguably constitute the single most significant event in human history, it also represents a *danger* to humanity of equal magnitude. Imagine the thought of people whose minds are bent on oppression and tyranny living forever. Imagine technologies vastly more powerful than those we have today in the hands of people who wish to inflict harm upon others. Human consciousness clearly has a long way to go to sufficiently sort out its *da'at tov vara*, to be able to distinguish between constructive and destructive thinking/action in this world, and to act in accordance with *da'at tov*.

And so it appears that the race is on. Will we reach the *Etz HaChaim* before we sufficiently work through our *da'at tov vara*? Will we harness the power of immortality before human consciousness is mature enough to use that power responsibly? This may be the greatest challenge humankind has ever faced, as well as our greatest opportunity for *tikun* (rectification, positive transformation). If we succeed in producing an overwhelming *da'at tov* in the world, if we focus our minds and our energies toward Life, conduct ourselves with *kedusha* in the life-affirming sense we spoke of earlier, we will effectively transform humanity into a *kli* for *chaim*, a people truly ready and fit to live forever. And all the fantastic advancements in technology and life-extension, instead of being something to fear, will constitute an unparalleled *bracha*.

כָּל זְמַן שֶׁהַנְּשָׁמָה בְקִרְבִּי, מוֹדֶה אֲנִי לְפָנֶיךָ
All the time that [my] conscious-identity is within me,
I gratefully yield before You

This part of the *bracha* is a restatement of themes discussed in the chapter on *Modeh Ani*. To summarize briefly: The word *modeh* connotes "yielding," admitting, in the sense of allowing something else to enter. To say "*modeh ani lefanecha*" expresses not only gratitude but also the willingness to yield and allow the fullness of life—and the will for Life—to enter within and penetrate our consciousness. It is to say, "As long as I am conscious, I will direct my conscious mind toward *life*."

רִבּוֹן כָּל הַמַּעֲשִׂים אֲדוֹן כָּל הַנְּשָׁמוֹת
Master of all the created-works, holder of all the neshamot

Ribon and Adon

The word *ribon* is generally understood as the Aramaic equivalent to the Hebrew word *adon*, "master." However, there are subtle differences. *Ribon* (רבון) is related to *ravav* (רבב),[65] becoming "great" in the sense of possessing an abundance. The word *adon* (אדון) connotes "holding," potentially related to *eden* (אדן),[66] a base or socket, that which secures or holds something in place. Both *ribon* and *adon* convey the idea of possession. But whereas *ribon* emphasizes the abundance aspect, referring to the multitude of creations in possession, *adon* emphasizes the holding aspect, as in a greater Consciousness that holds within it a multitude of subdivisions of that consciousness—i.e., the myriad *neshamot*.

בָּרוּךְ אַתָּה ה' הַמַּחֲזִיר נְשָׁמוֹת לִפְגָרִים מֵתִים
Be expanded, You Hashem, Who returns neshamot to dead bodies

Waking Up as Techiyat Hametim

The word *pegarim* (פגרים), corpses, comes from the root *pagar* (פגר), to be faint or exhausted.[67] As we discussed earlier, the tradition likens exhaustion and sleep to death.[68] Waking up from sleep is thus akin to resurrection, where the "lifeless" body has consciousness returned to it.

Besides suggesting that awakening from sleep constitutes a form of *techiyat hametim*, the ending of the *Elokai Neshama bracha* has other connotations as well. As we have been discussing, it is also a statement about the future, envisioning a day when death itself is eradicated. In addition, we might understand that even when we are alive and awake, we are still in need of a *techiyat hametim*. It is all too easy to go about our lives as the "walking dead." We easily fall into the state of mindlessness at times we would sooner be more aware, more present. And we too often suffer

---

[65] See entry for רבון in the *Dictionary of the Talmud*, M. Jastrow.

[66] See entry for אדן in the *Etymological Dictionary of Biblical Hebrew*, M. Clark.

[67] As it says, וַיַּעַמְדוּ מָאתַיִם אִישׁ אֲשֶׁר פִּגְּרוּ מֵעֲבֹר אֶת נַחַל הַבְּשׂוֹר, "Two hundred people stood in place, who were too exhausted to cross over the Besor stream" (*I Shmuel* 30:10).

[68] See p. 96.

from joylessness, numbness, lack of vitality and zest for life. *Techiyat hametim* is thus something we need on an ongoing basis, to wake ourselves up and embrace life.

Also, it is *Hashem* that is "*mechayeh hametim*," that brings life to the dead. Meaning, we look to Torah, with its underlying Life principle, as a vehicle for mindfulness, a catalyst for vitalizing our lives. And so the very process of our minds waking up to and embracing the will for Life, dedicating our energies toward the enrichment and betterment of life for ourselves and others—that itself constitutes a very real and profound *techiya*.

Birchot HaTorah
ברכות התורה

בָּרוּךְ אַתָּה ה' אֱ-לֹהֵינוּ מֶלֶךְ הָעוֹלָם, אֲשֶׁר קִדְּשָׁנוּ בְּמִצְוֹתָיו וְצִוָּנוּ לַעֲסוֹק בְּדִבְרֵי תוֹרָה, וְהַעֲרֶב נָא ה' אֱ-לֹהֵינוּ אֶת דִּבְרֵי תוֹרָתְךָ בְּפִינוּ וּבְפִי עַמְּךָ בֵּית יִשְׂרָאֵל, וְנִהְיֶה אֲנַחְנוּ וְצֶאֱצָאֵינוּ וְצֶאֱצָאֵי עַמְּךָ בֵּית יִשְׂרָאֵל, כֻּלָּנוּ יוֹדְעֵי שְׁמֶךָ וְלוֹמְדֵי תוֹרָתֶךָ לִשְׁמָהּ, בָּרוּךְ אַתָּה ה' הַמְלַמֵּד תּוֹרָה לְעַמּוֹ יִשְׂרָאֵל.

בָּרוּךְ אַתָּה ה' אֱ-לֹהֵינוּ מֶלֶךְ הָעוֹלָם, אֲשֶׁר בָּחַר בָּנוּ מִכָּל הָעַמִּים וְנָתַן לָנוּ אֶת תּוֹרָתוֹ, בָּרוּךְ אַתָּה ה' נוֹתֵן הַתּוֹרָה.

Before beginning one's Torah learning for the day, two *brachot* are said: one on the *mitzva* of Torah study (*La'asok Bedivrei Torah*), and the other on *Am Yisrael's* having been given the Torah (*Asher Bachar Banu*).

וְצִוָּנוּ לַעֲסוֹק בְּדִבְרֵי תוֹרָה
and commanded us to engage with words of Torah[1]

Learning through Engagement

The word *la'asok* (לעסוק) comes from *esek* (עסק), a late-Hebrew (post-Tanach) term meaning "involvement" or "business." The idea of associating Torah learning with business has a number of suggestive connotations. First, business implies that which a person is "busy" with, which occupies their time as well as their mind, and—assuming they are passionate about their business—their heart. The language of the *bracha* therefore suggests that our involvement in Torah should be imbued with a sense of intimacy and urgency, as a matter close to the heart.[2] Business also denotes an activity wherein a person acquires his or her "life bread," sustenance vital for living. So too, our Torah learning is ideally

---

[1] Note that the Sephardi *nusach* of the *bracha* reads "על דברי תורה," not לעסוק בדברי תורה.
[2] As in, לעסוק בתורה היינו עסק בלב (R. Tzadok HaKohen, *Pri Tzadik, Kedushat Shabbat* 7).

experienced such that when we learn, we see ourselves as imbibing vital nourishment.[3]

In addition, business is referred to in the tradition as *masa umatan*, "give and take" (lit., "take and give"), as for example providing a product or service and taking compensation in return. "Give and take" also relates to the idea of back-and-forth negotiations. *Masa umatan* corresponds to the Aramaic "*shakla vetarya*," an expression that is used in the context of Torah learning to describe Talmudic back-and-forth argumentation.[4] Indeed the word *esek* (עסק) is thought to perhaps derive from *asak* (עשק),[5] meaning to "contend" or "strive with."[6]

In this sense, the idea of the *bracha* is that we should not simply "busy" ourselves with words of Torah, but truly *engage* with them, even "contend" with them. If something bothers us in Torah, this is not something to simply accept passively. Rather, we are to take it as a call to explore the issue, to *strive* with it and negotiate a better understanding, employing a measure of give and take. Maybe we are missing something which further clarification of the Torah can provide, or maybe the common conception about a particular piece of Torah is missing something which *we* can provide. By applying our unique perspective to the material, by developing *chidushim* (novel ideas), not only do we participate in the *mitzva* of learning in the full sense of "*la'asok*," but we also contribute to the great legacy of Torah thought. The baton of Torah has been passed to us from previous generations, and it is in our hands to run with as far as we can, to contribute as much as we can, until we hand it over to the next generation.

Thus, the phrase *la'asok bedivrei Torah* can be thought of as implying a two-way relationship with Torah. When we contend with Torah, engage in give-and-take, not only do we become enriched ourselves, but we help bring greater clarity and understanding to Torah. Perhaps this is one of the reasons that the *bracha* does not say *vetzivanu* "*lilmod*" *Torah*,

---

[3] As in, לֹא עַל הַלֶּחֶם לְבַדּוֹ יִחְיֶה הָאָדָם כִּי עַל כָּל מוֹצָא פִי ה' יִחְיֶה הָאָדָם (*Devarim* 8:3).

[4] Rabbeinu Manoach (*Sefer Hamenucha*, laws of *brachot*) explains *esek* (עסק) as referring to Mishna and Talmud, wherein one needs משא ומתן in order to understand them.

[5] See the entry for עשק in the *Dictionary of the Talmud*, M. Jastrow, and in the *Brown-Driver-Briggs Lexicon*.

[6] As in, וַיִּקְרָא שֵׁם הַבְּאֵר עֵשֶׂק כִּי הִתְעַשְּׂקוּ עִמּוֹ, "And he called the name of the well 'Esek', because they contended with him" (*Bereshit* 26:20).

commanding us to "learn" Torah. Learning emphasizes the impact that the Torah has on us. "Engaging" however implies a two-way street, where we likewise have the capacity to impact Torah.[7]

וְהַעֲרֶב ... אֶת דִּבְרֵי תוֹרָתְךָ בְּפִינוּ
and harmonize ... the words of Your Torah in our mouths

The word *veha'arev* comes from the root *arav* (ערב), which implies the intermixing of two or more elements. For example, *erev* (עֶרֶב, evening) is the twilight period when dark mixes with light, or alternatively when the world darkens and objects appear to mix, blend in with one another, become indistinguishable.[8] An *arov* (עָרוֹב, swarm) is a wild mixture, chaotic and dangerous.[9] An *eruv* (עֵירוּב) is a mechanism in Halacha used to merge/mix adjacent areas into one domain.[10]

Am Yisrael and Torah as Guarantors

One of the ways that "*veha'arev*" in our *bracha* is classically interpreted has the word stemming from *arev* (עָרֵב), "guarantor," a third party who "mixes in" with one of the parties in a business transaction by providing the needed security, backing them up, assuming responsibility. According to this interpretation, the words of Torah are seen as a "guarantor" for us, serving as a kind of protection,[11] or providing security in our continuity from one generation to the next.[12]

---

[7] Cf., Maharal (*Derech Chaim* 3:3), who also asks why the word *la'asok* is used and not *lilmod*. He suggests that the *bracha* is directed to the individual, and that studying Torah on one's own is not called "learning" per se but merely "involvement."

[8] As opposed to the word *boker* (בקר), "morning," which shares its root with *levaker* (לבקר), to examine or inquire. *Levaker* implies the opposite of *erev*, mixing and darkness, since in order to conduct a proper inquiry, one must be able to discern and distinguish between things, an undertaking to which the light of day is more naturally suited.

[9] Related are the words *arava*, meaning "wild desert plains," and *Aravim*, the people who inhabit those plains.

[10] There is the *eruv chatzerot* (mixing of courtyards), allowing one to carry objects outside of a private domain on Shabbat, and *eruv techumin* (mixing of borders), which extends the distance one is allowed to walk outside of town on Shabbat. In addition, there is the *eruv tavshilin* (mixing of cooked foods), allowing one to cook for Shabbat during Yom Tov.

[11] As in, שהתורה מגנה (R. Yehuda Bar-Yakar on *Birchot HaShachar*).

[12] See R. Yehuda Bar-Yakar (Ibid.) and Abudraham on *Birchot HaShachar*, who cite the *pasuk*: וּדְבָרַי אֲשֶׁר שַׂמְתִּי בְּפִיךָ לֹא יָמוּשׁוּ מִפִּיךָ וּמִפִּי זַרְעֲךָ וּמִפִּי זֶרַע זַרְעֲךָ (*Yeshayahu* 59:21). This interpretation is echoed further on in the *bracha*: אֲנַחְנוּ וְצֶאֱצָאֵינוּ, "we and our offspring."

As a people, we are enjoined to be *arevim* to one another, to see ourselves in a relationship of mutual responsibility, as it says:

כל ישראל ערבים זה בזה.

"All of Yisrael are guarantors of one another."[13]

We are charged to look at ourselves as one another's guarantors, as being mixed in with one another, identified with each other's successes and hardships, bound to one another in the sense of:

וְנַפְשׁוֹ קְשׁוּרָה בְנַפְשׁוֹ

"And his nefesh is bound up with his nefesh"[14]

The *bracha* however is addressing the relationship between *Am Yisrael* and Torah. Indeed, Torah is bound up with our *nefesh*, as we discussed earlier about the *mitzvot* helping to regulate the various areas of the *nefesh*.[15] It is also bound to us in the sense of:

ג' דרגין אינון מתקשרן דא בדא,
קודשא בריך הוא אורייתא וישראל.

"There are three levels bound up with one another:
HaKadosh Baruch Hu, Torah and Yisrael."[16]

The tradition speaks of *Hashem*, Torah and *Am Yisrael* as being identified with one another—as being "one."[17] They are one in the sense of the *shem Hashem* being the legacy of Life, the Torah expressing that legacy in the form of specific detailed instruction, and *Am Yisrael* as being the ones who carry and live out that legacy and instruction, who bind it within our consciousness. So besides its relation to the *nefesh*, Torah is also understood as being the *neshama* (consciousness) of *Am Yisrael*.[18]

---

[13] *Shevuot* 39a; see also *Sanhedrin* 27b.

[14] *Bereshit* 44:30, referring to Ya'akov being intimately tied to his son Binyamin. See Alshich, *Shemot* 30, who links the concepts of ערבים זה לזה and נפשו קשורה בחברו.

[15] See p. 81.

[16] *Zohar* 3:73a

[17] As in: קוב״ה ואורייתא וישראל כולא חד (*Likutei Moharan* 251; R. Tzadok HaKohen, *Likutei Ma'amarim*, p. 153, and other places, based on the above citation from the *Zohar*). R. Tzadok adds: פירוש יחד׳ ממש אחד, that the word "one" here means "really/literally one."

[18] As in, כי התורה נשמותיהן של ישראל (Shelah/*Shnei Luchot Habrit, Parshat Kedoshim* and other places); כל הדברי תורה שהוא כלל נשמת ישראל (R. Tzadok HaKohen, *Pri Tzadik, Parshat Vayishlach*).

Am Yisrael and Torah are bound together, *arevim* to one another. *Am Yisrael* is responsible for Torah in the sense of making it our *esek*, being intimately involved in it, keeping it vibrant, dynamic and ever relevant. And Torah is responsible for essentially the same thing— keeping *us* alive as a people, vitalized and dynamic, a relevant force for humanity. We preserve the legacy of Life, and the legacy of Life preserves us.[19]

Harmony and Dissonance

The interpretation of *"veha'arev"* generally adopted in translations is not related to the concept of a guarantor, nor to any of the meanings of *arev* mentioned earlier. Rather, it sees *veha'arev* as stemming from a similar word *arev* (עָרֵב)[20] meaning "pleasing" or "sweet."[21] *Arev* in this sense connotes a taste that "mixes harmoniously," pleasantly, in one's palate.[22] The *bracha* suggests that the words of Torah we engage in should leave us with a sweet and pleasant taste. However, it is more than a mere hope or desire that this be the case. It is a declaration, an impassioned plea, a firm commitment that we must make it so. We are responsible for the words we speak, the interpretations we favor, and we will not rest until our understanding of Torah is sweet and harmonious, until we feel a resonance with Torah, not a dissonance.

The expanded phrase reads *"veha'arev na Hashem Elokeinu,"* to say in effect that in order to sweeten and harmonize the words of Torah, we need to take the Life principle as our conscious guide. It is when we take Torah to be the Tree of Life that its fruit (i.e., the words in our mouths) becomes sweet, as in:

---

[19] This relationship of *arevut* can be seen as encapsulated in the *bracha* preceding *Shema* at *Ma'ariv*: כי הם חיינו ואורך ימינו ובהם נהגה יומם ולילה. We contemplate the words of Torah day and night, and those words in turn serve as our life/vitality and the length of our days.

[20] Note however that not all instances of ערב may have originated from the same root. For instance, *arev* (sweet) may have once had a different root than *erev* (evening), the former initially possessing a "soft" *ayin* and the latter a "hard" (guttural) *ayin*. (See *How the Hebrew Language Grew*, Edward Horowitz, p. 104. Also see Note 71, p. 56.)

[21] See e.g. Koren Hebrew/English Siddur and Artscroll Siddur. The understanding of וְהַעֲרֶב as "sweeten" is also implied by the Maharsha (gloss on *Brachot* 11b).

[22] As opposed to the word *matok*, which more literally means "sweet" to the tongue, i.e., not bitter.

בְּצִלּוֹ חִמַּדְתִּי וְיָשַׁבְתִּי וּפִרְיוֹ מָתוֹק לְחִכִּי

"In its shadow I delighted and I sat, and its fruit was sweet to my palate."[23]

It follows from this idea that not only should Torah be sweet and palatable in our own mouths, but the words we speak should be palatable to others as well. As people who learn Torah and who are identified with Torah, our words and our actions in the world must convey this sweetness, and not leave others with a feeling that Torah is distasteful, harsh or disagreeable. As the Talmud states:

> *"If a person learns Torah and Mishnah and attends to Torah scholars, and he is honest in business, and speaks pleasantly to people, what do people then say about him? 'Happy is the father who taught him Torah! Happy is the teacher who taught him Torah! ... For this man has learned Torah; look how fine his ways are, how sweet his deeds are!' ... But [if] he is dishonest in business, and discourteous in his relations with people, what do people say about him? "Woe to him who learned Torah! Woe to his father who taught him Torah! Woe to his teacher who taught him Torah! For this man has learned Torah; look how corrupt his deeds are, how ugly his ways are.'"*[24]

As sweet as certain words of Torah may seem to us, if they do not translate into an overall sense of pleasantness in our words and actions, sensitivity and care in our dealings with other individuals, then something is gravely amiss. The sweetness is illusory, not genuine. This idea is reinforced by the plural grammar of the *bracha*, which says that the Torah should be sweet in *"our* mouths," meaning the mouths of the people. Therefore, even if one regards his or her own behavior as "sweet," if this same behavior is deemed contemptible, decidedly *unsweet*, by the people as a whole, then according to the *bracha* this should serve as a litmus test for determining whose palate is correct. This especially goes for actions done "in the name of Torah." For words of Torah or Torah-justified actions to be genuinely sweet, they must be perceived as sweet by the *Klal*, the greater community.

---

[23] *Shir HaShirim* 2:3. See R. Tzadok HaKohen, *Pri Tzadik, Devarim L'Rosh Hashana*, who cites this *pasuk*, referring to the sweet taste of the fruit as דברי תורה, and to the shade of the tree as אור פני מלך חיים.

[24] *Yoma* 86a

Dealing with Text – Sweetening or Souring

One sign of a Life-oriented religious society is that it will take even the harshest words of its source texts and go to great lengths to sweeten and harmonize them, or at the very least deemphasize them. This is as opposed to deliberately seeking out the darker verses of one's sacred texts and using them to create terrible dissonance, to justify horrific acts of violence and destruction. At face value, Torah is no less vulnerable to destructive manipulation than any philosophy or religion, but we are enjoined—as this *bracha* helps to remind us—to seek out sweetness, to wherever possible choose the gentle path, the path of civility and *derech eretz*, to cultivate pleasantness in our words and actions, as it says:

דְּרָכֶיהָ דַרְכֵי נֹעַם וְכָל נְתִיבוֹתֶיהָ שָׁלוֹם.
*"[The Torah's] ways are ways of pleasantness,
and all its paths are peace."*[25]

Ta'am – Taste and Reason

Torah should be pleasant to the palate—it should have a good *ta'am*. The word *ta'am* means "taste," and it also connotes "reason."[26] *Ta'amei hamitzvot* is the area of study devoted to identifying "reasons for the *mitzvot*"—referring to the overall purpose of the *mitzvot*, as well as specific reasons for individual *mitzvot*. The tradition itself however is conflicted as to the wisdom of delving into *ta'amei hamitzvot*.

For instance, regarding the *mitzva* of *shiluach haken* (shooing away the mother bird before taking her eggs), the Mishna issues a warning: If one says about this *mitzva* (regarding *Hashem*), "Your compassion extends to the bird's nest," that person must be silenced.[27] Why should that be? One opinion cited in the Gemara is that the person is declaring the *mitzvot*[28] to be about "compassion" when in fact they are "decrees." This could be taken to mean either that it is presumptuous to claim to know the reasons for *mitzvot* (i.e., they are decrees beyond human grasp), or that such a sentiment implies doing the *mitzva* only because of a specific

---

[25] *Mishlei* 3:17

[26] For instance, a person's "*ta'am*" refers to their faculty of reason, their sanity. See e.g., I *Shmuel* 21:14, where David disguises his *ta'am* (reason/sanity) before Achish, King of Gat.

[27] See *Brachot* 33b.

[28] The Gemara uses the word "*midotav*," which Rashi interprets as "*mitzvotav*." (See ibid., Rashi, ד״ה מדותיו.)

reason (in this case "compassion") rather than doing it because we are commanded.[29]

The first potential concern is that the attempt to identify the reasons behind the *mitzvot* is an exercise in futility, since they are decrees whose rationale is beyond the grasp of the human mind. The Torah itself however seems to go out of its way to state explicitly otherwise:

כִּי הַמִּצְוָה הַזֹּאת אֲשֶׁר אָנֹכִי מְצַוְּךָ הַיּוֹם
לֹא נִפְלֵאת הִוא מִמְּךָ וְלֹא רְחֹקָה הִוא.

"Because this mitzva that I command you today,
it is not beyond you, and it is not far away."

לֹא בַשָּׁמַיִם הִוא... וְלֹא מֵעֵבֶר לַיָּם הִוא...
כִּי קָרוֹב אֵלֶיךָ הַדָּבָר מְאֹד בְּפִיךָ וּבִלְבָבְךָ לַעֲשֹׂתוֹ.

"It is not in the heavens... It is not across the sea...
For the matter is very close to you, in your mouth and in your heart, to do it."[30]

The idea of *lo bashamayim hi* ("it is not in the heavens") is understood in the tradition to include not only our ability to observe the *mitzvot*, but also the ability to *grasp* them intellectually.[31] Far from being futile to comprehend, the *mitzvot* are indeed "very close" to us.

The second concern about *ta'amei hamitzvot* is more of a pragmatic one, that emphasizing "reasons" takes us away from doing a *mitzva* simply because we are commanded to do so. Not only that, but by providing a reason for a *mitzva*, it leaves open the possibility for people to say that the reason no longer applies, or does not apply to them, and therefore the *mitzva* need not be observed. The fear is that seeking out *ta'amei hamitzvot* may have a weakening effect on our observance.

---

[29] This second interpretation is implied in Rashi's words: להטיל על ישראל חקי גזרותיו להודיע שהם עבדיו ושומרי מצוותיו (see Rashi, ibid.).

[30] *Devarim* 30:11–14. The phrase "this *mitzva*" (כִּי הַמִּצְוָה הַזֹּאת) is generally interpreted to refer to Torah and *mitzvot* in general, and not merely to the *mitzva* of *teshuva*, which the Torah had just been discussing (see e.g., Ramban, Rabbeinu Bachye and Malbim, ibid.). Alshich explains that the previous *pasuk* (כִּי תִשְׁמַע בְּקוֹל ה') demonstrates that the theme has transitioned from *teshuva* to Torah and *mitzvot* as a whole. This understanding is also implied in *Eruvin* 54a.

[31] See Ba'al HaTurim (*Devarim* 30:14), who explains the word ובלבבך as referring to *svara*, understanding. Also see Alshich (Ibid.), who states that these *psukim* pertain to grasping the wisdom of Torah: ורבותינו ז"ל פירשו שהיא השגת חכמת התורה.

However, it all depends on how one interprets the word *ta'am*, reason. If we look at reason in the sense of justification, as in doing a *mitzva* "because of" a certain reason, then yes, it follows logically that if we do not have the reason then we no longer have the *mitzva*. But rather than think of *ta'amei hamitzvot* as "reasons for doing" a *mitzva*, we might instead see them as speaking to the "reasonableness" of a *mitzva*, the common sense, logic and even pragmatic spirit of a *mitzva*. This reasonableness may have to do with the historical development of the *mitzva*, its significance as part of our mindset as a people, its practical societal benefits, its contribution to personal meaning and well-being, or any number of other factors. Such insights help us appreciate the *ta'am*, the flavor of the *mitzva*. They impart taste to what can otherwise become bland, rote observance.

It is possible to go through life and simply "do," experience the *mitzvot*, without giving much thought to the *ta'am*. However, doing *and* understanding are both integral parts of our acceptance of Torah, as it says:

וַיֹּאמְרוּ כֹּל אֲשֶׁר דִּבֶּר ה'
נַעֲשֶׂה וְנִשְׁמָע

*"and [the people] said: Everything that Hashem has spoken
we will do and we will hear/understand"*[32]

Not only is striving to understand Torah and *mitzvot* not viewed as a threat to observance—it is seen as an essential component of the doing itself, part of our commitment and development in Torah.

Some commentators point out that the order in the aforementioned verse is *na'aseh* and then *nishma*.[33] Doing is seen as a prerequisite for understanding. This can be interpreted in a number of ways. First, there is something that real-life experience contributes to our understanding which abstract conceptual analysis alone cannot provide. Second, observance of the *mitzvot* is seen as the constant. It is in no way predicated upon understanding but rather provides a stable context that supports our continued inquiry over time. Furthermore, it says that while

---

[32] *Shemot* 24:7. Regarding the word ונשמע meaning "understanding," see *Sefat Emet* on *Shemot* 24:7: וזה פי' נעשה ונשמע שעי"י העשיה זוכין אח"כ לשמיעה שהיא ההשגה, whereby in doing we merit comprehension. Also see *Shem Mishmuel, Parshat Vayishlach*, which says, ונשמע' הוא מצד השכל.

[33] See e.g., *Sefat Emet*, previous note.

enrichment of the mind is crucial, what is even more fundamental is that the principles of Torah see the light of day in concrete application, having a practical impact via the *mitzvot*.

However, the relationship does not only go in one direction. Just as the tradition recognizes that doing leads to understanding, it also acknowledges the opposite—that understanding leads to action. *Limud Torah* leads to observance of the Torah.[34] So there is something akin to a "symbiotic" relationship between doing and understanding, whereby each fosters and strengthens the other.

In sum, the goal of *ta'amei hamitzvot* is two-fold: First, it is to sufficiently satisfy the mind and not leave it wanting, so that when we are involved in observance, in the experience of the *mitzvot*, we can do so with the mind at ease, knowing that the Torah does not force us to bypass common sense and reason. Second, an understanding of *ta'amei hamitzvot* can translate into a more enriched experience, bringing greater meaning to our observance. To understand Torah from a usability standpoint (e.g., learning practical Halacha) is an important endeavor in its own right. But *ta'amei hamitzvot* goes further. It is part of the lifelong quest to comprehend, to the greatest extent possible, the underlying principles and intent of Torah. To understand the "reasoning" behind the Torah is to more closely identify with its goals and purpose, to get into the mindset of the system. It is a path to intimacy and connection with Torah. That is the power of "*ta'am*"—not to justify observance, but rather to infuse it with meaning, relevance and a sense of connectedness.

וְנִהְיֶה... כֻּלָּנוּ יוֹדְעֵי שְׁמֶךָ וְלוֹמְדֵי תוֹרָתֶךָ לִשְׁמָהּ

May... all of us know Your legacy and learn Your Torah for its legacy

---

Learning Torah Lishma – for its Shem

Related to the idea of *ta'am*, and investigating the intent of Torah and *mitzvot*, is the concept of *Torah lishma*. The phrase is generally understood to mean "Torah for its own sake," meaning to exclude learning

---

34 See *Kiddushin* 40a, נענו כולם ואמרו תלמוד גדול שהתלמוד מביא לידי מעשה.

Torah for ulterior motives such as financial gain, honor or reward.[35] But "for its own sake" is not an exact translation. Rather, *lishma* is literally "for its *shem*." As the *bracha* says, "May we all become aware of Your *shem* and learn Torah for its *shem*." A *shem* is a name. In the wider sense it is a legacy. As we discussed earlier, the Midrash speaks about a *shem* as a sequence of *otiyot* (letters) which describe or define a "thing." It is a plan or program—a statement of *intent*.[36]

In this sense, learning Torah *lishma* does not simply mean learning "what" Torah says—it means learning Torah for its *intent*. It is a mindset that seeks to know the program or plan which underlies the instructions of the Torah. It relates to the motivating principles, function and purpose of Torah—what the Torah is designed to manifest. As we have discussed, the underlying intent and goal of Torah is to bring Life into the world. The Midrash states:

תורה נתתי לישראל שהיא חיים לעולם
"I gave Torah to Yisrael, which is life for the world"[37]

So if we have already identified the overall intent of the Torah to be "Life," what does it mean then to learn Torah *lishma*, to strive to understand its intent? Here we can refer back to the prior discussion on *ta'amei hamitzvot*. There is the more "general" approach to *ta'amei hamitzvot*, to understand what they are meant to accomplish overall. That is the question we have a proposed answer to—the goal is Life. However, "Life" is a very broad term, one which includes vitality, *simcha*, *ahava*, health, *bracha*, *kedusha*, growth, *shalom*—any number of factors that contribute to individual/societal "aliveness." It is identifying those factors, and examining exactly how they are meant to manifest in specific *mitzvot* as well as in specific teachings and texts, which needs to be worked out and clarified. To study *lishma* is to endeavor to understand the intent of the Torah *in fine detail*. This is an undertaking filled with great subtlety and complexity—more than enough material for a lifetime of study.

---

[35] As the Midrash explains, "Lest you say: I will learn Torah so that I will be wealthy, so that I will be called Rabbi, so that I will receive a reward in the World to Come" (*Yalkut Shimoni, Parshat Eikev*). See also Rashi on *Devarim* 11:13; Rambam *Hilchot Teshuva*, Ch. 10; *Sefer Abudraham, Birchot HaShachar*.

[36] See p. 121.

[37] *Sifri*, quoted by Rashi on *Devarim* 32:2.

The *bracha* states, "May we all know Your *shem*, and learn Torah for its *shem*." What this implies is that understanding the *shem Hashem* comes as a result of learning the *"shem"* of the Torah.[38] That is to say, *Hashem*'s name—program or legacy—is expressed in long-form through Torah.[39] When we learn Torah for its *shem*, involving ourselves in the *torat chaim* (life-instruction) and *chukei chaim* (life-laws),[40] by definition we come to know the *"shem hachaim,"*[41] the Life legacy or *shem Hashem*.

הַמְלַמֵּד תּוֹרָה לְעַמּוֹ יִשְׂרָאֵל
Who teaches Torah to His people Yisrael

Goading the Mind

The word *limud* (לימוד, learning/teaching) comes from the same root as *malmed* (מלמד), an "ox goad."[42] That is, *limud* stems from the idea of goading, prodding forward, guiding this way or that. To learn is to prod the mind, to stimulate and guide our thought. Thus *limud Torah*, aside from being about the acquisition of Torah knowledge, also means using Torah to goad or train the mind. The idea is for Torah to prod us, challenge us, help us to ask more refined questions, to think more clearly and sensitively, and to extend our book knowledge into real-world activity, for the betterment of ourselves and those around us.

The *bracha* describes *Hashem* as our *"melamed,"* our teacher. That is to say, how does one effectively use Torah to train the mind? By remembering that *Hashem/chaim* is the overarching principle—the intent and goal—of the system. The Life principle is the mindset that must prod us along the way, so that we keep moving in a healthy and positive direction during our lifelong journey of Torah learning.

---

[38] As in, כי לימוד לשמה היינו לשם ה' (R. Ya'akov Yosef HaKohen, *Sefer Ben Porat Yosef, Parshat Chayei Sara*).

[39] As quoted previously (see Note 34, p. 124), see Ramban, *Introduction to Sefer Bereshit*, כל התורה כולה שמותיו של הקב"ה, "The entire Torah consists of names of *HaKadosh Baruch Hu*."

[40] Both these expressions are employed later in the *Shacharit tefila*—*"chukei chaim"* in the *bracha* preceding the *Shema*, and *"torat chaim"* in the final *bracha* of the *Shemona Esrei*.

[41] As in, הכי קרא שמך יחיים' כי מוצאך מצא חיים (R. Yitzchak ben Sheshet, *Teshuvot HaRivash* 297).

[42] See *Brown-Driver-Briggs Lexicon*, entry for מַלְמֵד/למד. *Shoftim* 3:31 describes Shamgar striking down six hundred Philistines with a *"malmed."* Note also that the original pictograph for the letter *lamed* was an ox goad (╱ in Paleo-Hebrew script).•

Limud, Chinuch and Hora'ah

There are several Hebrew words that carry the meaning "teacher." These include *mechanech*, *moreh* and *melamed*—corresponding to *chinuch*, *hora'ah/torah* and *limud* respectively. *Chinuch* (חינוך) is "initiation," the kick-off or initial rite of passage in learning, becoming accustomed to Torah for the first time. The same root (חנך) is used in the term "*chanukat hamizbe'ach*," initiating the Altar for first use. *Hora'ah* (הוראה) is instruction, direction, from the root *yara* (ירה) meaning "point the way" or "shoot." *Limud* (לימוד) as we said above is goading, training, prodding.

To see how all three contribute to the learning process, we can employ the metaphor of learning how to drive a car. In this context, *hora'ah* would be learning the rules of the road, knowing where and where not to drive, studying the operating instructions for the vehicle. *Chinuch* would be starting the car and getting used to the controls, comfortable behind the wheel. *Limud* would be the ongoing process of learning and adapting to the various real-life scenarios that come up on the road, all the things that prod us to make spot decisions—brake, accelerate, turn left or right, signal, and so on. All three types of learning are therefore essential components in the process.

אֲשֶׁר בָּחַר בָּנוּ מִכָּל הָעַמִּים וְנָתַן לָנוּ אֶת תּוֹרָתוֹ

Who selected us from all the peoples and gave us His Torah

Chosenness and Restriction

The second *bracha* in *Birchot HaTorah* is *Asher Bachar Banu*, "Who has selected/chosen us." Where does the idea of being a "chosen people" come from, and how might we understand this concept? The Torah states:

כִּי עַם קָדוֹשׁ אַתָּה לַה' אֱ-לֹהֶיךָ וּבְךָ בָּחַר ה'
לִהְיוֹת לוֹ לְעַם סְגֻלָּה מִכֹּל הָעַמִּים

"For you are an Am Kadosh to Hashem Elokecha, and Hashem selected you to be, for Him, a people of prized-possession, out of all the peoples"[43]

We can make a number of observations from this verse. First, *Am Yisrael* is selected, chosen, to be an "*am segula*." The word *segula* is used in Tanach to refer to a treasure, like the precious metals and gemstones stored

---

[43] *Devarim* 14:2; see also 7:6.

away inside a palace.[44] As such, it can be taken to imply something of great value. However, the simple definition of the word *segula* is a "possession," a piece of "property," that which *belongs* to someone. The term *am segula* thus may best be understood in the sense of *Am Yisrael* being a "prized possession."[45] The idea of *segula* as property is suggested as well by the language *"am kadosh."* To be *kodesh laShem* is to "belong to *Hashem*" so to speak. It is to be restricted to *Hashem*'s domain, to be beholden to the Life principle. *Am Yisrael* is designated as consecrated property, and such property is subject to special rules and confined to limited use. "Chosenness" is thus a term that suggests possession and *hekdesh* (consecrated property). So rather than implying that there is something "better" about *Am Yisrael*, as it is sometimes characterized, what being "chosen" more accurately reflects is the self-identity of a nation that has undertaken a substantial set of restrictions and responsibilities, a nation that is dedicated and consecrated to the cause of Life.

Furthermore, there is another case where the Torah describes people as being "chosen":

כִּי בוֹ בָּחַר ה' אֱ-לֹהֶיךָ מִכָּל שְׁבָטֶיךָ
לַעֲמֹד לְשָׁרֵת בְּשֵׁם ה' הוּא וּבָנָיו כָּל הַיָּמִים.

"For Hashem Elokecha selected [the Levite kohen] out of all your tribes,
to stand to serve in the name of Hashem—him and his sons—for all days."[46]

Just as *Am Yisrael* is chosen, designated as restricted property, so too are the *kohanim* (priests) chosen.[47] But the choosing of *Am Yisrael* and the choosing of the *kohanim* are not simply two disconnected acts of selection. They are in fact very much linked, since *Am Yisrael* is chosen precisely in order to be *kohanim*:

---

[44] As in, כָּנַסְתִּי לִי גַּם כֶּסֶף וְזָהָב וּסְגֻלַּת מְלָכִים וְהַמְּדִינוֹת (*Kohelet* 2:8).

[45] See *Brown-Driver-Briggs Lexicon*, entry for סגולה, and M. Jastrow, *Dictionary of the Talmud*, סגולא, both of which define *segula* as possession or property. The possession aspect of *segula* is also indicated by the possessive *"לי,"* as in *Shemot* 19:5: וִהְיִיתֶם לִי סְגֻלָּה, "You will be *for Me* a prized-possession."

[46] *Devarim* 18:5; see also 21:5.

[47] The language of "choosing" is also employed in the narrative of Korach, which again concerns the *kohanim*. It says: וְהָיָה הָאִישׁ אֲשֶׁר אֶבְחַר בּוֹ מַטֵּהוּ יִפְרָח...וְהִנֵּה פָּרַח מַטֵּה אַהֲרֹן, "And it will be that the man whom I will choose, his staff will blossom... And behold, the staff of Aharon blossomed" (*Bamidbar* 17:20 and 17:23).

וִהְיִיתֶם לִי סְגֻלָּה מִכָּל הָעַמִּים...
וְאַתֶּם תִּהְיוּ לִי מַמְלֶכֶת כֹּהֲנִים וְגוֹי קָדוֹשׁ

*"and you will be for Me a prized-possession out of all the peoples...
And you will be for Me a kingdom of kohanim and a kadosh nation"*[48]

Once again, we have the term *"segula"* juxtaposed with *"goy kadosh,"* indicating possession. In addition, these two concepts are linked with *kehuna*, designating *Am Yisrael* as a *mamlechet kohanim*, a "kingdom of priests." Meaning, the very notion of *Am Yisrael* being "chosen," being a *segula*, an *am kadosh*, a people subject to restrictions, is connected to being a nation of *kohanim*.

Mamlechet Kohanim – A Radical Experiment

The peoples of the ancient world each had their priests, their *kohanim*. The Torah itself mentions priests in Midian, Egypt and Canaan.[49] From what we know about priests throughout the ancient world, they functioned as bearers of knowledge, teachers of the law, healers for the people, and they presided over sacrifices and other temple rites. They lived under a stricter code of personal conduct than the rest of the nation — in some cases including special dietary restrictions, circumcision, as well as regular ritual immersion of the body in water.[50] A small and elite group, the priesthood in many ways represented the ideal, living according to the best practices of health and morality as they were understood in the day and in their particular culture.

The great and ambitious project of Torah and *Am Yisrael* might then be understood as follows: Rather than limit this ideal to a select few, a small group of *kohanim* who would follow the highest and best practices

---

[48] *Shemot* 19:5–6

[49] See e.g., *Shemot* 3:1 regarding Yitro, כֹּהֵן מִדְיָן; *Bereshit* 46:20 regarding Poti-fera, כֹּהֵן אֹן, of Egypt; *Bereshit* 14:18 regarding Malki-Tzedek, כֹּהֵן לְאֵ-ל עֶלְיוֹן, in the Canaanite city of Shalem. Cf., Rashi on *Bereshit* 47:22, who interprets *"kohen"* to mean a leader, a person of high stature, in the cases of Yitro and Poti-fera. Ibn Ezra (*Bereshit* 41:45) however understands the word *kohen* to mean עוֹבֵד הַשֵּׁם אוֹ עוֹבֵד עֲבוֹדַת גְּלוּלִים in all cases.

[50] Regarding the Egyptian priesthood for instance, Josephus states: "For [the Egyptian Priests], as is said, originally received two commissions from royalty: divine worship and the charge of learning. But all those priests are circumcised, and all abstain from swine's flesh" (*Against Apion* II 140–141). See also: Teeter, *Religion and Ritual in Ancient Egypt*, Cambridge University Press, 2011, pp. 22, 164; Bunson, *Encyclopedia of Ancient Egypt*, Facts on File, 2012, p. 230.

known to the society, *Am Yisrael* would seek to be a *mamlechet kohanim*, an *entire nation* committed to the highest and best mode of conduct. We would *all* take upon ourselves the strictures of *kohanim*... It was a radical idea, to say the least.

Relationship to the Nations

In addition to maintaining a higher set of standards, the task of the *kohanim* is to tend to the well-being of the people. As the Torah states:

וְנָשָׂא אַהֲרֹן אֶת מִשְׁפַּט בְּנֵי יִשְׂרָאֵל עַל לִבּוֹ לִפְנֵי ה' תָּמִיד

"and Aharon will carry the judgment of the Children of Israel upon his heart, before Hashem, continually"[51]

Aharon HaKohen is instructed to have the concern for the life and well-being of *Am Yisrael* on his mind (lit., "upon his heart"), always. That is to say, the task of the *kohanim* is to look after and care for the needs of "non-*kohanim*." The implication then should be fairly clear: If *Am Yisrael* is a *mamlechet kohanim*, a whole nation of priests, then the non-*kohanim* in this case would be literally *everyone else*—i.e., the rest of humanity. Thus, not only is *Am Yisrael* asked to achieve a high standard of personal and national conduct, but it is charged as well with attending to the well-being of the other nations, looking after the peoples of the world—a very ambitious assignment indeed.

This idea carries with it definite implications regarding the attitude that *Am Yisrael* is to have toward the world, and toward non-Jews. For one, despite the fact that the lifestyle of *kohanim* requires a certain degree of separation, they do not live in outright isolation but rather are directly involved with the people, tending to their needs. So too, we can extrapolate that *Am Yisrael* is meant not to isolate itself from the nations[52] but

---

[51] *Shemot* 28:30. Sforno says here, שיתפלל עליהם שיזכו במשפט.

[52] The *pasuk* says regarding *Am Yisrael*, "It is a people that will dwell alone, and it will not be reckoned among the nations" (*Bamidbar* 23:9). However, this is classically interpreted as referring to the future judgment of the nations (see Rashi, Rabbeinu Bachye, ibid.), or alternatively in the sense of *Am Yisrael* remaining distinct and unique, without any nation parallel to it (see *Shemot Rabbah* 15:7). Being distinct is a significant achievement not when one is isolated from others, but rather precisely when one is a part of the world and yet does not meld in and lose his or her identity. Moreover, *Am Yisrael* is charged with the task of being "לאור גוים," a light to the nations (see *Yeshayahu* 42:6, 49:6), and this is rather difficult to fulfill if we reside in isolation.

rather to work alongside peoples everywhere—helping to teach, inspire, heal, innovate, provide relief from suffering, and endeavor to raise up the consciousness of humanity.

Secondly, as incongruous as it would be for *kohanim* to look down their noses at or speak derogatorily about "*non-kohahim*," so too is it equally out of place to use epithets such as "*goy*" and "*shiksa*" to refer condescendingly to non-Jews. The whole purpose of a *kohen* is to attend to the welfare of others—thereby attending to *Hashem*, the Life principle. There is no *kohen* without the non-*kohen*, and there is no nation of *kohanim* without the other nations. It is our job to be there for *them*. Moreover, to deride the 99.8% of humanity who is not Jewish is quite simply to be anti-human, and arguably anti-Creation.[53]

Therefore, in the same way that the well-being of *Am Yisrael* is carried on Aharon's heart, the welfare of non-Jews must be on our hearts continuously, as a matter of dearest concern. This is integral not only to our identity as a *mamlechet kohanim*, but also to the very idea of being "chosen." Because while the *bracha* of *Asher Bachar Banu* is certainly about embracing our unique identity, that identity does not exist in a vacuum. Our true uniqueness is found in the unique and tangible *contribution* that we make to people's lives throughout the world.

Choosing Life

When we consider the idea of chosenness, we might then conclude that it is not so much about being *inherently* special as it is about accepting a *special assignment*, something that should evoke within us a sense of gravity and responsibility—not self-satisfaction.[54] The tradition explains that we were originally selected for this assignment against our will,[55]

---

[53] The Netziv (*Ha'emek Davar*, introduction to *Sefer Bereshit*) states that people who appear religiously "righteous," but who lack concern for fellow human beings, in fact work to "destroy the Creation." He explains that the greatness of the *avot* is that they displayed love, tolerance and *derech eretz* even in their dealings with idolaters and corrupt people: מכל מקום היו עמם באהבה וחשו לטובתם באשר היא קיום הבריאה, "Nevertheless [the *avot*] dealt with them with love and were concerned for their welfare, since that constitutes the continuity of Creation."

[54] Although to the extent that we successfully *fulfill* such an assignment, that is certainly cause for great celebration.

[55] See the following chapter, Note 38, p. 169, regarding *Matan Torah* originally being foisted upon *Am Yisrael* by force. Thus, being "chosen" can also have the connotation of

but in the end it is we who have to make the choice. The other famous instance of "choosing" in the Torah relates to the choice placed in the hands of *Am Yisrael*, the opportunity to choose that which we have been chosen for, to choose to embrace the Torah and embrace Life:

וּבָחַרְתָּ בַּחַיִּים לְמַעַן תִּחְיֶה אַתָּה וְזַרְעֶךָ

"and choose life, so that you will live—you and your offspring"[56]

In sum, the *bracha* of *Asher Bachar Banu* is about the great responsibility we have in being the bearers of Torah—in embodying the legacy of Life. We are charged not only with conducting ourselves in an elevated manner but also with actively looking after the well-being of people throughout the world. This is a task that we choose for ourselves, each day, with a sense of responsibility, determination and joy.

---

being taken against one's will, as the Torah says elsewhere, וַיִּקְחוּ לָהֶם נָשִׁים מִכֹּל אֲשֶׁר בָּחָרוּ, "And they took for themselves women from whomever they chose" (*Bereshit* 6:2).

[56] *Devarim* 30:19

Birchot HaShachar
ברכות השחר

בָּרוּךְ אַתָּה ה׳ אֱ-לֹהֵינוּ מֶלֶךְ הָעוֹלָם...

אֲשֶׁר נָתַן לַשֶּׂכְוִי בִינָה לְהַבְחִין בֵּין יוֹם וּבֵין לָיְלָה... שֶׁלֹּא עָשַׂנִי גוֹי... שֶׁלֹּא עָשַׂנִי עָבֶד... שֶׁלֹּא עָשַׂנִי אִשָּׁה / שֶׁעָשַׂנִי כִּרְצוֹנוֹ... פּוֹקֵחַ עִוְרִים... מַלְבִּישׁ עֲרֻמִּים... מַתִּיר אֲסוּרִים... זוֹקֵף כְּפוּפִים... רוֹקַע הָאָרֶץ עַל הַמָּיִם... שֶׁעָשָׂה לִי כָּל צָרְכִּי... הַמֵּכִין מִצְעֲדֵי גָבֶר... אוֹזֵר יִשְׂרָאֵל בִּגְבוּרָה... עוֹטֵר יִשְׂרָאֵל בְּתִפְאָרָה... הַנּוֹתֵן לַיָּעֵף כֹּחַ.

The following set of fifteen *brachot* (including *HaMa'avir Sheina* in the following chapter) is referred to collectively as *"Birchot HaShachar."*[1] The focus throughout these *brachot* is on the transformation from the sleeping state to waking state, from being bound by unconsciousness to becoming mindful and aware, free to choose our path on this new day.

אֲשֶׁר נָתַן לַשֶּׂכְוִי בִינָה לְהַבְחִין בֵּין יוֹם וּבֵין לָיְלָה
Who gave the rooster/heart discernment to distinguish between day and night

---

This *bracha* is based on the following *pasuk*:

מִי שָׁת בַּטֻּחוֹת חָכְמָה אוֹ מִי נָתַן לַשֶּׂכְוִי בִינָה.

"Who set wisdom in the covered places, or who gave discernment to the sechvi?"[2]

This is the only instance of the word *sechvi* in Tanach, and it is not clear what it means in this *pasuk* except that it parallels the word *tuchot,* "covered places," a term which is also obscure. *Tuchot* may refer to clouds or alternatively to bodily innards.[3] The latter meaning has led to the

---

[1] Not to be confused with the entire set of morning *brachot*, which is sometimes referred to on the whole as *"Birchot HaShachar."*

[2] *Iyov* 38:36

[3] See the entry for טֻחוֹת in the *Brown-Driver-Briggs Lexicon*.

interpretation of the plural *tuchot* as "kidneys,"[4] with the singular *sechvi* as "heart"[5] (all of which are spoken of in the tradition as seats of wisdom and discernment in the body). In Talmudic sources however, *sechvi* means "rooster,"[6] which clearly fits the context of the *bracha*. Namely, the rooster crows when the light of dawn appears, distinguishing between night and day.

That said, the term *sechvi* in the *bracha* may be deliberately ambiguous. Although we appreciate the great service performed by the rooster, the *bracha* speaks about the faculty of *bina*—drawing distinctions in the mind—which is something we generally attribute to human beings, not to our fine-feathered friends nor to any other members of the animal world. The rooster can thus be seen as a metaphor for our own capacity for *bina*—comparative reasoning, conceptual analysis, *din* (judgment) and self-reflection. *Bina* is an integral part of what makes our consciousness uniquely human.[7]

Are We Awake or Asleep?

On the most basic level, the *bracha* expresses appreciation for something that largely goes unnoticed—our ability to know when dawn breaks, so that we wake up at the start of the new day. This may not seem like a difficult feat, but on a more figurative level, knowing day from night can in no way be taken for granted. It is a *bracha* to be able to discern light from darkness, to distinguish enlightenment, awareness and freedom from the lack thereof. Attaining such discernment can often be exceedingly difficult.

We tend to underestimate the effect that our surroundings have on us, the limitations they impose on our thinking. The world is a hypnotic place. We are relentlessly bombarded by messages and attitudes around

---

[4] See e.g., *Bamidbar Rabbah* 10:8, also Rashi and Radak on *Tehilim* 51:8.

[5] See e.g., Ibn Ezra, Malbim and *Metzudat Tzion* on *Iyov* 38:36. Also see the entry for שֶׂכְוִי in the *Gesenius Lexicon*. Cf., *Brown-Driver-Briggs Lexicon*, which renders שֶׂכְוִי as a celestial phenomenon (corresponding to *tuchot* as "clouds"), or alternatively as a rooster.

[6] As in, יאו מי נתן לשכוי בינה׳ זה תרנלול (*Rosh Hashana* 26a). Also see M. Jastrow, *Dictionary of the Talmud*, entry for שֶׂכְוִי.

[7] In addition, the *bracha* does not say that the *sechvi* distinguishes "between night and day" (בֵּין לְיְלָה וּבֵין יום, as one would expect, where the rooster's call marks the transition from night to day) but rather "between day and night," which perhaps is intended to highlight the ambiguity of "*sechvi*," so as to refer both to rooster *and* heart.

us which influence and even define the way we look at things. So while we may perceive ourselves as being free to think as we wish, we are in fact trapped within a very limited worldview, greatly biased by our immediate culture and surroundings, and inescapably influenced by the time in history in which we live. We look back in wonderment and ask how brilliant and enlightened people in centuries past could have owned slaves or done other things that we would find appalling today. But consider: People in the future may wonder about *us* how we could live happily, comfortably, even lavishly, while millions on the planet suffer from disease, hunger and oppression. How can we sleep at night, let alone go a lifetime worrying primarily about ourselves and our families, without making it a top priority to end mass suffering or assist others in need?

This question is especially pertinent for a people who identifies itself as being chosen for a higher calling. Surely a nation that considers itself to be an *am segula*, *mamlechet kohanim* and *goy kadosh* must be especially sensitive to matters of human suffering, and should be vigilant never to become numb to it nor cease in our efforts to promote peace and justice, and to help those in need. Certainly such a nation would make every effort to push itself and the world to "break the spell" as it were, to wake up, get our priorities in order, truly care about the welfare of one another and aspire to ever higher modes of thinking and conduct.

Yet day-to-day life puts us in a trance from which it is extraordinarily difficult to awaken. Thus we consider ourselves awake when in many ways we are very much asleep. We are imprisoned in our own minds, but we are unaware of it, since the mind cannot "go outside the mind" to perceive it. It is like being a prisoner inside a box, but not knowing that there is any outside world beyond the box. It is thinking we are already in the state of *ge'ula* (redemption) when really we remain in *galut* (exile). It is not possessing the *bina* to distinguish day from night.

And this lack of *bina* can work the opposite way as well—i.e., thinking we are in *galut* when really we are in the process of *ge'ula*, being so used to the long, bitter night that we cannot recognize or fully appreciate when dawn has arrived.[8] This is what is at stake when we talk about recognizing day and night. It is a true *bracha* to possess *bina*.

---

[8] An example would be not sufficiently waking up to and appreciating the extraordinary historic/religious/*halachic* significance of the establishment, populating and building up of the

שֶׁלֹּא עָשַׂנִי גּוֹי... עָבֶד... אִשָּׁה / שֶׁעָשַׂנִי כִּרְצוֹנוֹ
Who did not make me a non-Jew... a slave... a woman /
Who made me according to His will

Shelo Asani – Embracing the Self and the Other

Most of the *brachot* in *Birchot HaShachar* are brought in the Talmud as being associated with specific morning activities.[9] However, the three *brachot* regarding not having been made a non-Jew, a slave or a woman constitute a separate unit and are brought elsewhere in the Talmud:

חייב אדם לברך שלש ברכות בכל יום, אלו הן:
שעשאני ישראל, שלא עשאני אשה, שלא עשאני בור.

"A person is obligated to make three brachot every day, and they are:
'Who made me a Yisrael', 'Who did not make me a woman',
'Who did not make me a brute'."[10]

Notes in the Vilna edition point out that the correct wording of the first *bracha* is not "*she'asani Yisrael*" but rather "*shelo asani goy.*"[11] As for "*shelo asani bur,*" the Talmud itself goes on to change it from *bur* (brute) to *eved* (slave).[12] As such, we have the three traditional *brachot* of *shelo asani goy*, *shelo asani aved* and *shelo asani isha*.

The Talmud elsewhere states explicitly that the reason for saying *shelo asani isha* is that women are not obligated in the *mitzvot* to the same degree as men.[13] And indeed the tradition recognizes all three *brachot* as relating to categories of people who are not obligated in some or all of

---

State of Israel, and the new era it ushers in for the Jewish people. One does not have to say it is "the" *ge'ula*, but it is without a doubt a *ge'ula*, in a very profound and concrete way.

[9] E.g., saying "*poke'ach ivrim*" when opening one's eyes, "*malbish arumim*" when getting dressed, etc. See *Brachot* 60b, which mentions eleven of the fifteen *brachot* in *Birchot HaShachar* as corresponding to activities associated with waking up. The "*shelo asani*" set is another three, and the last (sourced much later than the Talmud) is "*hanoten laya'ef ko'ach.*"

[10] *Menachot* 43b

[11] This is according to the wording of the *Tosefta Brachot*, *Perek* 6, as well as the Rif, Rosh.

[12] According to Rashi, it was deemed improper to make a *bracha* that one was not made a brute, either because it sounds arrogant or because even a brute is obligated in the *mitzvot*. (See ahead regarding the theme of *mitzvot* obligation.) There is however a Midrashic tradition that includes both *bur* and *aved*, making it a series of four *brachot* in total (see *Pirkei Rabbeinu HaKadosh* 4:13).

[13] See *Yerushalmi Brachot* 9:2.

the *mitzvot*.[14] A non-Jew is exempt from all *mitzvot*, aside from the seven *mitzvot* of *Bnei Noach*. Both an *eved kena'ani* (lit., "Canaanite slave") and a woman are exempt from positive time-bound *mitzvot*.[15]

Many commentators ask the question: Wouldn't it have been more straightforward, and in fact more fitting, to express these *brachot* in the positive (e.g., *she'asani Yisrael*, *she'asani ben chorin*, *she'asani ish*), rather than emphasizing what a person is *not*?[16] One answer given is that if we were to say *she'asani Yisrael*, this would include (and thus render superfluous) the next two *brachot*, since "*Yisrael*" already implies not being an *eved kena'ani*, and it implies being a male (feminine form would be "*Yisraelit*"). Formulating it in the negative therefore allows a person to say all three *brachot*.[17] Others cite an idea brought in the Talmud that it may have been better for human beings not to have been created at all, so therefore we do not express gratitude for "being made" per se, but rather we speak about how we were *not* made, i.e., in an indirect manner.[18] Still others respond that the negative functions as a sort of positive, since saying "*she'asani*" only acknowledges the creation of oneself, whereas "*shelo asani*" also recognizes the creation—and therefore the inherent value—of others.[19]

To expand on the last explanation, perhaps we can understand the way these *brachot* are formulated as relating to the theme of the previous *bracha* (*Hanoten Lasechvi Bina*) and the capacity for *bina*, being able to distinguish between one thing and another, the self and the other.[20]

---

[14] As in, מברכין שלא עשני גוי שאינו בר מצות כלל (Shelah, *Chulin*, *Perek Derech Chaim*). See also Abudraham, R. Yehuda Bar-Yakar and Ra'aven on *Birchot HaShachar*.

[15] Although some understand "*shelo asani aved*" to include an *eved ivri*, a Jewish indentured servant (see Ra'aven, ibid.), it is generally accepted that the *bracha* refers exclusively to an *eved kena'ani*, a Canaanite slave acquired or captured in war. Whereas an *eved ivri* was obligated in all the *mitzvot*, like any Jew, an *eved kena'ani* was seen as having a special status as part of *Bnei Yisrael*, observing most of the *mitzvot* but being exempt from "*mitzvot aseh shehazman grama*," positive time-bound *mitzvot*.

[16] As in, לכאורה קשה דלא תני לכולהו ברכות דהיינו שעשני ישראל, שעשני בן חורין, שעשני זכר (*Tzlach*, *Brachot*, *Perek Haro'eh*). See also *Magen Avraham* (*Orach Chaim* 46:9).

[17] See *Bach* (*Orach Chaim* 46), *Aruch Hashulchan* (Ibid., 46:10), *Magen Avraham* (Ibid., 46:9).

[18] See *Magen Avraham* (Ibid., 46:9), *Aruch Hashulchan* (Ibid., 46:10), *Tzlach* (*Brachot*, *Perek Haro'eh*), based on *Eruvin* 13b: נוח לו לאדם שלא נברא יותר משנברא.

[19] As in, ואילו היה מברך 'שעשני ישראל' היה משמע שעשיית האחרות אינה עשייה כלל (*Aruch Hashulchan*, *Orach Chaim* 46:9).

[20] This is the idea of "*havdala*," acknowledging distinctions. It has been suggested that these *brachot* were in fact formulated as part of a polemic regarding distinctions, brought

Meaning, it is a kind of recognition of self that is achieved by acknowledging the existence of another.[21] And it is appreciating one's obligation to the *mitzvot* by acknowledging others who have less of an obligation.

Now, the question we might reasonably ask is: Are the above explanations truly sufficient? Many certainly feel that they are and regard the *"shelo asani"* *brachot* as positive affirmations of identity, no more and no less. However, there are those who deem *Shelo Asani Goy* and *Shelo Asani Isha* to nonetheless be problematic, since the negative formulation of the *brachot* has the potential to come across as a slight—as if to imply that being made a woman or a non-Jew is an "undesirable" thing. To use an analogy: If another religion were to include in its liturgy a prayer of thanks for "not making me a Jew," we might understandably raise our eyebrows as Jews—*despite* any positive explanations we were offered—simply because of the way such a prayer sounds at face value.

What this highlights is a tension that sometimes exists between the way we *understand* our tradition and the way it is *perceived*. While we endeavor to interpret the tradition "sweetly,"[22] this interpretation may not always be apparent in the plain meaning of the text, creating the possibility that despite our best efforts, the tradition will leave others with a bitter taste. There may be no way to entirely resolve this tension. Indeed as a matter of practice, individuals are sometimes forced to choose either to let go of concerns about way the tradition is perceived in the eyes of others, or to let go of parts of the tradition itself. However, we can still appreciate that ideally our goal is to maintain *both*—to honor the tradition by conceptualizing it as sweetly/pleasantly as possible, and also to honor people's

---

against the Christian doctrine of Paul, who is quoted as saying, "There is neither Jew nor Greek, there is neither slave nor free man, there is neither man nor woman, for you are all one..." (See e.g., *Jews, Greeks and Barbarians* by Martin Hengel, Fortress Press, 1980, p. 79.) That is, whereas this doctrine sought to blur distinctions of identity, to bring people into the ideological fold under the banner of unity, the *"shelo asani"* *brachot* aimed to affirm identity boundaries and thus rebuff the doctrine.

[21] To illustrate the point, we can look at *Brachot* 43b, which mentions another *bracha* formulated in the negative: ברוך שלא חיסר בעולמו כלום וכו׳, said upon seeing fruit trees in bloom in the month of Nisan. Rather than say more directly, "Who gave the world everything," we say, "Who did not cause anything to be lacking in the world." By invoking the idea of lack, the experience of fullness and bounty becomes all the more magnified. Likewise, it can be argued that our experience of self is magnified when we think about ourselves as distinct from others.

[22] See p. 143, regarding the concept of "sweetness" in our words and interpretations.

sensibilities, to recognize that no tradition is fully *"shalem"* (complete) unless it succeeds in imparting that *"ta'am,"* that pleasant taste, to others.

Kirtzono – the Will for Life

It is clear that the *"shelo asani"* *brachot* were not originally formulated for women to recite. However, over time it became the custom for women to say these *brachot*, but with *she'asani kirtzono* ("Who made me according to His will") in place of *shelo asani isha*.[23] The will of *Hashem*, as we have suggested, is the "will for Life." Therefore, to state that a woman is created *"kirtzono"* is to say that she is the very embodiment of the *retzon hachaim*. Her special vitality, her capacity to give forth another human life—her very being—manifests and radiates the will for Life.

Gender and the Zachar-Nekeiva Distinction

The above *brachot* relate to three distinctions—between *Am Yisrael* and the nations, between free people and slaves, and between women and men. However, it should be emphasized that "man" and "woman" are not equivalent to "maleness" and "femaleness" as conveyed in the concepts of *"zachar"* and *"nekeiva."* The Torah states:

זָכָר וּנְקֵבָה בְּרָאָם וַיְבָרֶךְ אֹתָם
וַיִּקְרָא אֶת שְׁמָם אָדָם בְּיוֹם הִבָּרְאָם.

"Male and female He created them, and He blessed them,
and He called their name 'adam' on the day they were created."[24]

The straightforward meaning of *zachar* and *nekeiva* here is clearly male and female of the species, referring to gender—man and woman.[25] However, when the *pasuk* says, "He called *their* name 'adam'," we might also view this in more conceptual terms, implying that *adam* is really *zachar* and *nekeiva* put together. That is, only with a combination of male and female attributes can one be considered truly "human." Indeed, the

---

[23] Some women also have the custom of saying *"shelo asani shifcha"* instead of *"aved,"* and *"shelo asani goya"* instead of *"goy"* (see *Yalkut Yosef, Orach Chaim* 46:17). The *bracha* of *She'asani Kirtzono* is not sourced in the Talmud and is a custom that appears to have been introduced many centuries later. Early mentions of the *bracha* appear in the *Tur* and *Sefer Abudraham* (late 13th to early 14th centuries).

[24] *Bereshit* 5:2

[25] The phrase "He called their name *adam*" thus does not refer to the personal name "Adam" but rather to the common noun *adam*, "humankind," which includes both male and female.

Midrash cites this *pasuk* to state that Adam was originally created androgynous, a combination of *zachar* and *nekeiva*. Only afterwards did the two genders split off from one another and become two separate beings.[26]

Beyond their use as designations of gender, *zachar* and *nekeiva* are understood in the Kabbalah tradition as having conceptual and functional meanings. *Zachar* is the projecting outward of one's energy or raw vitality, and *nekeiva* is the channeling, guiding and containing of that energy, in order to put it to productive use. We have already spoken about this distinction, albeit not in male-female terms. *Zachar* and *nekeiva* are expressed in the concepts of *ohr* and *kli*, *chesed* and *gevura*, *rachamim* and *din*, *chochma* and *bina*, *netzach* and *hod*, and *mashpia* and *mekabel* respectively.[27] It is not one but *both* aspects that are necessary for any system to function and thrive.

That does not mean however that there cannot be dominances of *zachar* or *nekeiva* which localize in one area or another, one person or another, or one time or another. There is a place for the dominance of compassion, as well as the dominance of judgment. There is a place for the dominance of assertion, and the dominance of deference. There is a place for inspiration to dominate, and for critical analysis to dominate. There is a place for giving to dominate, and for withholding or receiving to dominate.[28] These all map onto *zachar* and *nekeiva* dominances respectively, and we know from real-life experience that each of these dominances—whether the *zachar* variety or *nekeiva* variety—can localize in both women and men alike.

Point being, *zachar* and *nekeiva* can by no means be mapped exclusively onto gender distinctions. They are essential, complementary functions that coexist within *any* system, in every man and every woman, and are present at all times in a relationship. Whether man or woman, there is a time to be "male" and a time to be "female," a time to give and a time to receive, a time to extend outward and a time to focus inward, a time to put forth one's energy and a time to weigh, consider and ana-

---

[26] See *Bereshit Rabbah* 8:1.

[27] *Zachar* and *nekeiva* are understood throughout Kabbalah literature in this frame. See e.g., the Ramak's *Pardes Rimonim* 23:22.

[28] We might understand this as similar to *Kohelet*'s לַכֹּל זְמָן וְעֵת (3:1), that there is a time and season for everything—love and hate, breaking down and building up, etc. That is to say, dominances are recognized as having their appropriateness and relevance as a part of life.

lyze. So notwithstanding the man-woman norms adopted by society, the notion of "fixed roles" based on gender is conceptually inconsistent with the idea of *zachar* and *nekeiva* as outlined above. Roles are necessarily *dynamic*, reflecting what is called for in a given moment in order to complement the other, to bring success to the system, and to foster *shalom*, *bracha*, and *simcha*—all the critical signs of life.

Fig. 30   Zachar/Nekeiva conceptual correspondences

Zachar	Nekeiva
Chochma	Bina
Chesed	Gevura
Netzach	Hod
Mashpia	Mekabel
Rachamim	Din
Hashem	Elokim
Etz HaChaim	Etz HaDa'at
Ohr	Kli
Energy	Consciousness
Being/Experiencing	Self-reflection/Analysis
Radiating	Channeling/Directing

פּוֹקֵחַ עִוְרִים / מַלְבִּישׁ עֲרֻמִּים
Who opens [the eyes of] the blind / Who clothes the naked

Adam and Chava – Awakening the Tzelem Elokim

The *brachot* of *Poke'ach Ivrim* (giving sight to the blind) and *Malbish Arumim* (clothing the naked) are highly suggestive of the primordial "awakening" described in the Garden of Eden story. After Adam and Chava eat from the *Etz HaDa'at*, the Torah states:

וַתִּפָּקַחְנָה עֵינֵי שְׁנֵיהֶם וַיֵּדְעוּ כִּי עֵירֻמִּם הֵם
וַיִּתְפְּרוּ עֲלֵה תְאֵנָה וַיַּעֲשׂוּ לָהֶם חֲגֹרֹת.

"The eyes of the two of them were opened, and they were aware that they were naked, and they sewed a fig leaf and made for themselves loin coverings."[29]

---

[29] *Bereshit* 3:7. R. Yehuda Bar-Yakar, Abudraham and Ra'aven on *Birchot Hashachar* all cite this *pasuk* or related *psukim* (Ibid., 3:5, 3:21) as the source for *Poke'ach Ivrim/Malbish Arumim*.

When the Torah says that their eyes were opened, it is undoubtedly speaking figuratively. Prior to eating from the *Etz HaDa'at*, Adam and Chava were clearly not walking around with their eyes closed—rather, they were not fully *conscious*. It is to say that humankind lacked a certain capacity for self-awareness. We were in a quasi-sleeping state, such that we could not "see" or perceive in a fundamentally human way. That is, while the first part of the Creation narrative relates to the emergence of *adam*, the human "species," the eating from the *Etz HaDa'at* is seen as marking the beginning of the story—the history—of *human beings*.

The distinction of humanity, according to the Torah, is our having been created in the *tzelem Elokim*. But this distinction is only fully realized after eating from the *Etz HaDa'at*, after the dawn of conscious self-awareness.[30] Prior to that, the *tzelem Elokim* is dormant, *da'at* and the conscious mind still in a state of incubation, in potential. The *pasuk* states explicitly that Adam and Chava would not be like *Elokim* until they ate from the fruit of *da'at*:

כִּי יֹדֵעַ אֱ-לֹהִים כִּי בְּיוֹם אֲכָלְכֶם מִמֶּנּוּ
וְנִפְקְחוּ עֵינֵיכֶם וִהְיִיתֶם כֵּא-לֹהִים יֹדְעֵי טוֹב וָרָע.

"Because Elokim knows that on the day of your eating from it,
your eyes will be opened, and you will be like Elokim, knowing good and bad."[31]

Ingesting the fruit of the *Etz HaDa'at* is the conceptual origin of the human faculty of judgment, the ability to analyze and reflect, to distinguish between good and bad, and between the self and the other. *Da'at* is the mark of the human being.

The Dawn of Consciousness as the Beginning of History

This is perhaps why, according to Torah tradition, history and the counting of years is thought to begin from the time of Adam and Chava. Only once humankind is "reborn" as it were with *da'at*, and attains a sufficient level of abstract self-reflection, can there exist any notion of "history." In other words, history begins when we realize that we *have* a history, when we begin to reflect on (tell tales of, record) our past and think

---

[30] As such, the concept of the *tzelem Elokim* is understood in Kabbalah to be associated with *"da'at"* and *"mochin,"* i.e., cognitive functioning (see the Arizal's *Likutei Torah, Parshat Bereshit*; also *Etz Chaim* 25:1).

[31] *Bereshit* 3:5

ahead to the future.[32] Simply "being," living, might be described as our *"tzelem Hashem,"* a property that we share with all other animals, but *pondering* that being and existence is the exclusive domain of the *tzelem Elokim*, a capability that belongs to human beings alone.

Three Phases of Development

We are all familiar with the three-act play. The first act is the setup, introduction of the characters, setting, and so on. The second act is where the protagonists undergo a crisis, a challenge, where pressure and suspense are introduced within the story. The third act is the time of resolution, when equilibrium is restored, pressure is alleviated, and when the protagonists have—we hope—risen to the challenge, emerged successful, and undergone a positive transformation in the process.

This is very much the same developmental structure that runs through concepts in Torah: setup, shakeup and transformation. Phase One is the setup, characterized by our existing in a natural state of flow. Phase Two is the shakeup, when consciousness is awakened, the natural flow is disrupted, and new challenges—indeed great pain and suffering—are experienced. Phase Three is when we overcome our challenges, when our labor and toil pay off, and we emerge anew, transformed, fundamentally evolved, and far better off than we were originally.

The paradigm for Phase One is "Eden," humankind in its primordial, "proto-conscious" state. Eden represents our intellectual infancy, wherein we simply experience the natural rhythms of life without self-reflection. We may be "intelligent," but we are essentially creatures of instinct. Phase One is characterized by *Hashem* and the *Etz HaChaim*.[33]

Human history per se really begins with the start of Phase Two, as our conscious minds awaken and we are "banished" from Eden. Phase Two is *galut* (exile), disconnection from the source of life, from our natural

---

[32] This relates to the concepts of Creation and *tzimtzum*. Before there is an initial distinction, there is no "time" per se. Likewise, before Adam is capable of making the conscious distinctions that allow humankind to reflect on the self and the other, good and bad, past and future, there is no "historical time" in the sense of the human perception thereof, the marking of calendars, etc. So when we refer to the Hebrew year, as in "the year 5700 from the creation of the world," we might understand this "creation of the world" as reflecting a *tzimtzum* of sorts in the mind of human beings, the first faint echoes of our historical memory, our very earliest distinctions in time. (See p. 58, regarding the concept of *tzimtzum*.)

[33] See p. 74, on the concepts of *Hashem/Etz HaChaim* and *Elokim/Etz HaDa'at*.

state of flow. It is the time when we must go it on our own, learn how to handle the conscious mind—its awesome power and its capacity for both creation and destruction, *tov* and *ra*. It is a learning process that entails immeasurable hardship and bloodshed, one that spans the entirety of human history until today. Phase Two is characterized by *Elokim* and the *Etz HaDa'at*.

Finally, assuming we rise to the challenge and emerge intact, we arrive at Phase Three, *ge'ula* (redemption). We reach a level of conscious maturation where the great power of the human mind is used predominantly for constructive, creative, life-enhancing purposes. We cease attempting to destroy one another, either in our drive for survival or in the name of perverse ideologies. Instead, we find ways to come together in creative collaboration, to explore and discover, remake ourselves, and unlock the secrets of life itself. Phase Three is characterized by *Hashem-Elokim*. It is a return to the *Etz HaChaim*—only this time by way of the *Etz HaDa'at*, equipped with full awareness, and as the result of our own efforts. Phase Three is about using the mind for the advancement of Life.

What begins as disconnection results in independence. The same consciousness that starts as a curse becomes the basis for great transformation and growth. This accords with the opinion in the Talmud that the same *Etz HaDa'at* that served as an agent of destruction was later used as the agent of rectification:

שבדבר שנתקלקלו בו נתקנו

"For with the thing through which they were damaged, they were rectified."[34]

Da'at is thus the address for *"tikun."* Human consciousness, which might be termed "ground zero" for the problems that afflict humankind, is also the arena with the greatest potential for rectification and advance.

The three-phase pattern we have outlined above in fact localizes in numerous themes throughout the Torah tradition. We will now explore several of these: The three Temples, the three names in the *pasuk* of *Shema Yisrael* in relation to the three calls of the *shofar*, the three sons of Noach, the three phases in relation to the *bechor* (firstborn), the three

---

[34] *Brachot* 40a. This opinion says that the *Etz HaDa'at* is a fig tree, whereby the same tree that provides the fruit also provides the leaves with which Adam and Chava cover themselves. (See also Rashi on *Bereshit* 3:7.)

phases of questioning, and finally the question of "Why do the righteous suffer?" and the three phases within the *Book of Iyov* (Job).[35]

Three Phases: Three Temples

Bayit Rishon (the First Temple) corresponds to Phase One. According to some classical sources, *korbanot* (sacrifices) were instituted to keep *Am Yisrael* away from idolatry.[36] In the ancient world, having a temple and sacrifices was a natural extension of human consciousness and society. Every people served its god(s), used sacrifices to gain divine favor and to restore equilibrium, neutralizing the worry and guilt weighing on the mind. To bring a *korban* in *Bayit Rishon*—like during the prior days of the *Mishkan*—was to engage in a highly physical, visceral, intuitive experience. This is mirrored by descriptions in Tanach of the *Anan* and *Kevod Hashem*, manifestations of the *"Shechina"* (localization of *Hashem*), which are depicted in visual, tangible terms following the construction of *Bayit Rishon*, just as they are in relation to the *Mishkan* in the desert.[37]

Phase One/*Bayit Rishon* can be understood in this sense as an extension of the *Mishkan* and of *Matan Torah* (the giving of the Torah). *"Matan"* implies *matana*, a "gift" that *Am Yisrael* is given, top-down, at Sinai. Indeed Chazal depict Mount Sinai as being held over our heads, such that the Torah is presented to us as a gift we cannot refuse.[38] That is to say, during *Matan Torah*, there is little choice involved or decision made. Torah is simply imposed upon us. We are as children, given a set of rules to follow on the basis of *emuna*, on faith, without the prerequisite of first understanding the rationale of the Torah. It is a period that is dominated by *"na'aseh"* ("we will do") and less so by *"nishma"* ("we will hear/understand").[39] Phase One is about intuition, experience, simply

---

[35] This pattern is also expressed in the *bracha* of *Elokai Neshama* (see p. 117): Life is given, then subsequently taken, and finally restored—only to a far greater level than the original.

[36] See *Vayikra Rabbah, Parshat Acharei Mot* 22:8, אמר הקב״ה יהיו מקריבין לפני בכל עת קרבנותיהן באהל מועד והן נפרשים מעבודת כוכבים. Also see Rambam, *Moreh Nevuchim* 3:32.

[37] See I *Melachim* 8:10–11 and compare to *Shemot* 40:34–35. Also see p. 104, on the concept of *"Kevod Hashem."*

[38] See *Shabbat* 88a. Chazal interpret the *pasuk,* "They stood at the bottom of the mountain" (ויתיצבו בתחתית ההר, *Shemot* 19:17), to mean that Mount Sinai was hoisted over their heads "like a barrel." *Am Yisrael* is given an ultimatum: "If you accept the Torah, it is well; if not, there [underneath the mountain] will be your burial."

[39] See p. 147, regarding the concept of *"na'aseh venishma."*

going with the flow and following the rules—or not following them and then dealing with the consequences.

Bayit Sheni (the Second Temple) is Phase Two. Despite this period involving a return from exile, it retains many aspects of *galut*. The ten northern tribes (most of *Am Yisrael*) are absent, having been exiled some 200 years earlier by Assyria. Of the remaining tribes (referred to collectively as the *Yehudim*, the "Jews"), only some 43,000 return to the land of Israel, a small fraction compared to the vast majority who remain in Babylonia.[40] Unlike the time of Shlomo HaMelech and the building of the First Temple, there is no account of "Clouds" or the *Kevod Hashem* appearing at the completion of the Second Temple. In fact there is no *Aron* (Ark of the Covenant), which has been missing (or hidden) since the first destruction.[41] *Kehuna* (priesthood) in the Second Temple is infamously marked by politics, corruption and bribery.[42] The notion of a *korban* as an intuitive vehicle for personal/societal rectification gradually becomes overshadowed by Greek thinking, the *Mikdash* and its proceedings viewed instead in the light of cultural aesthetics.[43]

At the same time however comes an intellectual renaissance unparalleled in our people's history. The Anshe Knesset Hagedola ("Great Assembly" of sages), schools of Hillel and Shamai, the Tanaim of the Mishna—the great early sages of Chazal—are a product of Second Temple times. The piercing logic of the Gemara, the legal analysis of Halacha, the Rabbinic Judaism which has come to characterize the Torah world until today, including most of the *tefilot* and *brachot* we have been discussing—all these are the great works of Chazal, products of their bold and visionary thinking. This is the time of the great pouring forth

---

[40] As in, ואף בזמן בית שני נשארו רוב ישראל בגלות תחת יד מלכי אומות העולם (R. Tzadok HaKohen, *Machshavot Charutz* 20).

[41] As the Talmud states: חמשה דברים שהיו בין מקדש ראשון למקדש שני ואלו הן, ארון וכפורת וכרובים, אש, ושכינה, ורוח הקודש, ואורים ותומים (*Yoma* 21b).

[42] See e.g., *Yevamot* 61a and *Yoma* 18a, which relate the story of money being paid to nominate Yehoshua ben Gamla as *Kohen Gadol*. Also, the Midrash speaks about only eighteen people who were *Kohen Gadol* during the period of the First Temple, as opposed to eighty in the Second Temple (*Yoma* 9a says three hundred), the reason being that during the Second Temple the *kehuna* was sold for money, so the *kohanim* did not merit long tenures (see *Sifri Bamidbar* 131).

[43] See J. Levinson, *Chanukah: A Light to the Future*, 2010, p. 21.

of the Oral Torah.[44] It is an era understood in the tradition as initiating with the statement *"kimu vekiblu"* at the time of Purim:

קִיְּמוּ וְקִבְּל הַיְּהוּדִים עֲלֵיהֶם... אֶת שְׁנֵי הַיָּמִים הָאֵלֶּה

"The Jews established and accepted upon themselves… these two days"[45]

After hearing the directive to celebrate Purim, we officially affirm our desire to observe it as a holiday. Chazal however interpret the words *kimu vekiblu* to mean, "They established what they had accepted already,"[46] i.e., at the time of *Matan Torah*. That is, we solidified and made firm (were *mekayem*) our connection to Torah, which we had already received (were *mekabel*) at Sinai. At Sinai, Torah was thrust upon us from the top-down. On Purim, we "rose up" (*kimu*) and received (*kiblu*) Torah, from the bottom-up. That "bottom-up" orientation of *kimu vekiblu* relates to the great intellectual heritage of the Oral Torah.[47] We reach up to grasp Torah with our minds, to connect with it not as a compulsory gift but as a result of being *"koneh"* the Torah, "acquiring" it out of our own volition and our own understanding. This period represents our transition to the *"nishma"* component of *"na'aseh venishma."*

Thus, Phase Two at once constitutes a disconnection from the vitality of Phase One, as well as a considerable *upgrade* from Phase One. *Bayit Sheni* is a far cry from *Bayit Rishon*,[48] but it is a departure that, while painful, creates the opportunity for us to evolve into something greater.

Bayit Shlishi (the Third Temple) is Phase Three, a projection into future times, the era of redemption. What exactly such a structure is envisioned to be, and what kinds of activities would theoretically be done there, are the subject of much conjecture. Some sources suggest that *korbanot* would be all but eliminated in a future *Bayit Shlishi*.[49] The

---

[44] See R. Tzadok HaKohen, ועיקר יסוד תורה שבעל פה התחיל אז מאנשי כנסת הגדולה (*Machshavot Charutz* 17). Also see *Kedushat Levi,* וממרדכי ואילך התחילו אנשי כנסת הגדולה ויסוד התפלה (*Shemot, L'Purim*).

[45] *Esther* 9:27

[46] קיימו מה שקיבלו כבר, *Shabbat* 88a.

[47] See R. Tzadok HaKohen and *Kedushat Levi* (Ibid.).

[48] See *Ezra* 3:12, which speaks of the elders, who had seen the glory of *Bayit Rishon*, weeping at the sight of *Bayit Sheni*.

[49] The Midrash relates: לעתיד לבא כל הקרבנות בטלין וקרבן תודה אינו בטל, that in the future, all *korbanot* will be eliminated except for the *korban todah* (*Vayikra Rabbah* 9:7, 27:12; *Tanchuma, Parshat Emor* 19; *Yalkut Shimoni, Parshat Tzav*).

predominant view however is that *korbanot* would resume as before.[50] Conflicting pictures of the future notwithstanding, we might speculate the following in accordance with the three-phase developmental model: The First Temple is about *korban*. The Second Temple is about the introduction of *tefila* (prayer) in conjunction with *korban*, which eventually becomes *tefila bimkom korban*, prayer in place of sacrifice. The transition is from a highly physical, visceral, intuitive and centralized process of rectification and giving of one's life-energy, to a more conscious, intellectual, abstracted, internal and individual process. It is a shift from the predominance of *chaim* to the predominance of *da'at*.

From a conceptual standpoint, Phase Three and *Bayit Shlishi* should be expected to comprise a sort of synthesis of *Bayit Rishon* and *Bayit Sheni*, the integration of *chaim* and *da'at*. Although the traditional view would see that synthesis as once again being the presence of both *korban* and *tefila* simultaneously,[51] the three-phase model is not one of A + B = AB, but rather A + B = C. In other words, Phase Three is not simply a combination of Phases One and Two, nor is it (as commonly thought) a return to the "good old days" of Phase One. Phase Three is something *new*, an "*ohr chadash*." It is the culmination of all the hard work of Phase Two, producing something that one might see as "analogous" to Phase One in the sense of vitality and *shalom* being restored, but it is vitality on a plane that is qualitatively and quantitatively different from anything in our prior experience. Phase Three is about a quantum leap, an evolutionary shift in the development of humankind. It is *chaim* reclaimed by *da'at*, Life reclaimed—that is, extended and enriched—by human understanding.

Phase Three existence is a world where the intellect is used toward the advancement of life—for the understanding of life itself, and for the betterment of humanity. It is a world ripe with developments in science

---

[50] *Yechezkel* 40–47 gives a vision of the final *Mikdash* (וְשָׁכַנְתִּי בְתוֹכָם לְעוֹלָם, 43:9) and discusses the sacrifices to be performed therein, including וְהַמִּנְחָה וְהַחַטָּאת וְהָאָשָׁם (42:13). *Yirmiyahu* 33 speaks about the future era (בַּיָּמִים הָהֵם וּבָעֵת הַהִיא, 33:15), which includes sacrifices, מַעֲלֶה עוֹלָה וּמַקְטִיר מִנְחָה (33:18). The Rambam states regarding the times of *Mashiach*, ובונה מקדש, that the *Mikdash* will be built, and מקריבין קרבנות כשהיו מקודם, that *korbanot* will be reinstated "as they were before" (*Hilchot Melachim* 11:1). Also, our daily *tefila* anticipates the restoration of *korbanot* (see e.g., the *bracha* of *Avoda* in *Shemona Esrei*).

[51] As it says, עוֹלֹתֵיהֶם וְזִבְחֵיהֶם לְרָצוֹן עַל מִזְבְּחִי כִּי בֵיתִי בֵּית תְּפִלָּה יִקָּרֵא לְכָל הָעַמִּים (*Yeshayahu* 56:7). Likewise, the *bracha* of *Avoda* states, וְאִשֵּׁי יִשְׂרָאֵל וּתְפִלָּתָם בְּאַהֲבָה תְקַבֵּל בְּרָצוֹן (*Shemona Esrei*).

and technology so revolutionary that they will fundamentally transform the human being.[52] So it stands to reason that the needs of the *nefesh* and *neshama* in Phase Three/*Bayit Shlishi* would be managed using methodologies that far surpass both *korban* and *tefila*.[53] But this is pure speculation. We cannot say with any certainty what lies in store for humankind, nor what a theoretical *ge'ula* (redemption) or *Bayit Shlishi* would comprise.[54] What we might contend, however, is that the *transition* from Phase Two to Phase Three is the critical component. Will human consciousness indeed mature to the point where we choose life and creativity over oppression and destruction? That, it would appear, is our great challenge ahead.[55]

Three Phases: Shema Yisrael and Tekiot

Phase One is characterized by *Hashem*, *rachamim* and *chaim*. Phase Two is *Elokim*, *din* and *da'at*. Phase Three is a return to *Hashem*. The *pasuk* says:

אֲנִי ה׳ רִאשׁוֹן וְאֶת אַחֲרֹנִים אֲנִי הוּא

"I Hashem am first, and I am with the last"[56]

Hashem is first and last—with *Elokim*/*din* in between, during "*galut.*"[57] This structure is expressed in the *Shema*: "*Hashem, Elokeinu, Hashem Echad.*" It also follows the order of *shofar* blowing on Rosh Hashana: *tekia, terua, tekia.* Indeed, *Elokim* and *Hashem* are associated with *terua* and *tekia* respectively:

עָלָה אֱ-לֹהִים בִּתְרוּעָה, ה׳ בְּקוֹל שׁוֹפָר.

"Elokim ascended with the terua, Hashem with the sound of the shofar."[58]

The phrase "*kol shofar*" here is interpreted as "*tekia.*"[59] Classical sources likewise associate the *tekia* with *rachamim* and the *terua* with *din.*[60] In *shofar*

---

[52] See p. 131, regarding life-extending/enhancing technologies expected in the future.

[53] Indeed the Midrash states that both *korban* and *tefila* (aside from expressions of thanks) will be eliminated in the future (see *Vayikra Rabbah* 9:7).

[54] As the Rambam states regarding the future era: וכל אלו הדברים וכיוצא בהן לא ידע אדם איך יהיו עד שיהיו (*Hilchot Melachim* 12:2), that no one knows how this future will unfold until it actually comes to pass.

[55] See also p. 135, discussing this challenge in the context of conquering death.

[56] *Yeshayahu* 41:4; see also 44:6, 48:12.

[57] See Alshich (*Yeshayahu* 3 and other places), who states, שם א-להים הוא שכינה שבגלות.

[58] *Tehilim* 47:6

[59] See Alshich on *Tehilim* 47:6; and Maharsha, glosses on *Rosh Hashana* 32a.

[60] As in, תקיעה שהיא פשוטה, ופשוטה (Ramban, *Bamidbar* 10:6); כי התרועה רמז למדת הדין, רמז למדת הרחמים (Rabbeinu Bachye, *Bamidbar* 10:2).

blowing, the *tekia* is a single, unbroken tone—one uninterrupted *neshima*, breath. It expresses *chaim* and *rachamim*,[61] the state of wholeness and fullness of life—characteristic of *Hashem*. The *terua*, by contrast, is a staccato tone, breath starting and stopping. It conveys *din*,[62] *tov* and *ra*, energy and lack, life and death—characteristic of *Elokim*.

The *tekia* (*chaim/rachamim*) is first and last. But the final *tekia* is not the same as the first. The final blast is a *"tekia gedola,"* a tone that in theory goes on without end, except that in practice the *ba'al tokea* (*shofar* blower) eventually runs out of air. Likewise, in the *Shema* it is *Hashem, Elokeinu, "Hashem echad."* We extend the word *"echad."* All this suggests a future era of extended *chaim*, life that does not end but rather becomes continually enriched.[63] *Hashem echad* and the *tekia gedola* point to Phase Three.

Three Phases: Cham, Yefet and Shem

The three sons of Noach—Shem, Cham and Yefet—can be understood to represent three strands of civilization, each of which dominates in one of the three developmental phases. Phase One is Cham-dominated. The word *cham* literally means "hot." Heat is a form of kinetic energy, movement whose nature is to spread out in all directions. It is pure, unbridled flow, similar to what we discussed earlier regarding *chesed*.[64] A Cham-dominated society is characterized by great vitality and movement, but in the raw, instinctive, primal sense, where the focus of one's

---

[61] As in, ופשוטה רמז למדת הרחמים (see previous note).

[62] The word *terua* in Tanach means a "shout," "war cry" or "sound of alarm," and the Talmud associates it with "wailing" (see *Rosh Hashana* 34a)—all of which is evocative of *din*.

[63] The Talmud in fact associates the extending of the word *echad* with an increase in *chaim*/life: כל המאריך ב׳אחד׳ מאריכין לו ימיו ושנותיו, "Whoever extends 'echad', they extend for him his days and years" (*Brachot* 13b).

[64] See p. 110. Aside from corresponding to developmental phases, Shem, Cham and Yefet can also be viewed as corresponding to different *sephirot*. Cham and Yefet might be understood as overdominances of *chesed* and *gevura* respectively, and Shem as *tiferet*, the synthesis. Cf., the Arizal, who puts forward a similar set of correspondences, linking Cham with *gevura* (relating to *Mitzraim*, oppression), Yefet with *tiferet* (*yofi* and *tiferet* both relating to "beauty"), and Shem with *chesed* (whereby *Am Yisrael* is associated with "loving-kindness"). (See *Pri Etz Chaim, Sha'ar Rosh Chodesh-Chanuka-Purim* 6.) Note however that there is no one fixed set of correspondences between the sons of Noach and the *sephirot*, even within the Arizal. He also links Shem, Cham and Yefet to *netzach, hod* and *yesod* respectively (*Likutei Torah, Parshat Bereshit*, פ׳ חכמה נקרא ראשית), and elsewhere to *netzach, yesod* and *hod* respectively (Ibid., *Parshat Noach*, ברוך ה׳ אלקי שם וגו׳).

energies is to satisfy the immediate physical drives.[65] It is in-the-moment experience without a great deal of self-reflection. In sum, Cham possesses a dominance of *chaim* over (and at the expense of) *da'at*.

Phase Two is Yefet-dominated. Yefet is from *yofi*, "beauty." That is, Yefet is focused primarily on beauty of form, structural elegance — the realm of aesthetics. Yefet begat Yavan, the father of Greek civilization, which embodies perhaps more than any other society the legacy of aesthetics. Yefet/Yavan is the great designer, an intellectual powerhouse. A Yefet society is motivated by the quest for the perfect design, attaining the Platonic "ideal," the most elegant, magnificent structure (physical or conceptual), and this drives Yefet's many and varied achievements in the arts, science and technology, architecture, logic, mathematics, socio-political thought, and the building of empires. Even when Yefet emphasizes the body, the focus is on beauty of form. It indulges in sensory pleasures in order to achieve a certain cultural aesthetic, doing that which it believes a "higher society" should embrace. Yefet is associated explicitly with *Elokim*, as the *pasuk* says:

יַפְתְּ אֱ-לֹהִים לְיֶפֶת

"Elokim will expand for Yefet [his inheritance/legacy]"[66]

Elokim encompasses all that is mind-related — logic, judgment, philosophy, ethics, *da'at tov vara*. These are all Phase Two attributes. Indeed, the influence of Greek civilization, as we spoke about earlier, characterizes Phase Two.[67] It is a dominance of *da'at* over (and at the expense of) *chaim*.

Yefet is the polar opposite of Cham. Whereas Cham is in tune with the body, natural rhythms and energy-flow, the realm of the *Etz HaChaim*, Yefet is all but divorced from these, filtering all experience through the

---

[65] Cham and his son Kena'an are cursed for their lewd behavior. Cham is described as seeing his father Noach lying naked (and not covering him, see *Bereshit* 9:22), or as the Talmud suggests, he saw his son Kena'an sodomize or castrate Noach (see *Sanhedrin* 70a). Later in the Torah, Yitzchak is instructed not to marry a Canaanite woman (the descendants of Kena'an), because they were known to be lewd and morally underdeveloped (see *Drashot HaRan*, Drush 5). Morality is a function of *da'at tov vara*, and Cham is *chaim*-dominated to the point where *tov vara* is largely eclipsed.

[66] *Bereshit* 9:27

[67] See p. 170, regarding the Second Temple period. The Talmud in fact speaks of the Second Temple as being built by Yefet, the progenitor of the Persians (see Rashi on *Yoma* 10a, ד"ה אעפ"י שיפת).

mind, the *Etz HaDa'at Tov VaRa*. Yefet regards Cham and those of a "lower intellectual order" as savages, to be enslaved for its own benefit, and considers slavery to be part of the "ideal" aesthetic.[68] Thus, he not only subjugates and brutalizes others but rationalizes it ideologically. Whereas Cham-oriented societies kill with hot-blooded, primal fervor, Yefet-oriented societies kill with cold-blooded premeditation, philosophical justification, or simply for sport—another cultural aesthetic.[69]

So for all the mind-power of Yefet—all his sophistication and technology—without input from the *Etz Chaim*, Yefet degrades into killing, conquest and oppression. Without an overarching sensitivity to life, all structural beauty is for naught, as it says:

שֶׁקֶר הַחֵן וְהֶבֶל הַיֹּפִי

"Grace is a lie, and beauty is a fleeting-nothingness"[70]

In short, Cham-oriented societies are characterized by unstructured energy, tremendous vitality lacking sufficient guidance by the mind. Yefet-oriented societies are like magnificently elaborate yet empty shells, possessing a great deal of structure and sophistication but without being sufficiently conducive to life. Cham possesses an overdominance of *chesed*, Yefet an overdominance of *gevura*.

Phase Three is about the reign and influence of Shem. Like Yefet, Shem places primary emphasis on the conscious mind, occupying himself with intellectual endeavors, bringing order to the mind and structure to the world. But the difference is that whereas Yefet builds with an eye toward aesthetics, the goal being perfection of *form*, Shem builds such forms to serve as *kelim* (conduits) to channel and house *life*. Life is

---

[68] See for example Aristotle, who discusses the idea of "natural slavery," wherein it is deemed proper for those of greater intellect to enslave those who are predisposed to the passions: "From the hour of their birth, some are marked for subjection, others for rule... And it is clear that the rule of the soul over the body, and of the mind and the rational faculty over the passionate, is natural and expedient" (*Politics* 1:5). "It is clear, then, that some men are by nature free, and others slaves, and that for the latter, slavery is both expedient and right" (Ibid., 1:13).

[69] Killing human beings for sport was a feature of the Roman world, which arose out of the Greek Empire and adopted much of its culture (hence the term "Greco-Roman"). So despite the fact that Yavan and Edom (traditionally identified with Greece and Rome respectively) have different Biblical progenitors, they are conceptually connected, as in נתחברו יון ואדום יחד (R. Tzadok HaKohen, *Likutei Ma'amarim*, p. 125).

[70] *Mishlei* 31:30

at the center of Shem's world; it is the target, the overarching impetus and motivation of his work. For Shem, structure and aesthetics are either a means to an end or an enjoyable byproduct, but they are not the focus. The mind is not something to be worshipped or in which to build elaborate castles, but rather to be leveraged as a potent tool for the increase of life, tangible good and well-being.[71] Stated in Eden terminology, whereas Yefet is based in the *Etz HaDa'at*, and Cham based in the *Etz HaChaim*, Shem uses the *Etz HaDa'at* in order to connect with the *Etz HaChaim*.

Shem of course means "name." As we discussed earlier, a *shem* is understood in the tradition to express the content or legacy of its bearer.[72] It can also imply a plan or program by which something is created. A *shem* represents a creative technology. It suggests intelligence and know-how applied/directed toward the goal of life, creation. This is the legacy carried by Shem—the use of the mind and intellect for purposes of cultivating life. It is within the mind-work of Shem that Yefet has a role, as it says:

וְיִשְׁכֹּן בְּאָהֳלֵי שֵׁם

"[Yefet] will dwell in the tents of Shem"[73]

That is, beauty and aesthetics have a value when utilized within the creative work of Shem—when the product of that work is *life*. And indeed, is not life the most *beautiful* thing there is to behold?

Am Yisrael carries the legacy of Shem. It is seen as being destined for *shem* (renown) and *tiferet* (splendor), as it says:

וּלְתִתְּךָ עֶלְיוֹן עַל כָּל הַגּוֹיִם... לְשֵׁם וּלְתִפְאָרֶת

"and to place you above all the nations... for shem and for tiferet"[74]

We might see this as envisioning not the dominion of *Am Yisrael* per se, but rather the preeminence of the *life-legacy* we bear. It is about the reign of *tiferet* and *kedusha*, the constructive channeling of human energies. The

---

[71] Shem is identified in the Talmud with Malki-Tzedek (see *Nedarim* 32b), who was king of "Shalem" as well as a *kohen* (both of which indicate a predisposition toward *shalom*). The Midrash also speaks about him as presiding over a *beit midrash* (see *Bereshit Rabbah* 63:6) and a *beit din* within which the *Shechina* (*ruach hakodesh*) was said to reside (see *Makkot* 23b). All these elements—*kehuna, shalom, Shechina*—are indicative not simply of intellect, but intellect applied for the purpose of *chaim*, intellect wherein Life is at the center.

[72] See p. 106 and 121, regarding the concept of "*shem*."

[73] *Bereshit* 9:27

[74] *Devarim* 26:19. See p. 112, on the concept of "*tiferet*."

future Phase Three occurs when our consciousness is focused predominantly on Life—on the welfare and advancement of humankind.

Three Phases and Bypassing of the Firstborn

In the Torah (largely in the stories of the book of *Bereshit*), a conspicuous and persistent pattern emerges regarding the firstborn. Namely, the status of *bechora*/firstborn (of the father, regarding inheritance and *bracha*) is consistently uprooted from the elder child and given to the younger. The original *bechor* is systematically rejected, bypassed.

- Kayin is bypassed in favor of Hevel.[75]
- Yishmael is bypassed in favor of Yitzchak.[76]
- Esav is bypassed in favor of Ya'akov.[77]
- Reuven is bypassed in favor of Yosef.[78]
- Zerach is bypassed in favor of Peretz.[79]
- Menashe is bypassed in favor of Ephraim.[80]
- The firstborn of *Bnei Yisrael* are bypassed in favor of the Levites.[81]
- Amalek is bypassed in favor of *Am Yisrael*.[82]

Why is the Torah so intent on bypassing the firstborn?

It should be clarified that there are two types of *bechora*—that of the mother and that of the father.[83] It is only the *bechora* of the father which can be "bypassed," transferred, whereby the younger child receives the greater inheritance and *bracha*. The status of firstborn of a mother is an inherent, immutable state—it is not a question of *bracha* but rather *kedusha*. The Torah requires the first fruit of the womb to be sanctified/restricted to *Hashem*, as it says:

---

[75] *Hashem* turns to Hevel's *korban*, and does not turn to Kayin's (see *Bereshit* 4:4–5).

[76] Yishmael will be a great nation, but Yitzchak gets the covenant (see *Bereshit* 17:20–21).

[77] Esav sells his birthright, is told Ya'akov will rule over him (see *Bereshit* 25:33, 27:37).

[78] Reuven's birthright is lost, given to Yosef (see *Bereshit* 49:4, I *Divrei HaYamim* 5:1).

[79] Zerach emerges first from the womb, but Peretz overtakes him (see *Bereshit* 38:28–29).

[80] Ya'akov places his right hand on Ephraim instead of Menashe (see *Bereshit* 48:17–20).

[81] *Hashem* takes the *Levi'im* in place of the *bechorei Yisrael* (see *Bamidbar* 3:12, 3:41, 3:45).

[82] The Torah says, רֵאשִׁית גּוֹיִם עֲמָלֵק, "*First of the nations is Amalek*" (*Bamidbar* 24:20), and yet, כֹּה אָמַר ה' בְּנִי בְכֹרִי יִשְׂרָאֵל, "*Thus said Hashem: My firstborn child is Yisrael*" (*Shemot* 4:22).

[83] The Mishna refers to the *bechor* of the mother as the "*bechor lekohen*" (for the *kohen*), and the *bechor* of the father as the "*bechor lenachala*" (for inheritance). (See *Bechorot* 8:1.)

קַדֶּשׁ לִי כָל בְּכוֹר פֶּטֶר כָּל רֶחֶם
בִּבְנֵי יִשְׂרָאֵל בָּאָדָם וּבַבְּהֵמָה לִי הוּא.

*"Sanctify/Restrict to Me, every firstborn, first out of every womb
of the Children of Israel, of a person and of an animal—it is Mine."*[84]

The requirement to designate the mother's firstborn as *"kodesh laShem"* is traced to the *makat bechorot* (plague of the firstborn) in Egypt.[85] What is it about this plague that was so severe and decisive that it finally broke Egypt and allowed *Bnei Yisrael* to leave? Some suggest that striking the firstborn of Egypt, leaving it bereft of the *bechor*, was seen as draining Egypt of its power, its strength.[86]

Indeed we see that the Torah considers the *bechor* as being given the largest endowment of the parent's vitality. For instance, Ya'akov says regarding Reuven:

רְאוּבֵן בְּכֹרִי אַתָּה, כֹּחִי וְרֵאשִׁית אוֹנִי
יֶתֶר שְׂאֵת וְיֶתֶר עָז.

*"Reuven, you are my firstborn, my power and the first of my vigor,
extra preeminence and extra strength."*[87]

The vitality of the *bechor* is understood however to be a volatile one, difficult for a person to control and to channel constructively. Kayin kills Hevel. Yishmael is a "wild man."[88] Esav lives by the sword.[89] As for Reuven, Ya'akov continues:

פַּחַז כַּמַּיִם אַל תּוֹתַר
כִּי עָלִיתָ מִשְׁכְּבֵי אָבִיךָ אָז חִלַּלְתָּ

*"Chaotic like water, you will no longer have extra,
since you ascended your father's bed, at that point you desecrated/depleted"*[90]

Reuven is chaotic or impetuous "like water," in the sense that water has no defined borders, runs to wherever there is a *kli* (vessel) that will accept it. It is all *chesed* and no *gevura*. The metaphorical "water" that Ya'akov speaks about refers to Reuven's erratic sexually-related impro-

---

[84] *Shemot* 13:2

[85] As in, כִּי לִי כָּל בְּכוֹר בְּיוֹם הַכֹּתִי כָל בְּכוֹר בְּאֶרֶץ מִצְרַיִם (*Bamidbar* 3:13).

[86] As in, כי אבד כח הקליפה העצום שהוא בחינת בכור (*Ohr HaChaim* on *Shemot* 11:5).

[87] *Bereshit* 49:3

[88] See ibid., 16:12.

[89] See ibid., 27:40.

[90] Ibid., 49:4; see p. 57 on the concept of *"chilul."*

prieties, which in the end cost him the *bechora*.[91] Instead, it is Yosef who is granted the *bechora*, given a double portion in the land of Israel.[92] Yosef succeeds precisely where Reuven fails. Like Reuven, Yosef also has the *kedushat bechora* from his mother.[93] However unlike Reuven, Yosef is able to contain this energy—most notably in the sexual domain, where he maintains exceptional restraint. Yosef is repeatedly targeted for seduction by the wife of Potifar in Egypt and declines each time.[94] Whereas Reuven's energy is called "excess" (יתר), Yosef's energy is merely "additional" (נוסף). It adds vitality without making him unstable. Thus the tradition refers to him as "Yosef the *tzadik*," the righteous or balanced one.

A *tzadik* is one who exerts conscious control over the body, over the emotions and physical drives. It is a self-mastery that prevents internal pressures from building up, such that the person maintains a state of *shalom*, dynamic equilibrium. A system that is in equilibrium, whose structure is balanced and stable, provides the *yesod* (foundation) for *bracha*, where growth and expansion can take place, where life can thrive and propagate. Yosef is associated with the *sephira* of *yesod*. He builds a *yesod* in Egypt that eventually becomes the very womb of *Am Yisrael*.[95]

This is the overarching pattern regarding the *bechor*. The child with a greater proclivity toward inward, conscious focus and control is chosen over the outwardly energetic one who lacks the ability to channel their energies constructively. The *bechor* is seen as being particularly susceptible to such volatility due to the extra vitality they are understood to possess. Thus, the reins are passed to the younger child, the one who can exercise better control. Or in the case of the *bechorei Yisrael* in general, who originally served as *kohanim*,[96] that task is given over to the tribe of Levi. Levi is understood as embodying *gevura/din*, the strength of self-

---

91 See Radak on *Bereshit* 49:3, who explains פחז כמים to mean that like water, which flows quickly and loosely, Reuven was quick to follow his drives. Ya'akov essentially tells Reuven that instead of exercising *gevura* over his inclinations, וגבר יצרך עליך ולא עמדת לפניו, "Your inclination overpowered you, and you did not stand [strong] before it."

92 Ephraim and Menashe are given the status of sons of Ya'akov for purposes of inheritance. (See *Bereshit* 48:5, כִּרְאוּבֵן וְשִׁמְעוֹן יִהְיוּ לִי; 48:22 with Rashi, שיטלו בניו שני חלקים.)

93 Yosef is the firstborn of Rachel, and Reuven is the firstborn of Leah.

94 See Bereshit 39:7–12.

95 As in, וכן נתברר יוסף במצרים במדתו צדיק יסוד עולם (R. Tzadok HaKohen, *Pri Tzadik*, *Parshat Ki Tavo*).

96 See *Zevachim* 115b, עד שלא הוקם המשכן, הבמות מותרות ועבודה בבכורות.

restraint, the power of the mind.[97] Regarding the nations, whereas Amalek was "first,"[98] its warlike, aggressive nature was diametrically opposed to the task of carrying the legacy of Life. Vitality, when misdirected, can be anti-Life. Therefore, *Am Yisrael*, whose nature is to be more cognitively predisposed, and more inclined toward *chaim* and *rachamim*, is chosen as the *bechor* over Amalek.

Phase One corresponds to the *bechor*, the dominance of vitality without sufficient structure and self-discipline. Phase Two is where that vitality and life-energy are bypassed in favor of conscious control. It is in a sense a comedown, a drop in vitality, but also fully necessary in order to stem the tide of chaos, rein in our energies, and build more robust conscious *kelim* (tools/capabilities). Phase Three, one might speculate, is when human consciousness will be developed and strengthened to the point where the level of vitality that is characteristic of the *bechor* may be safely reintroduced.[99] It is being able to hold that enhanced vitality, and channeling our energies toward positive, creative ends.

Three Phases: Emuna, She'eila and Teshuva

The three developmental phases can also be framed in terms of the process of questioning. Phase One is pure *emuna*—an existence based on flow, trust, unquestioning reliance, pure experience, wherein the assumptions of one's reality are not challenged and perhaps not even reflected upon. It is the state of an infant or small child in relation to the parent, where the child simply draws nourishment and influence from the parent.[100] This is the Eden/*Etz Chaim* state.

Phase Two is when a *she'eila* (question) first comes to mind about what was previously assumed: "But is it *really* true?" This is the Serpent in Eden who asks Chava to stop and question her assumptions regarding the prohibition of the Tree of Knowledge.[101] It is the phase of later

---

[97] As in, לוי בחינת גבורה (R. Tzadok HaKohen, *Pri Tzadik, Bamidbar, L'Chag Shavuot*).

[98] As in, שהוא הראש והשורש לכל הגוים כולם (R. Tzadok HaKohen, *Yisrael Kedoshim* 7).

[99] See *Ohr HaChaim* (*Bamidbar* 3:45), who suggests in accordance with Chazal that in the future era, the *avoda* in the *Mikdash* will return to the *bechorot*.

[100] The word *emuna* shares its root with *omen/omenet*, a nurse or caregiver from whom a child draws support and nourishment. See p. 34, on the concept of *emuna*.

[101] The Serpent poses the *she'eila* to Chava: "But did *Elokim* really say: 'You shall not eat from every tree in the Garden'?" (*Bereshit* 3:1). Meaning: "Aren't *all* trees there for the taking? Would *Elokim* have planted a tree whose fruit you are forbidden to eat?" The Serpent

childhood, culminating in adolescence, characterized by the emergence of and continual quest for *da'at*, conscious independence. It is a phase of alienation, pain, disillusionment, confusion, separation and exile, but also one of tremendous growth.

Phase Three is about *teshuva* ("answer," lit., "return"), where probing and questioning leads a person to answers—greater conceptual coherence and understanding. As a result, either what was once trusted unquestioningly is now returned to on the basis of understanding, or else a new path is forged—the conclusion being that the initial assumptions were not entirely correct, or at least not correct for that person. In either case, a flow in life is regained. This is *da'at* used to return to *chaim*, *she'eila* bringing forth *teshuva*. It is the phase of adulthood and maturity, the time when a person attains sufficient understanding and coherence to make his or her unique creative contribution in the world.

She'eila and Creation

Coming up with a *she'eila*, a question, can be understood metaphorically as opening up a new space in consciousness, a vacuum in the mind. The more urgent and relevant the question, the greater the pressure of the vacuum to pull thought-energy (i.e., information, answers) into this space. When coherent thought is drawn to the question-space, we have *teshuva*—pressure is alleviated and new structures are built in consciousness, creating greater order and understanding.[102]

Fig. 31   She'eila and Teshuva – building in the mind

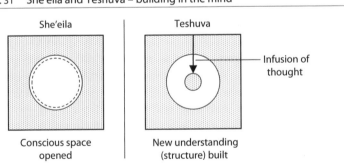

represents the questioning thought that first comes up in the mind: "Maybe what we have been told and simply assumed to be true, is in fact *not* entirely true."

[102] See p. 57, regarding pressure states and Creation.

As such, *she'eila* can be understood as a mechanism for *briya* (creation). Asking a question may be seen as creating a conscious space inside which worlds can be built, *chidushim* (new understandings) constructed. *She'eila* occurs when a person is made aware of something that does not fit within his or her present frame of reference, when the current model of understanding is challenged. This is in part why the preferred method of learning Torah is via *chavruta* (study partner). When faced with a partner who brings to the table a different bank of experiences, different thinking and perspectives, a person has the opportunity to significantly refine and build upon existing thought structures — or dismantle them entirely and reconstruct their understanding from the ground up.[103]

Thus the goal in a *chavruta* is not for the two sides to agree or meld with one another. It is actually the *machloket* (division) between the two that generates a dynamic synergy, an engine for creative activity. Rabbi Nachman of Breslov[104] refers to *machloket* as the *"ikar briyat ha'olam"* (basis for creation of the world).[105] He describes *machloket* as a separation of *ohr* (light/energy) into two divisions, leaving a *chalal panui* (empty vacuum) in between. That is, one person is on each side, with a *she'eila* (question-space) in between. As they exchange ideas, this is akin to projecting *ohr* into the *chalal* and building a new "world" of conceptual understanding.

The Mishna in Avot states that the hallmark of a *machloket l'shem shamayim* (a "disagreement for the sake of heaven," i.e., conducted with integrity, with genuine interest in gaining understanding or advancing the *retzon Hashem*, the will for Life) is that *"sofa lehitkayem,"* it is destined to stand/remain.[106] Where there is a mutual desire for both *emet* and *shalom* (truth and peace), the two sides of a debate will build rather than destroy. Using the Creation metaphor, in a *machloket l'shem shamayim*, the thought-energy projected into the conscious space between the two sides will achieve a *"kiyum"* — it will solidify into lasting, coherent conceptual

---

[103] R. Tzadok HaKohen speaks about a *chavruta* as producing חידוד, sharpening or refinement, which then binds the *chavruta* together (see *Tzidkat HaTzadik* 186).

[104] 18–19th century Torah luminary

[105] See *Likutei Moharan* 64:4.

[106] See *Avot* 5:20.

structures upon which later generations can build. Such is the legacy, the Mishna states, of Beit Hillel and Beit Shamai.[107]

Destructive She'eila

What does the same Mishna offer as an example of a debate that is not *l'shem shamayim*, not destined to stand? It is Korach and his assembly, whose *machloket* is rooted in the following *she'eila* to Moshe and Aharon: "Why do you lift yourselves above the congregation of *Hashem*?" This is understood not to be a question stemming from a genuine desire for clarification, as in: "Moshe, could you please explain the wisdom behind the leadership structure?" Rather, Korach is thought to be simply projecting his own thirst for power onto Moshe and Aharon, accusing them of unfairly taking the mantle of leadership for themselves.[108] It is a pseudo-question, a *she'eila* formed with the syntax of a real question, but which is really just a statement reflecting Korach's jealousy and desire for honor.[109]

In the end, Korach, his assembly and all their possessions meet their downfall (figuratively and literally), as the earth opens up and swallows them:

וַיֵּרְדוּ הֵם וְכָל אֲשֶׁר לָהֶם חַיִּים שְׁאֹלָה

"And they fell—they and all that was theirs—alive, toward the She'ol."[110]

The *pasuk* does not merely state that they died, but that they fell into the *she'ol*, the "pit" or "grave."[111] In effect, their *she'eila* (שאילה) turned into a *she'ol* (שאול).[112] Their pseudo-question against Moshe and Aharon consumed them. Their *"chaim,"* all of their life-energy, was sucked into it.

---

[107] The Talmud (*Yevamot* 14a–b) points out that despite the fact that they maintained differences in areas of Halacha that could pose practical complications for intermarrying between families, daughters of Beit Shamai married sons of Beit Hillel and vice-versa. By conducting themselves with dearness and friendship toward one another, they exemplified the *pasuk*, וְהָאֱמֶת וְהַשָּׁלוֹם אֱהָבוּ, "Love truth and peace" (*Zecharya* 8:19).

[108] The Midrash explains that Korach was upset at not having been appointed head of the tribal family of Kehat (see *Bamidbar Rabbah* 18:2).

[109] As in, והם קרח ועדתו שקנאו למשה ולאהרון (*Metzudat David* on *Tehilim* 106:16); קרח נתקנא בנשיאות אליצפן וביקש כבוד (R. Yochanan Luria, *Meshivat Nefesh*, Bamidbar 16:1).

[110] *Bamidbar* 16:33

[111] In Tanach, the *she'ol* is understood to be an underworld where people descend to upon death and where their spirits continue to dwell. See e.g., *Yeshayahu* 14:9. Also see *Gesenius Lexicon* and *Brown-Driver-Briggs Lexicon*, entry for שְׁאוֹל.

[112] In other words, read it not as "שְׁאֹלָה," but rather "שְׁאֵלָה."

Also curious is Moshe's use of the word *briya* (creation) when anticipating Korach's demise:

וְאִם בְּרִיאָה יִבְרָא ה'... וְיָרְדוּ חַיִּים שְׁאֹלָה...

"If Hashem creates a creation… and they fall alive, toward the She'ol…"[113]

As we discussed, a *she'eila* can be looked at as a kind of *briya*, carving out a space in the mind. This space can either be used to build positive, lasting structures, or it can create a vortex, sucking into it a person's life-energy with nothing to show for it in the end. It all depends on the question which is asked.

Fig. 32   She'eila as a vortex – wasted mental energy

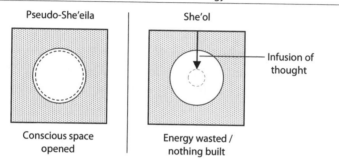

Interestingly, the Haftara (portion of Navi) for *Parshat Korach* is about Shaul HaMelech (King Saul). The name Shaul (שאול) literally means "asked for" (or "borrowed"). Indeed Shaul emerged out of *she'eila* (שאילה) — when the people asked for a king "like all the nations."[114] Because this *she'eila* was deemed a rejection of the reign of *Hashem*[115] (i.e., a rejection of *chaim*/Life as the organizing principle of society), this *malchut* was not destined to stand/survive, as it says:

וְעַתָּה מַמְלַכְתְּךָ לֹא תָקוּם

"And now, your kingdom will not stand"[116]

---

[113] *Bamidbar* 16:30

[114] See *I Shmuel* 8:5. Shmuel later refers to this question as a *"she'eila"* (Ibid., 12:17).

[115] As it says: אֹתִי מָאֲסוּ מִמְּלֹךְ עֲלֵיהֶם, "They rejected Me from reigning over them" (Ibid., 8:7).

[116] Ibid., 13:14

In other words, just as a *machloket* that is not *l'shem shamayim* will not have *kiyum*, will not stand in the end, so too is Shaul's kingship born out of a *she'eila* that is not *l'shem shamayim* and is fated not to stand.

Romanticizing the Vortex

Not all pseudo-questions are based on ulterior motives or lack of integrity. Some are asked in earnest, only they function as a vortex by their inherent inability to yield answers. These include philosophical and theological conundrums, where the utter impossibility to wrap the mind around them, instead of leading the person to the conclusion that they are not worth expending one's time and energy on, have the exact opposite effect. Namely, the unanswerable nature of such questions (e.g., How does a mortal/finite human being attach to the Infinite?) is thought to enshroud the questions with a "divine" quality, such that people see it as their sacred duty to wrestle with them, enter the paradox, embrace the discomfort, seek out that which is impossible to touch, which is always just beyond human grasp. It is an outlook that romanticizes existential angst and loneliness, the thirst that is never entirely quenched, the connection that is never fully made, and so forth.

But what does the Torah itself state? *Achalta vesavata*—"You will eat, and you will be satisfied."[117] Meaning, we are meant to derive concrete satisfaction, not be left wanting. This is true not only for our physical being but also for our intellect. If we find ourselves continually confounded by a question, this indicates either that we lack sufficient information (or brainpower) to be able to answer it, or that the question is by definition unanswerable—that is, it leads the questioner in circles, into an endless loop that draws in the person's energy and provides nothing tangible in return. It is neither Godly to throw oneself into philosophical conundrums, nor is it sublime to be lonely, hungry or despairing.

Rabbi Nachman speaks about people who, by confounding others, appear to possess great depth and profundity. But he calls such words "wisdoms that are not wisdoms" and goes so far as to call it a branch of *apikorsut*, a type of heresy, and that one should not respond to such questions. As an example of this type of misleading question, Rabbi Nachman quotes a piece of Talmud that describes Moshe Rabbeinu,

---

[117] *Devarim* 8:10

foreseeing the brutal murder of Rabbi Akiva at the hands of the Romans, posing the she'eila to Hashem: "This is Torah and this is its reward?!"[118] That is to say, Moshe asks the age-old question of tzadik v'ra lo—Why do bad things happen to good people? According to Chazal, Moshe is the author of the Book of Iyov (Job),[119] the classic Biblical case study of "tzadik v'ra lo," a righteous person who suffers.

Iyov's She'eila

Iyov is a tzadik, a righteous person. He possesses every manner of bracha and then loses it all—his wealth, his children and finally his own physical health. In his great suffering he becomes disillusioned by the lack of Divine justice:

$$תָּם וְרָשָׁע הוּא מְכַלֶּה$$

"He destroys the innocent and wicked alike"[120]

Visitors come to Iyov to comfort him, and their contention is that despite the way it might appear to Iyov, in reality there is no breach of Divine justice—there cannot be by very definition.[121] What this means is that Iyov must have done something wrong—he cannot be a tzadik. Iyov retorts that if this is the case, "The tzadik is made into a laughingstock."[122] Meaning, if when a tzadik suffers we are all required to assume he/she must have "hidden wrongdoings," this makes a mockery of tzidkut (righteousness). Iyov feels betrayed by his friends—they have only added insult to his injury.[123] Not only has Iyov suffered terribly, but now he is told that he is actually to blame for it. The exchange between Iyov and his visitors takes up the bulk of the book.[124] Then Hashem enters the story once again to settle the score, saying in a speech to Iyov:

---

[118] See *Likutei Moharan* 64:3, quoting *Menachot* 29b.

[119] See *Bava Batra* 14b.

[120] *Iyov* 9:22

[121] As in, "Would E-l pervert judgment or Sha-dai pervert justice?" (Ibid., 8:3); "For He knows falsehood and sees iniquity" (11:11); "Is your evil not great, and is there no end to your sin?" (22:5).

[122] Ibid., 12:4

[123] As in, "How long will you torment me and crush me with words?" (Ibid., 19:2).

[124] The initial exchange (Ch. 3–26) includes Eliphaz, Bildad and Tzophar, each of whom speaks to Iyov several times, unsuccessfully. Then, after a few chapters of Iyov speaking,

אֵיפֹה הָיִיתָ בְּיָסְדִי אָרֶץ, הַגֵּד אִם יָדַעְתָּ בִינָה.

"Where were you when I laid the earth's foundation?
Tell, if you have known discernment."[125]

At first glance, it appears that *Hashem* is taking the side of the visitors, as if to say: "Do you claim to know the mysteries of the Creator and Divine justice, to be able to proclaim yourself innocent and say that what happened to you is undeserved?"[126] But in fact nowhere in the conclusion of the *Book of Iyov* does *Hashem* ever say that Iyov "sinned," that he was not a *tzadik,* and nowhere does Iyov ever admit to any sin that would have warranted his suffering. On the contrary, the text says quite explicitly (twice in fact) that Iyov is right, and that it is the *visitors* who are wrong:

חָרָה אַפִּי בְךָ וּבִשְׁנֵי רֵעֶיךָ
כִּי לֹא דִבַּרְתֶּם אֵלַי נְכוֹנָה כְּעַבְדִּי אִיּוֹב

"My anger has been roused against you and your two companions,
because you did not speak correctly of Me, as My servant Iyov did"[127]

The visitors did not speak correctly about *Hashem.* What was their main point? That everything which happens to a person is the result of Divine justice, and so Iyov's suffering shows that he cannot be a true *tzadik.* According to the visitors, there is no such thing as *"tzadik v'ra lo,"* no suffering that does not come as a result of sin. The narrative says very clearly that they are *wrong.* Iyov is correct in maintaining his innocence, insisting that there *is* such a thing as *tzadik v'ra lo.* A perfect *tzadik* can experience *yisurin* (suffering, hardships), and it does not mean he or she has any "hidden wrongdoings."[128] The visitors' words are thus empty and self-righteous, a religious façade. If anything, it is the *visitors* who com-

---

the three visitors "saw that Iyov was righteous in his own eyes" (32:1), and a fourth visitor, Elihu, enters and makes a long speech to Iyov (Ch. 32–37).

[125] Ibid., 38:4

[126] Indeed, Eliphaz states something similar earlier on: "Are you the first person to be born, and were you brought forth before the hills?... Are you privy to God's secret counsel?... What is it that you know..?" (Ibid., 15:7–9).

[127] Ibid., 42:7. The statement, "You did not speak correctly of Me, as My servant Iyov did," is then repeated in in the next verse.

[128] This principle is stated explicitly in the Talmud: שמע מינה יש מיתה בלא חטא ויש יסורין בלא עון – "Hear from this [i.e., that what was just stated proves the following]: There is death without *cheit,* and there is suffering without *avon*" (*Shabbat* 55b).

mitted a transgression—*Hashem* tells them to bring a *korban* for *kapara* and instructs Iyov to pray on their behalf.[129]

But if Iyov is right, how do we understand *Hashem's* admonishment to Iyov: "Where were you when I created the world?"

Iyov's Teshuva and Escape from the Vortex

To answer the question, we need to recognize that Iyov and his visitors do share something in common—the belief in a just universe. That is, Iyov holds that the universe is run by justice, which is why he is so disillusioned when such tragedy befalls him—*Where is the justice?* The visitors hold that the universe *was* just and *remains* just—and where we can't see the justice in a person's suffering, this is due to our limited, earthly perspective. As we saw above, the visitors' position is false—they were wrong to ascribe sin to Iyov's suffering. Iyov was correct that he suffered without wrongdoing. However, he was wrong to be *resentful* for his suffering, to see it as "unjust." Why? Because that resentment is only possible if one assumes that the world is run purely by justice. What *Hashem* comes to tell Iyov is the following: *The world is not run by justice alone.*

The speech *Hashem* gives to Iyov focuses on nature—the land and sea, rain and dew, constellations, clouds and lightning, and the animal kingdom.[130] *Hashem* essentially tells Iyov: You want to get a little perspective on the universe? Look anywhere outside your species, outside that tiny sliver of Creation that human beings and their penchant for *din* and *tov vara* inhabit. Where do you see justice? Is it justice that commands the movement of the sun and stars, that creates weather systems, that makes the land teem with life? Is it justice that forms the tenderness with which a mother cares for her young, or the cruel indifference with which an ostrich abandons her eggs, "hardened against her offspring as if they were not hers"?[131] "Would [a Leviathan] make a covenant with you?"[132] Look around, Iyov—where in all of nature do you see justice?

---

[129] See *Iyov* 42:8.

[130] Elihu likewise draws from the natural world in his speech. But he ultimately ascribes sin to Iyov just like the other visitors did: "He adds upon his transgression with rebelliousness...arguing with God" (Ibid., 34:37). In other words, Iyov's arguments against God are only "adding" to the sins he already committed which brought about his suffering in the first place.

[131] Ibid., 39:16

[132] Ibid., 40:28

Where is the fairness and equity, the *quid pro quo*? Being a human being with a human mind, you naturally get snared within *da'at tov vara*, caught up in good/evil delineations. You assume that the way your mind operates is a reflection of how the rest of the universe works. But you are projecting! You were not there when I fashioned the Creation, and so you do not have the full picture. In truth, throughout the entirety of the cosmos, it is only in the tiny realm of human affairs where justice plays a role at all.[133] And even there, it is only one component of the human experience. In the world I have built, creatures endure pain, and it is not because of sin. It is a part of *life*. And you, like them, are part of that world—do not forget that. So there is no need to doubt your own righteousness, but there is no need to resent Me either!

This is *Hashem*'s admonishment to Iyov—that his concept of human suffering as being the exclusive product of Divine justice is both myopic and presumptuous. It led him to a place of terrible bitterness, indeed cursing his own life.[134] His presumptions made *Hashem* into a *rasha*, as one who punishes cruelly and unjustly, while he, Iyov, self-righteously assumed the role of the victimized *tzadik*.[135] Yes, Iyov is a *tzadik*, but he is no one's "victim." He was not punished. His suffering is no more a function of *Hashem*'s "*din*" than any occurrence of pain throughout the natural world.[136]

What Iyov becomes aware of is that in addition to *din*, there is another paradigm at work—*rachamim/chaim*. *Rachamim* means "compassion" but more generally implies acting "irrespective of deservingness."[137]

---

[133] One might ask, why then does the *pasuk* say, "כִּי כָל דְּרָכָיו מִשְׁפָּט" (*Devarim* 32:4), that all of *Hashem*'s ways are justice? We might respond that this *pasuk*, and similar *psukim*, are concerned with the question of "justice" versus "injustice," and that in all matters related to justice, *Hashem* is not "unjust" ("אֵין עָוֶל," as the above *pasuk* goes on to say). But that does not mean that everything resides in the domain of justice. Indeed much of life does not.

[134] As in, "Why did I not die from the womb, expire as I left the belly?" (*Iyov* 3:11).

[135] As in, "Would you even annul My judgment, make Me wicked in order that you be righteous?" (Ibid., 40:8).

[136] The first chapter of *Iyov* describes *Hashem* giving the Satan (prosecuting angel) permission to wreak havoc in Iyov's life in order to test his *tzidkut* (see 1:6–12), so one might argue that Iyov was indeed "victimized." However, the Satan, like the Serpent in Eden, is best understood as a literary device to explain the events that follow—in this case, explaining the fact that suffering that is entirely unrelated to justice is "allowed" to happen in the world. It is simply the way of the world.

[137] As in, אע"פ שאינו הגון, even though the person is not worthy (see *Brachot* 7a).

Rachamim and *chaim* constitute a *different system entirely* than *din* and *tov vara*. It is a paradigm where "merit" and "justice" are simply bypassed—and once you introduce such a framework into the mix, yes, life can be *given* regardless of a person's deeds, but it can also be *taken* regardless of one's deeds or what a person "deserves." It is a paradigm that reflects the world *as it actually is*—a world that Iyov now perceives for the first time.

Moshe and Iyov – the Resolution

We spoke earlier about Moshe's question: "This is Torah and this is its reward?!" What does the Talmud cite as *Hashem*'s response? "*Shtok!*" ("Silence!"), which we might understand to mean, "Don't go there, Moshe. Do not pose that *she'eila*—it is a trap, a vortex."[138] Likewise, Iyov says in response to *Hashem*'s speech, "I place my hand against my mouth... I spoke once... and I will not continue."[139] Iyov is silenced by the stunned realization that all this time he was working from an entirely misplaced set of assumptions. He was so sure that the universe is run solely based on *din*, pure justice, when in fact the reality is different, profoundly different.

When does Moshe's moment of "realization" come? Moshe petitions *Hashem*, "Show me Your glory,"[140] which the Talmud understands as Moshe asking the question of *tzadik v'ra lo*: Why do some righteous people suffer, and some wicked people prosper?[141] *Hashem* responds:

וְחַנֹּתִי אֶת אֲשֶׁר אָחֹן, וְרִחַמְתִּי אֶת אֲשֶׁר אֲרַחֵם

"I will have chein wherever I have chein,
and I will have rachamim wherever I have rachamim"[142]

The response to Moshe comes not with a language of *din* but a language of *rachamim*. In essence, Moshe is told, like Iyov, that asking the question of *tzadik v'ra lo* itself indicates that he is coming from the wrong set of

---

[138] The full phrase reads, שתוק, כך עלה במחשבה לפני, "Silence! Such is what arose in the mind before Me." This may be interpreted to mean that "such" (i.e., Rabbi Akiva's death) arose to *Hashem*'s mind, meaning it is *Hashem*'s will. Alternatively, it might be understood to mean that "such" (i.e., the notion that Rabbi Akiva was being unjustly punished) is what arose to *Moshe*'s mind, "before *Hashem*"—confronting and impugning *Hashem*. Meaning, it is merely a thought that came into his mind, and in no way does it reflect the reality.

[139] *Iyov*, 40:4–5

[140] *Shemot* 33:18

[141] See *Brachot* 7a.

[142] *Shemot* 33:19. Cf., *Brachot* 7a, where Moshe is answered: צדיק ורע לו צדיק שאינו גמור, וגו'.

assumptions. To understand *"Hashem,"* he needs to get out of the *din/tov vara* paradigm and instead enter the *rachamim/chaim* paradigm.

Furthermore, the response is given in an unusual form: "I will have *rachamim* wherever I have *rachamim.*" The other language that is similar to this in the Torah is the name *Ehyeh Asher Ehyeh,* "I will be whatever I will be." Both indicate a sense of indeterminacy. Meaning, *rachamim* cannot be calculated and predicted like *din.* And neither can it be predicted whether a *tzadik* or a *rasha* will suffer or prosper.

Hashem goes on to say, "You will see My back, and My face will not be seen."[143] That is, the entire paradigm of *rachamim, Hashem,* and the *Etz HaChaim* can only be seen "from the back," observed as part of the experience of life. They are nearly impossible to pick apart and understand, predict, or even adequately articulate—hence Moshe and Iyov's "silence." This is unlike *din, Elokim,* and the *Etz HaDa'at,* which can be seen "from the front," analyzed directly, predicted in advance, and articulated with a high degree of specificity.

In sum, Iyov/Moshe becomes aware of the reality of *chaim* and *rachamim.* This is a reality in which the ostrich is kind to her eggs and then abandons them. It is a world of kindness and cruelty, of tremendous beauty and fulfillment, as well as untold pain and suffering. And it can neither be predicted nor calculated. It comes without advance notice and without justification. That is after all the definition of *rachamim.* It is something that defies justification. It comes irrespective of "deservingness." Likewise, *tzadik v'ra lo,* the suffering of the righteous, is a part of life and has nothing to do with deservingness—and it does not imply "hidden sin." That is the great discovery Iyov and Moshe, which helps them to emerge out of the *she'eila* of resentment, out of the *she'ol.* The question of "Why do bad things happen to good people?" is answered simply by dissolving the assumptions underlying the question. It is revealed to be a pseudo-question and can now be filed away with other philosophical conundrums that hold no possibility of bearing fruit. The weight that this pseudo-question once placed on the psyche is now lifted, thus freeing up the mind for better and more productive endeavors.

That is not to say, however, that when we experience suffering, we cannot not take it as an occasion to introspect. On the contrary, there is a

---

[143] *Shemot* 33:23

rich tradition in Judaism for doing just that.[144] But to identify areas in one's life that need improvement does not have to presuppose "causality," to imply that the person is "to blame" for their suffering. Rather, it is leveraging a difficult situation, one where a person might otherwise be mired in feelings of hopelessness and victimhood, and using it as a vehicle for something constructive—to emerge from the experience feeling stronger, more empowered, and with a sense of positive resolve for the future.[145]

The Three Phases in Iyov

This brings us back to the idea of three-phase development, which as it turns out is built into the very structure of the Book of Iyov. The book begins with Iyov in a state of *emuna*. Life is flowing well, and he has no reason to question his underlying assumptions about the world. This is his state of "Eden," or Phase One. He is then tested by the Satan to see how his assumptions would stand in the face of suffering, much like the Serpent challenges Chava to question her assumptions.[146] Iyov is thrown into *galut*, into questions of *tov* and *ra*, becomes fixated on *din*, tormented and disillusioned by the lack of justice. This is Phase Two. Finally, Iyov's question is answered, by being *dissolved*, identified as a philosophical pseudo-question, by virtue of there being another paradigm altogether at work in the world—*rachamim* and *chaim*. Now that he is relieved of this terrible burden on the mind, Iyov experiences a personal redemption and an abundance of *chaim*. This is Phase Three, where Iyov is more enriched and has more *bracha* than he did even at first:

וַה׳ בֵּרַךְ אֶת אַחֲרִית אִיּוֹב מֵרֵאשִׁתוֹ

"And Hashem blessed the last [days] of Iyov more than his first"[147]

---

[144] As in, אם רואה אדם שיסורין באין עליו יפשפש במעשיו (*Brachot* 5a).

[145] The Talmud (Ibid.) states that a person who examines his or her deeds and finds no shortcomings should view the suffering as "יסורין של אהבה." Rashi describes this as suffering intended to increase a person's merit in the next world. But perhaps it can also be understood as more of a mindset. When people suffer, they can be plagued with feelings of "judgment." What "*yisurin shel ahava*" says is not to feel judged, but rather as having been given a precious *opportunity*—a chance to reap something positive and transformative from the experience.

[146] Indeed the Serpent and the Satan are understood in the tradition to be conceptually related, e.g., וידוע שהשטן הוא הנחש הנזכר בחטא אדם הראשון (Abarbanel on *Bereshit* 22).

[147] *Iyov* 42:12. See also 42:10: וַיֹּסֶף ה׳ אֶת כָּל אֲשֶׁר לְאִיּוֹב לְמִשְׁנֶה, "And *Hashem* added onto everything of Iyov's twice over."

Shemot Hashem in Iyov

For more explicit evidence of the Three Phases in Iyov, one can simply look at the use of the *shemot Hashem* throughout the text.

The Book of Iyov begins with the predominant use of name *Hashem* (ה-ו-ה-י). However, as soon as we enter into the debate between Iyov and his visitors, the name switches to *Elokim* and its various forms (*E-l, E-loah, E-l Sha-dai*, etc.). In the 886 *psukim* of back and forth (a long and arduous "*galut*"), variations on the name *Elokim* appear in excess of 100 times. By contrast, the name *Hashem* is mentioned only once, and by Iyov. (Perhaps we can construe from this single instance of the *shem Hashem* that Iyov has at least some inkling, some spark of awareness, that there is more to the universe than *Elokim*, than justice alone. Iyov is more tuned into the reality. Yes, Iyov is resentful and bitter, but at least he calls the world like it is: *Tzadik v'ra lo* does exist. The visitors on the other hand are willing to *distort* reality, make Iyov into a *rasha*, in order to sustain their pristine model of a universe run exclusively by *din*. And of course, only Iyov evolves out of the strict *din/Elokim* perspective and perceives something more.) Then, after dialogue upon dialogue wherein the name *Elokim* carries all but exclusive dominance, it is "*Hashem*" that responds to Iyov:

וַיַּעַן י-ה-ו-ה אֶת אִיּוֹב

"And Hashem answered Iyov"[148]

Indeed, "*Hashem*" *was* the answer. Iyov was answered by *chaim*, by *rachamim*. His eyes perceived what had been right in front of him all along—a world beyond *tov* and *ra*, and brimming with the singular, all-pervasive flow of Life, a world of immense beauty, and yes, sometimes cruelty, of awesome grandeur and sheer unpredictability. It is a world where both intense joy and great suffering are an integral part of the life experience—and none of it proves a person's "worthiness" or lack thereof. This knowledge served not only as a comfort and weight off the mind for Iyov, but ultimately as the gateway to great *bracha*.

The stories of Iyov and Moshe are about a simple yet profound discovery—that being open to what the reality is (i.e., being willing to shed one's cherished preconceptions about reality), and asking the right kinds of questions (i.e., questions asked from a genuine desire for knowledge,

---

[148] *Iyov* 38:1

and ones that are capable of yielding answers) are the keys to freeing up one's energies for more creative, productive ends. It is the difference between having one's life-energy sucked into the *she'ol*, the abyss, and having a *she'eila* that has the capacity to *generate* life-energy, in the sense of:

חַיִּים שָׁאַל מִמְּךָ נָתַתָּה לּוֹ

"He asked for Life from You; You gave it to him."[149]

In sum, the *brachot* of *Poke'ach Ivrim* and *Malbish Arumim* encompass the transition from Phase 1 to Phase 2, wherein we become conscious and grapple with the power of the mind. This mirrors our experience as individuals, as we transition from the sleeping to waking state. It also sets the stage for the current period of *tikun* (positive transformation), as we endeavor to advance toward Phase 3 and a new era for humanity.

Fig. 33   Three-Phase Model conceptual correspondences

Phase 1	Phase 2	Phase 3
Setup	Tension	Resolution
Childhood	Adolescence	Maturity
Eden	Exile	Redemption
Emuna	She'eila	Teshuva
Bayit Rishon	Bayit Sheni	Bayit Shlishi
Hashem	Elokim	Hashem-Elokim
Chochma	Bina	Da'at
Chesed	Gevura	Tiferet
Netzach	Hod	Yesod
Free-flowing Energy	Borders/Structure	Focused Flow
Cham	Yefet	Shem
Life-energy	Intellect	Intellect used for Life
Instinct	Ethics of good/bad	Life Principle
Tekia	Terua	Tekia Gedola
Hashem	Elokeinu	Hashem Echad
Zachar	Nekeiva	Basar Echad
Chaim	Tov/Ra	Chaim Le'olam

---

[149] *Tehilim* 21:5

מַתִּיר אֲסוּרִים

Who frees the bound

Freedom of Body and Mind

In the verse from which this *bracha* is taken, the phrase *matir asurim* refers to the freeing of prisoners.[150] Our *bracha* borrows from the *pasuk* to say that during sleep, we are considered as prisoners—our bodies are constrained, held down, and our eyes are bound shut.[151] What's more, the conscious mind is bound, held prisoner as it were. Our portal to the world is blocked, our awareness and reasoning blunted. Waking up thus constitutes a release—the mind is freed, the portal reopened, and we once again reenter the world, able to perceive and interact, discern and judge, and choose which direction we wish to take the new day.

Of course, even while awake we must exert effort in order to keep the mind from being held prisoner—from being bound by habit and by the influences of our surroundings, and from being effectively unconscious at times that would benefit from mindfulness. *Matir asurim* is thus a beneficial *kavana* (intent) to carry throughout the day—to continue to open and expand the mind, so that it is not unnecessarily bound or limited, and to keep it from going into an undesired "sleep" mode when we would rather be fully conscious.

Mutar and Asur vs. Right and Wrong

The word *matir* (מתיר) is from the root *natar* (נתר), to loosen, untie or free up. *Asurim* (אסורים) is from *asar* (אסר), meaning to bind, chain or tie down. These words are used in the *bracha* to express appreciation for having been freed from the bonds of sleep. But *matir asurim* is also suggestive of the words *mutar* and *asur*, terms used in Halacha to connote "permitted" and "forbidden" respectively. The question is, why does the tradition use language of "loosening" and "binding" in order to convey legal permissibility and forbiddenness?

---

[150] See *Metzudat David* on *Tehilim* 146:7.

[151] The *bracha* of *Matir Asurim* is related conceptually to the *bracha* said when going to sleep at night, המפיל חבלי שינה על עיני, "Who casts the bonds/ropes of sleep upon my eyes." When we awaken in the morning, these ropes are "untied," our eyes "freed" once again. (See R. Yehuda Bar-Yakar, commentary on *Birchot HaShachar*.)

Perhaps we might understand it as helping to prevent us from conceiving of Halacha as a set of norms and taboos, whereby things are inherently "good" or "bad" in the absolute sense. Rather, what is permitted should be thought of as "freed up" and available in a given context, and what is forbidden should be understood as merely "bound," tied up and unavailable in that particular context. Meaning, if circumstances change, and what was previously bound is now freed up, we should not have a visceral reaction against it, as if it were intrinsically "wrong" or "forbidden." Instead, when we engage in the process of deriving practical Halacha, we might try to shed our a priori biases and understand that there is a healthy, appropriate time and place for just about all things.

זוֹקֵף כְּפוּפִים
Who raises up the bent-over

Zokef (זוקף) is from *zakaf* (זקף), to raise up. *Kafuf* (כפוף) means bent or bowed, relating to *kaf* (כף),[152] the hollow or curve of one's hand, or a hollowed vessel like a bowl or spoon. In Tanach, *kafuf* connotes being curled up on the ground in fear or distress,[153] and *Hashem* is described as "*zokef kefufim*," raising up such a person from that position, removing the distress and allowing the person to once again stand straight and tall.[154]

Conscious Awareness and Standing Tall

Whereas *matir asurim* expresses being freed from captivity, *zokef kefufim* might be said to convey what happens immediately following one's release. Even once the shackles are undone, the person may still be on the ground, curled up, essentially broken of body and spirit. This *bracha* is about having the wherewithal to rise up, to transform from the mentality of someone held captive into a person who is able to stand tall, move forward, and embrace their new-found freedom.

Not only does standing erect evoke freedom from captivity—it signifies that which makes us distinctively human. There are many other

---

[152] See the entries for כַּף and כָּפַף in the *Gesenius Lexicon*.

[153] See *Tehilim* 57:7, רֶשֶׁת הֵכִינוּ לִפְעָמַי כָּפַף נַפְשִׁי, being bent over in fear of one's enemies.

[154] As it says, ה' זֹקֵף כְּפוּפִים (*Tehilim* 146:8); see *Metzudat David*.

animals that are "bipedal," but their knees are bent and their trunks sloped to varying degrees. Only humans truly stand and walk erect. Likewise, whereas other animals are bound purely by instinct, stimulus-response mechanisms, human beings have freedom of the mind, the freedom to choose, to rise above instinct. The *bracha* of *zokef kefufim*, the gift of standing upright, thus reminds us of the fact that the type of freedom we possess is a uniquely human one.

רוֹקַע הָאָרֶץ עַל הַמָּיִם
Who spreads out the land over the waters

The word *roka* (רוֹקַע) is from *raka* (רקע), beating or flattening so as to spread something out, as in hammering a piece of metal to expand its surface area.[155] Related is the term *rakia* (רקיע), which connotes an "expanse" or extended area.[156] In Day Two of the Creation narrative, a *rakia* (horizontal expanse) is created in the midst of the existing water, pushing the water apart to form the distinction between upper *mayim* (skies/clouds) and lower *mayim* (seas), with an empty/dry space in between. Then on Day Three, the seas themselves are pushed back, exposing the dry land underneath. The question is, what does pushing aside water and producing land have to do with the idea of waking up in the morning?

The Expanse of Consciousness

In the very straightforward sense, if we are to get up and go about our day, we need a surface, dry ground, on which to stand and walk. We therefore acknowledge the creation of that ground.[157] On a more conceptual level however, pushing back water to create a space of inhabitable land might be taken as a metaphor for pushing back *unconsciousness* (the "great sea" that envelops us during sleep) to create an expanse of *consciousness* (the "dry land" of the rational mind, which gives us the footing to think and function in the waking world).

This very much mirrors the idea of the "*tzimtzum*," where the boundless "sea" of *ohr* is pushed back to create an empty space, the

---

[155] As in, וַיְרַקְּעוּ אֶת פַּחֵי הַזָּהָב, "And they beat out the plates of gold" (*Shemot* 39:3).
[156] See the entry for רָקִיע in the *Brown-Driver-Briggs Lexicon*.
[157] See Abudraham and Ra'aven, commentaries on *Birchot HaShachar*.

"conscious space" of Creation.[158] Waking up thus constitutes a *tzimtzum*. It is consciousness opened up and distinguished from unconsciousness, *eretz* distinguished from *mayim*—an initial distinction that endows *us* with the ability to form distinctions and thereby create our world.

Fig. 34   Eretz and Mayim as states of consciousness

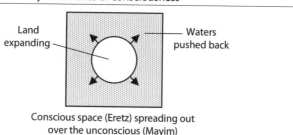

Conscious space (Eretz) spreading out
over the unconscious (Mayim)

Our *bracha* makes a clear reference to Day Three of Creation, which speaks of the appearance of dry land. However, whereas in the Creation narrative water is gathered together, exposing the dry land which had previously been submerged *beneath* the sea,[159] our *bracha* gives a different picture—that of land being spread out *above* the sea, "over the waters" (עַל הַמָּיִם). Perhaps this description is apt when thinking about the *bracha* in terms of consciousness. Namely, the land is a layer that sits above the water in the same way we might visualize consciousness as a layer that sits above the unconscious. And while our waking consciousness gives us a sense of concrete footing in the world, in truth we stand over both layers simultaneously. Meaning, the unconscious—as imperceptible and deep below the surface as it is—has a profound impact on us as well.

הַמֵּכִין מִצְעֲדֵי גָבֶר
Who directs a strong-person's footsteps

Kavana – Directing Our Thoughts and Actions

This *bracha* follows from the previous one. Once land, conscious space, has been created, we can move and build within it. The question is, now

---

[158] Indeed, in Kabbalah, *ohr* is likened to water, e.g., מֵי אוֹר הָעֶלְיוֹן, "the waters of the *ohr ha'elyon*" (R. Yehuda Ashlag, *Talmud Eser Sephirot* 2:1). See p. 57, on the concept of *tzimtzum*.
[159] See *Bereshit* 1:9, יִקָּווּ הַמַּיִם מִתַּחַת הַשָּׁמַיִם אֶל מָקוֹם אֶחָד וְתֵרָאֶה הַיַּבָּשָׁה.

that we have freedom of movement, and a ground on which to move, where do we go, and what do we build? We need some direction. Thus the *bracha* uses the word *"hamechin,"* that which "gives direction."[160] *Hamechin* (המכין) is from the root *kun* (כון), meaning to direct, fix firmly, or prepare the way by setting a course. The words *nachon* (נכון, "correct") and *ken* (כן, "yes") stem from the same root. While colloquially these words communicate an answer in the affirmative, more precisely what they describe is something firmly fixed in the right *kivun* (כיוון), the right direction. Also from the same root is the word *kavana* (כוונה), a term often used in connection with *tefila*, referring to "intent" but really meaning to set the heart/mind in a particular direction, as in:

וְהָכִינוּ לְבַבְכֶם אֶל ה' וְעִבְדֻהוּ לְבַדּוֹ

"and direct your hearts to Hashem and serve Him alone"[161]

The idea of *kavana* is to hold a particular direction of thought and not allow the mind to stray to things that are irrelevant or otherwise counterproductive. To use *kavana* is to exercise *gevura*, to restrain the mind from wandering in any direction it chooses. Concentration takes great strength. It is the work of a *gever*, a person with *gevura*. Hence, the word used in the *bracha* to refer to a person is not *ish*, *enosh* or *adam* but "*gever*."[162]

But the *bracha* is not speaking per se about a person's *"kavanat halev"* (lit., "direction of the heart"), the ability to focus the mind—rather, it pertains to the *kavana* of a person's "footsteps." In the same way that it is easy for the mind to wander off, it is likewise easy for us to be pulled in other directions when it comes to moving and acting in the world. So in order to stay on the desired path, one likewise needs to be a *gever*. Furthermore, it is *Hashem* that gives direction to the *gever*. Meaning, we look to the Torah system and its overarching Life principle to hone our focus, channel our strengths, and help guide our way forward.

---

[160] There is a different *nusach* of this *bracha* which concludes אשר הכין מצעדי גבר, "Who directed/prepared a person's footsteps," i.e., in the past tense. The present-tense formulation of המכין is the wording used in the Talmud (*Brachot* 60b).

[161] I *Shmuel* 7:3

[162] The *bracha* is inspired by several *psukim*: מֵה' מִצְעֲדֵי גֶבֶר כּוֹנָנוּ וְדַרְכּוֹ יֶחְפָּץ (*Tehilim* 37:23), יָדַעְתִּי ה' כִּי לֹא לָאָדָם דַּרְכּוֹ לֹא לְאִישׁ הֹלֵךְ (*Mishlei* 20:24), and מֵה' מִצְעֲדֵי גָבֶר וְאָדָם מַה יָּבִין דַּרְכּוֹ (*Yirmiyahu* 10:23). The word "*gever*" is used to indicate one whose footsteps are given direction, whereas the terms *adam* and *ish* describe people who do not know their way.

שֶׁעָשָׂה לִי כָּל צָרְכִּי
Who produced for me my every need

Need, Desire and Action

The Talmud associates this *bracha* with putting on one's shoes.[163] Why are shoes considered to represent a person's "every need"? Perhaps very simply, at the time this *bracha* was composed (and indeed today, in many places in the world), to own even a simple pair of shoes was something that one could in no way take for granted. So as we put on our shoes, we acknowledge that "all our needs" have been provided—i.e., *even* including shoes. Some however understand that shoes themselves are not the "need" that the *bracha* acknowledges, but rather that shoes enable a person to *act*, to go out and attend to all their needs.[164] Others stress "*kol*" *tzorki*, "all" of a person's needs, to mean that with shoes on one's feet a person is able to reach any desired destination.[165] In this sense, wearing shoes might be seen as symbolic of possessing the adequate tools or vehicles to see our will come to fruition. Having our basic needs met allows us to more freely pursue our higher needs, to achieve our goals and desires.

Need as a Catalyst for Creativity

The straightforward understanding of the *bracha* relates to our needs being met. However, the phrase "produced for me my every need" also carries a degree of ambiguity, so as to perhaps also mean that we appreciate having been created with "needs" in the first place. This would be something akin to the *bracha* of *Borei Nefashot*:

בּוֹרֵא נְפָשׁוֹת רַבּוֹת וְחֶסְרוֹנָן עַל כָּל מַה שֶׁבָּרָאתָ
לְהַחֲיוֹת בָּהֶם נֶפֶשׁ כָּל חַי

"Who creates numerous living things, and their lacks, upon all that You created,
to enliven within them the life-energy of every living thing"[166]

---

[163] See *Brachot* 60b. For this reason, some customs place this *bracha* before the previous one, so that the order would be first putting on one's shoes (*she'asa li kol tzorki*) and then walking (*hamechin mitzadei gaver*).

[164] See *Sefer Abudraham*, commentary on *Birchot HaShachar*.

[165] See *Levush* on *Orach Chaim* 46; also see *Mishna Berura* 554:32.

[166] The *Borei Nefashot bracha* is said after consuming food or drink that does not require the *bracha* of *Me'ein Shalosh* or *Birkat HaMazon*. The word for "need" used in *Borei Nefashot*,

That is to say, we were created in such a way that the fulfillment of a lack or need is enlivening, energizing. Not only does it give us momentary pleasure and satisfaction, but it propels us forward in our process of discovery and advance. As the saying goes, "necessity is the mother of invention."[167] The existence of need, that desire within us for something more, can serve as a great catalyst for creativity and growth.

אוֹזֵר יִשְׂרָאֵל בִּגְבוּרָה / עוֹטֵר יִשְׂרָאֵל בְּתִפְאָרָה
Who girds Yisrael with gevura / Who crowns Yisrael with tiferet

Invoking the National Calling

The *bracha* of *Ozer Yisrael Bigevura* is associated in the Talmud with tying a belt around one's waist, and *Oter Yisrael Betifara* with wrapping a cloth/turban around one's head.[168] Some suggest that covering the waist relates to *Am Yisrael*'s self-restraint/*gevura* where it comes to matters of sexuality, and that covering the head reflects *yirat Hashem*, whereby the watchfulness and care we put into Torah and *mitzvot* is our "*tifara*," our crowning splendor.[169]

These items of clothing also bring to mind the *avneit* (waist sash) and *mitznefet* (turban) worn by a *kohen*,[170] and so perhaps the reason the term "*Yisrael*" is used in these *brachot*, referring to *Am Yisrael* as a nation (as opposed to the preceding *brachot* which are focused on the individual), is to invoke the idea that we are a *mamlechet kohanim*. We are part of a larger national mission—to be a nation of priests, to embody the will for Life, to strive for higher standards personally and interpersonally, and to contribute meaningfully to the world, such that we leave it in a better state

---

and predominantly throughout Tanach, is *chesron* (or *machsor*), from the root חסר, connoting lack. The root צרך is a late-Hebrew term, appearing in only one *pasuk* in Tanach, וַאֲנַחְנוּ נִכְרֹת עֵצִים מִן הַלְּבָנוֹן כְּכָל צָרְכֶּךָ (II *Divrei HaYamim* 2:15). This *pasuk* is understood as inspiring the phrase כָּל צָרְכִּי in our *bracha* (see Abudraham on *Birchot HaShachar*).

[167] Originally from Plato's *The Republic*: "Necessity, who is the mother of invention..."

[168] See *Brachot* 60b. The *brachot* are based loosely on the *psukim* מֵכִין הָרִים בְּכֹחוֹ נֶאְזָר בִּגְבוּרָה (*Tehilim* 65:7) and עַבְדִּי אָתָּה יִשְׂרָאֵל אֲשֶׁר בְּךָ אֶתְפָּאָר (*Yeshayahu* 49:3). (See R. Yehuda Bar-Yakar, Abudraham, and Ra'aven, commentaries on *Birchot HaShachar*.)

[169] See Bach and Taz on *Orach Chaim* 46.

[170] The *Shulchan Aruch* itself uses the word "*mitznefet*" in connection with the *bracha* of *Oter Yisrael Betifara* (see *Orach Chaim* 46:1). R. Tzadok HaKohen associates the *avneit* of the *kohen* with the *bracha* of *Ozer Yisrael Bigevura* (see *Pri Tzadik, Devarim L'Rosh Chodesh Elul*).

than when we came into it. This ambitious project requires much *gevura* on our part, much strength of focus, resolve and determination. When we attend to it properly, we exude *ohr/chaim* and shine with great *tifara*.

From Gevura to Tiferet

The Sefat Emet[171] suggests that these two *brachot* relate to the periods of *galut* and *ge'ula*. *Ozer Yisrael Bigevura* is about the state of exile, wherein our task is to win out over the darker, anti-life human inclinations.[172] This requires us to be as a *gibor*, to summon heroic strength and self-restraint. The "belt" in this sense is that of a warrior, and *ozer* is the idea of girding, equipping oneself for battle.[173] The root *azar* (אזר) also means to encompass, surround. When we surround something, we keep it in bounds. To say that *Hashem* is *ozer Yisrael bigevura* can thus be understood to mean that we are held/bound by the will for Life. Girding and constraining ourselves with the Life principle requires *gevura*—the strength of restraint. When this is done successfully, the result is *tiferet*, the shining splendor of vitality—we arrive at "*Oter Yisrael Betifara*," our *geula*/redemption. *Gevura* corresponds to the battle, *tiferet* to the final triumph. That same feeling of being bound and limited ("*ozer*") is later experienced as being enveloped, wrapped ("*oter*"). Limitation, when used judiciously and effectively, can function as an embrace.

To more concretely visualize *gevura* and *tiferet*, we might look at the contraction and relaxation of muscles. *Gevura* is analogous to the state of a muscle in contraction. It is an exertion of effort, strength, wherein blood is drawn to the muscle, constrained to it. When the muscle is subsequently relaxed, blood rushes from the muscle, leaving the person with a feeling of warmth and tingling, a rush of energy and invigoration. That is analogous to *tiferet*. We thus encounter *gevura* and *tiferet* in a very palpable sense every time we undergo physical exertion, and we experience it in the larger sense whenever we put forth effort and determination, focus our energies, and come away with a feeling of vitalization from the end result as well as the process.

---

[171] R. Yehuda Aryeh Leib Alter (1847–1905), author of the work, *Sefat Emet*.

[172] See *Sefat Emet* on *Parshat Shemot*, starting במדרש ואלה שמות. He also suggests that the two *brachot* correspond to the arm and head *tefilin* respectively.

[173] See *I Melachim* 2:5 and *Yeshayahu* 8:9, among other examples in Tanach, where "belt" and "girding" relate to war.

הַנּוֹתֵן לַיָּעֵף כֹּחַ
Who gives strength to the weary

The *bracha* of *HaNoten Laya'ef Ko'ach* is based on the *pasuk*:

נֹתֵן לַיָּעֵף כֹּחַ וּלְאֵין אוֹנִים עָצְמָה יַרְבֶּה.

"He gives strength to the weary,
and to those with no vigor He increases might."[174]

One who is *ya'ef* is weary, faint or light-headed due to the lack of energy or fuel (e.g., food and water) in one's system.[175] It is the kind of light-headedness that causes a person to feel as if he or she is drifting up and away. The word *ya'ef* (יעף) is thus thought to be related to *uf* (עוף), "flight,"[176] and to *to'afa* (תועפה), "lofty height."[177] This is as opposed to the word *yage'a* (יגע), which implies exhaustion due to one's labors.[178]

Hashem as Ko'ach

The word *ko'ach* is "power" in the sense of the energy to act or move, and also in the sense of know-how and capability. In our case, the *bracha* is speaking in terms of energy, giving *ko'ach* to the weary. *Hashem* is "*noten laya'ef ko'ach*," meaning *Hashem* is the *chaim*, the energy and animating force—the *ko'ach*—that drives all creatures. The equating of *Hashem* and *ko'ach* is made explicitly in the story of Shimshon (Samson). When Shimshon's hair is cut by Delilah, all his strength is depleted, as the *pasuk* says:

---

[174] *Yeshayahu* 40:29. This *bracha* is not sourced in the Talmud, nor did it exist at the time of the Geonim. It is cited in the *Machzor Vitry* (11th century French work; note that the *Vitry* also includes two other *brachot*, "מגביה שפלים" and "סומך נופלים," in *Birchot HaShachar*). The *Shulchan Aruch* recommends against saying this *bracha*, יש נוהגין לברך...ואין דבריהם נראין, and the Rama states that the basic Ashkenazi custom is to say it (see *Orach Chaim* 46:6). Today however it has become the Sephardi custom to say it as well (see *Yalkut Yosef, Kitzur Shulchan Aruch, Orach Chaim* 46:16).

[175] See e.g., *Shoftim* 8:15, II *Shmuel* 16:2.

[176] See *Gesenius Lexicon*, entry for עוּף. Also cf., יעף and עיף.

[177] See *Brown-Driver-Briggs Lexicon*, entry for יעף.

[178] As in, הוּא קָם וַיַּךְ בַּפְּלִשְׁתִּים עַד כִּי יָגְעָה יָדוֹ (II *Shmuel* 23:10).

וַתְּגַלַּח אֶת שֶׁבַע מַחְלְפוֹת רֹאשׁוֹ
וַתָּחֶל לְעַנּוֹתוֹ וַיָּסַר כֹּחוֹ מֵעָלָיו

"and she shaved the seven locks of his head,
and she began to diminish him, and his power withdrew from him"[179]

His "power" withdrew from him. Then, in the very next *pasuk*, when Shimshon awakens, it says:

וְהוּא לֹא יָדַע כִּי ה׳ סָר מֵעָלָיו

"and he did not know that Hashem withdrew from him"[180]

Shimshon did not realize that "*Hashem*" had withdrawn from him. In other words, the terms "*koach*" and "*Hashem*" are used here more or less interchangeably, which reflects the understanding of *Hashem* we have been suggesting—that *Hashem* conveys *chaim*, life-energy.

Another way to think about *Hashem* giving strength to the weary is that the very will for Life itself, the desire to press on and survive amidst trying circumstances, has the capacity to impart near miraculous *ko'ach* to those who are otherwise exhausted—even when there appears to be no remaining physical fuel from which to draw. That is the great power of the human spirit.

---

[179] *Shoftim* 16:19

[180] Ibid., 16:20. Rabbeinu Bachye (on *Bamidbar* 6:3, speaking about Shimshon in the context of *nezirut*) explains: וּמִיָּד סָר כֹּחוֹ מֵעָלָיו וְהוּא כֹּח ה׳.

HaMa'avir Sheina
המעביר שינה

בָּרוּךְ אַתָּה ה' אֱ-לֹהֵינוּ מֶלֶךְ הָעוֹלָם הַמַּעֲבִיר שֵׁנָה מֵעֵינַי וּתְנוּמָה מֵעַפְעַפָּי. וִיהִי רָצוֹן מִלְּפָנֶיךָ ה' אֱ-לֹהֵינוּ וֵא-לֹהֵי אֲבוֹתֵינוּ, שֶׁתַּרְגִּילֵנוּ בְּתוֹרָתֶךָ וְדַבְּקֵנוּ בְּמִצְוֹתֶיךָ, וְאַל תְּבִיאֵנוּ לֹא לִידֵי חֵטְא וְלֹא לִידֵי עֲבֵרָה וְעָוֹן, וְלֹא לִידֵי נִסָּיוֹן וְלֹא לִידֵי בִזָּיוֹן, וְאַל תַּשְׁלֶט בָּנוּ יֵצֶר הָרָע, וְהַרְחִיקֵנוּ מֵאָדָם רָע וּמֵחָבֵר רָע, וְדַבְּקֵנוּ בְּיֵצֶר הַטּוֹב וּבְמַעֲשִׂים טוֹבִים, וְכֹף אֶת יִצְרֵנוּ לְהִשְׁתַּעְבֶּד לָךְ וּתְנֵנוּ הַיּוֹם וּבְכָל יוֹם לְחֵן וּלְחֶסֶד וּלְרַחֲמִים בְּעֵינֶיךָ וּבְעֵינֵי כָל רוֹאֵינוּ וְתִגְמְלֵנוּ חֲסָדִים טוֹבִים, בָּרוּךְ אַתָּה ה' הַגּוֹמֵל חֲסָדִים טוֹבִים לְעַמּוֹ יִשְׂרָאֵל.

There is a risk involved in becoming conscious, possessing *da'at*—the risk that rather than be a tool for creativity and life, the mind will lure us into thinking and actions that are destructive to ourselves and others. This *bracha*, the last of the fifteen *Birchot HaShachar*, calls on us to be proactive—to attach ourselves to Torah, engage in constructive activity, and be guided by the inclination toward Life. In so doing, we hope to overcome the obstacles in our path, become masters of the conscious mind, be mature and responsible bearers of *da'at*, and advance toward the next phase of human development—one which is marked by independence and unsurpassed *bracha*.

הַמַּעֲבִיר שֵׁנָה מֵעֵינַי וּתְנוּמָה מֵעַפְעַפָּי
Who removes sleep from my eyes and drowsiness from my eyelids

---

Stages of Awakening

The *bracha* of *HaMa'avir Sheina* is sourced in the Talmud,[1] and this first phrase is based on a *pasuk* in Tanach.[2] The phrase contains two parts—removing sleep from the eyes, and removing drowsiness from the eyelids.

---

[1] See *Brachot* 60b, which connects the phrase "Who removes sleep from my eyes" with washing one's face in the morning.

[2] The *pasuk*: אִם אֶתֵּן שְׁנַת לְעֵינָי לְעַפְעַפַּי תְּנוּמָה (*Tehilim* 132:4). See also *Mishlei* 6:4.

Perhaps this can be understood to suggest a two-stage process of awakening. The first stage is emerging from the state of sleep (*sheina*), where we are no longer completely unconscious but still feel drowsy, prone to dozing off again. There is still "slumber on our eyelids," so to speak. The word for eyelid is *afaf* (עפעף), related to *ohf* (עוף, a winged creature), likely in the sense of "fluttering," which is characteristic of the eyelids when drifting in and out of sleep.[3] The second stage of awakening is when the drowsiness (*tenuma*) passes and we become fully conscious—alert and present.

The stages of removing *sheina* and *tenuma* might also be likened to states of awareness in waking life. To first become aware of something is akin to removing "sleep" (*sheina*) from our eyes, awakening to a certain reality of which we had no prior awareness at all. However, even after having been made aware, that reality can easily drift in and out of our minds. We have spells of dozing off when we temporarily forget, lose track of what we know to be true and/or important, effectively reentering a state of sleep. To remove this "slumber" (*tenuma*), to stay on track and keep the reality in mind, requires a continuous effort on our part to remain conscious.

One might in fact think of daily *tefila* in this way—as functioning to help keep us aware of that which we already know is important, but which if we did not make a concerted, regular effort to focus on would quickly fall off the radar of our consciousness. *Tefila* thus has the capacity to keep us from slumbering.

וִיהִי רָצוֹן ... שֶׁתַּרְגִּילֵנוּ בְּתוֹרָתֶךָ וְדַבְּקֵנוּ בְּמִצְוֹתֶיךָ
*And may it be [Your] will... that You regulate us in Your Torah
and attach us to Your commands*

Torah and Mitzvot – Regularity and Intimacy

Now that we are fully conscious, we express the desire to direct that consciousness toward Life, via Torah and *mitzvot* (the *torat chaim* and *chukei chaim*). The word *targileinu* (תרגילנו, "regulate/accustom us") is from *regel* (רגל, leg/foot), connoting walking and going, as well as

---

[3] See the entry for עפעף in the *Brown-Driver-Briggs Lexicon*. Also cf., יעף and עיף in the previous chapter, p. 204.

groundedness and stability. The hope is that we are as comfortable with and accustomed to the learning of Torah as we are with walking, and it should move us, propel us forward, help guide us in our thoughts and actions, and also provide us with grounding, balance and structure.

The word *dabekeinu* (דבקינו, "attach us") is from *davak* (דבק, cling, attach), which conveys a sense of desire and intimacy, as in the *pasuk*:

וְדָבַק בְּאִשְׁתּוֹ וְהָיוּ לְבָשָׂר אֶחָד

"and he will attach to his wife, and they will be one flesh"[4]

This is as opposed to *chibur* (חיבור), as in *chaver* (חבר, "friend"), where although the attachment may be strong, it is less intimate than *davak*. *Chibur* can also include alliances made for convenience or strategic purposes.[5] Our attachment to the *mitzvot* should be that of "*davak*"—it should come with intimacy, whereby a person engages them not simply through force of habit, but also out of genuine interest and enthusiasm, the desire to connect.

Achieving a Balanced Relationship

The orientations of *targileinu* and *dabekeinu*, regularity and desire, are both vital in a relationship, and they are in fact complementary to one another. In an ideal relationship, a person "shows up" consistently, regularly, demonstrates commitment, and at the same time is passionate, has his or her heart in it, truly desires the other. Regularity without passion is cold and robotic—all structure, devoid of any real vitality. Passion without commitment is narcissistic and immature—all spontaneous energy with no structure to ground it, direct it.

It is therefore precisely with regard to the *mitzvot*, to which we can easily become habituated and perform by rote, that we say "*dabekeinu*," that we wish to maintain passion. And it is in relation to Torah learning, wherein there is no particular "*shiur*" (specified amount or time required), and we may decide to involve ourselves in Torah only when we feel the desire and inspiration, that we say "*targileinu*," that we

---

[4] *Bereshit* 2:24

[5] As in, וְאַחֲרֵי כֵן אֶתְחַבַּר יְהוֹשָׁפָט מֶלֶךְ יְהוּדָה עִם אֲחַזְיָה מֶלֶךְ יִשְׂרָאֵל (*II Divrei HaYamim* 20:35).

wish to accustom ourselves to learning Torah, to immerse ourselves in Torah on a regular basis.[6]

וְאַל תְּבִיאֵנוּ לֹא לִידֵי חֵטְא וְלֹא לִידֵי עֲבֵרָה וְעָוֹן
and do not bring us to error, and not to transgression and crookedness

---

Cheit and Avon – Two Types of Deviation

The words *cheit*, *aveira* and *avon* all refer in general to misconduct, particularly as it pertains to the *mitzvot*. *Aveira* means "transgression" in the sense of going beyond the line of the law. The words *cheit* and *avon* both connote a kind of "deviation" from that which is straight, a departure from proper, upright behavior. The deviation of *cheit* is that of missing the mark, as it says:

כָּל זֶה קֹלֵעַ בָּאֶבֶן אֶל הַשַּׂעֲרָה וְלֹא יַחֲטִא
"each one could sling a stone to a hairsbreadth and not miss"[7]

Although *cheit* can sometimes imply habituated indecency (as when the term is used to describe the people of Sedom[8]), the tradition looks at *cheit*—in relation to the *mitzvot*—as inadvertent transgression, which in certain cases can be rectified by bringing a *korban* (sacrifice). In this sense, *cheit* can be said to "crouch at the door,"[9] sneak up on a person who may be temporarily "slumbering" and is not mindful of his or her thoughts, emotions or actions.

Whereas *cheit* is associated more with action per se, *avon* (עָוֹן) connotes a deviation that is as much *within* the person as it is expressed outwardly. It connotes "crookedness," criminality, possibly from *ava* (עוה), meaning bent or twisted,[10] as in the *pasuk*:

---

[6] Torah and *mitzvot* in this sense are similar to the concepts of *ohr* and *kli* respectively. *Ohr* needs bounds to channel it, and a *kli* needs energy to give it life. Indeed the *pasuk* says explicitly, כִּי נֵר מִצְוָה וְתוֹרָה אוֹר (*Mishlei* 6:23), that a *mitzva* is likened to a *kli* and Torah to *ohr*.

[7] *Shoftim* 20:16

[8] As it says, וְאַנְשֵׁי סְדֹם רָעִים וְחַטָּאִים לַהֹ' מְאֹד (*Bereshit* 13:13).

[9] See *Bereshit* 4:7, regarding Kayin.

[10] See entry for עָוָה in the *Gesenius Lexicon*. Cf., *Brown-Driver-Briggs Lexicon*, which suggests two separate roots for עוה, one meaning "twist" and the other "iniquity."

חָטָאתִי וְיָשָׁר הֶעֱוֵיתִי

"I have erred, and straightness/uprightness I have twisted"[11]

As such, of all the terms relating to transgression, *avon* is the type that is the most internalized, that lingers, as in the phrase *"nosei avono,"* the idea that a person "carries" their *avon*.[12]

Korban Chatat – Returning What Was Taken

As we said above, inadvertent *cheit* can be resolved via *korban*. The conditions for this are described in the Torah as follows:

נֶפֶשׁ כִּי תֶחֱטָא בִשְׁגָגָה מִכֹּל מִצְוֹת ה'
אֲשֶׁר לֹא תֵעָשֶׂינָה וְעָשָׂה מֵאַחַת מֵהֵנָּה...

"A living-person who errs inadvertently from any of the commands of Hashem
that a person should not do, and he did one of them..."[13]

The option of a *korban* is available when the *cheit* is done inadvertently (i.e., without knowledge or premeditation), and when the person has transgressed a *"lo ta'aseh,"* a negative command.[14] That is to say, there was something *"asur,"* bound up and prohibited, and the person was *"matir"* it, inadvertently released the binds and took it for him or herself. In effect, breaking a negative command might be conceptualized as *taking* something that does not belong to us.

So perhaps we can understand the *korban chatat* as follows: If the act was done inadvertently, then what the person "took" they don't really feel is owed to them and are fully prepared to "give back." This giving back can then be done by way of a *korban*. If however it was done with knowledge and/or premeditation, then the person in essence did so out of a rationalized sense of entitlement and felt it was theirs to unbind and take. If they feel it was "owed" to them, and there is nothing for them to give back, a *korban* is pointless. Such a person requires

---

[11] *Iyov* 33:27

[12] See e.g., *Bereshit* 4:13, *Vayikra* 5:1, 17:16. This is to be distinguished from *"nosei avon"* in the sense of exoneration, where *Hashem* "carries" a person's transgression. The latter sense is used to refer to *avon* as well as to *cheit* and *pesha*, as in: נֹשֵׂא עָוֹן וָפֶשַׁע וְחַטָּאָה (*Shemot* 34:7). The "carrying" we are speaking about here however is only used in conjunction with *avon*.

[13] *Vayikra* 4:2

[14] See Rambam *Hilchot Shegagot* 1:1.

teshuva, "return" to *Hashem,* to the life-orientation, via personal trans-formation.[15]

Cheit as Plus-charge

We spoke earlier about *tuma* as a lack or depletion of life-energy, ex-pressed conceptually as a "minus-charge" on the person.[16] In this model, *cheit* could be characterized as an unhealthy excess or "plus-charge." By having taken something that is not ours, there is something "extra" that now weighs on the *nefesh.*

The idea of *cheit* as plus-charge (excess) may also explain the seem-ingly paradoxical meanings of "sin" and "purify" as emerging from the same root, *chata* (חטא). For instance, the Torah says regarding the water mixture containing the ashes of the *para aduma* (red cow):

הוּא יִתְחַטָּא בוֹ בַּיּוֹם הַשְּׁלִישִׁי וּבַיּוֹם הַשְּׁבִיעִי יִטְהָר
*"He will purify himself with it on the third day,
and on the seventh day he will be tahor"*[17]

How can *"chata"* convey both sin and purification? We might say as fol-lows: The root *chata* as "sin" means to accrue plus-charge *harmfully,* whereby it sits as an imbalance, an unhealthy excess, within the person (weighing upon the psyche), and requires a discharge. *Chata* as "purify" however means to accrue (or impart) plus-charge *beneficially,* to add it to that which is *tamei*/minus-charged, so as to effect *kapara*/neutralization, replenishing the depleted life-energy. The above *pasuk* refers to what is elsewhere called *"mei chatat,"*[18] the water mixture that is sprinkled on a person who is *tamei meit* (*tamei* from contact with the dead) in order to render the person *tahor* and cancel out the minus-charge. The *para aduma* procedure can thus be seen as a means of applying excess to lack, plus to minus, in order to have a neutralizing effect.[19]

---

[15] Today of course we have no *korban chatat.* Regarding other means of *kaparat cheit,* see ahead, p. 215. See also p. 171, on the concept of *Bayit Shlishi.*

[16] See p. 91.

[17] Bamidbar 19:12

[18] As in, הַזֶּה עֲלֵיהֶם מֵי חַטָּאת (*Bamidbar* 8:7). The mixture is also referred to as *"mei nida"* (see e.g., *Bamidbar* 19:9).

[19] There is an apparent paradox cited in the tradition regarding the *para aduma* (red cow). Namely, the ash mixture renders *tahor* the person who was *tamei,* yet at the same time puzzlingly renders *tamei* those who were *tahor* (i.e., the *kohanim* attending to the mixture

Fig. 35 Cheit ("Sin") – Adding plus-charge harmfully

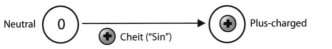

Neutral 0 → Plus-charged
Cheit ("Sin")

Fig. 36 Chitui ("Purification") – Adding plus-charge beneficially

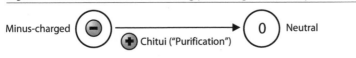

Minus-charged → 0 Neutral
Chitui ("Purification")

Kapara, widely defined as "atonement," in fact more precisely refers to the process of "cancelling out," nullifying or neutralizing.[20] Although the term *kapara* is used in connection with both *tuma* and *cheit*,[21] they employ opposite corrective methods to effect the neutralization. *Tuma* requires "plus" (replenishment) to be cancelled out or neutralized, since the person's *nefesh* is depleted. *Cheit* however requires "minus" (discharge) in order to be neutralized. A person with *cheit* needs to purge—discharge guilt, get rid of excess that is "carried" on the *nefesh*, give back that which has been taken.

---

and procedure). How can the same thing make one person *tahor* and others *tamei*? I offer the following speculation: The ash mixture, as we said above, is "plus-charged." The *kohanim* handling it become minus-charged (*tamei*). Perhaps these two things are very much connected. That is, the ash mixture becomes plus-charged precisely *as a result* of the *kohanim* becoming *tamei*. How so? Because the mixture is thought to draw/siphon off *nefesh* from each of the *kohanim* handling it. Hence the *kohanim* are each left with a slight minus-charge/*tuma*, while simultaneously the mixture itself becomes more and more plus-charged at each stage of the procedure. In other words, the *tuma* of the *kohanim* is not merely incidental to the procedure—the *nefesh* they lose becomes the very "fuel" for the *mei chatat*! This may account as well for the significance of the color "red," since red is equated with "*din*," drawing or pulling inward (as opposed to *chesed*, expanding outward)—i.e., it is seen as helping to draw the *nefesh* of the *kohanim* who handle it. In this understanding, the *para aduma* procedure is viewed as a very literal form of *mesirut nefesh*, wherein a number of *kohanim* contribute a bit of their *nefesh*, passing it on to someone else who is in a more severe state of depletion, in order to aid in their healing.

[20] The Midrash states explicitly: כפרה לשון ביטול, "*kapara* is a term of nullification" (*Midrash Aggadah Buber*, *Devarim* 21:7). See also Rashi (on *Bereshit* 32:21) who explains the phrase אֲכַפְּרָה פָנָיו to mean "אבטל רגזו." (Abarbanel and Ramban, ibid., explain the phrase similarly.)

[21] As in, וְכִפֶּר עָלָיו הַכֹּהֵן מֵחַטָּאתוֹ (*Vayikra* 14:19), and וְכִפֶּר עַל הַמִּטַּהֵר מִטֻּמְאָתוֹ (Ibid., 4:26).

Fig. 37   Kaparat Tuma – Neutralization by replenishing Nefesh

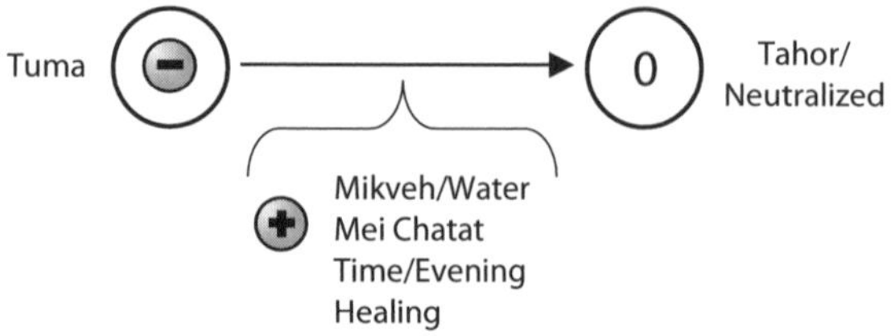

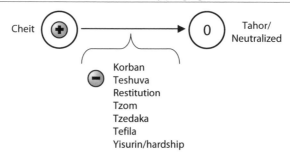

Fig. 38   Kaparat Cheit – Neutralization by purging Nefesh

Kaparat Cheit – Purging Excess Nefesh

We have spoken already about some of the methods for *kaparat tuma,* replenishing lost *nefesh.*[22] Now we will focus on *kaparat cheit.* The Torah itself speaks of the *korban chatat* as a *kapara* for *cheit.* It is a *kapara* because it constitutes a form of giving from one's *nefesh,* a purging of excess. Earlier in the book we discussed the idea of energy conservation as applied to the *Mikdash.*[23] In a similar spirit, we might look at the *korban chatat* as being analogous to the "recycling of energy." The process might be understood as follows: A person accrues "excess" in the form of *cheit.* This is energy that is unusable, weighing on the person in the form of guilt. When such a person brings a *korban chatat,* not only does this purge their excess energy, but rather than it being wasted, this energy is reintroduced to the system—to the *Mikdash*—for constructive use.[24]

---

[22] See p. 92, regarding water and time, and Note 19, p. 212, regarding the *para aduma.*

[23] See p. 57.

[24] How this process is perhaps understood: The person bringing the *korban* leans their hands on the animal, so that their *nefesh* and the *nefesh* of the animal become connected. (As in, והוא ענין הסמיכה בכל כחו ליחד נפשו לחבר בחינת נפשו עם נפש הבהמה, R. Pinchas Hor-

Aside from purging via *korban*, other traditional means of *kaparat cheit* (neutralization of *cheit*) include *tzom* (fasting), *tzedaka* (donating money), and doing *teshuva* (repentance, lit. "return"). *Teshuva*, when it involves interpersonal transgression, can include monetary restitution and/or obtaining *mechila* (forgiveness). Each of these methods is a means of giving, purging or diminution—effectively a "minus," done to counteract and neutralize the unhealthy "plus" which is *cheit*.

Tzom is a physical depletion by way of withholding food and water.[25] *Tzedaka* is drawing from one's life-energy/*nefesh* by way of giving money.[25] Returning illegally held property or money is a form of *teshuva* that involves purging the "excess" from one's possession. The word *mechila* (מחילה) comes from *chol* (חול), which implies depletion or lack.[26] When a person asks for *mechila*, they are requesting to be purged or depleted of the feelings of guilt that have been weighing on them. Likewise, doing personal *teshuva* is *not* about feel guilty, but in fact precisely the opposite—it is about purging/letting go of one's guilt by changing into the type of person who would no longer commit the original wrongdoing. *Teshuva* is the return to neutral, to equilibrium, to *shalom*.

All these are methods of deliberately effecting *kapara*, as opposed to *yisurin* (hardship/suffering), which although recognized in the tradition as a vehicle for *kapara*[27] is not something a person is meant to intentionally seek out. Rather, the idea of *yisurin* as having a corrective function simply means that if suffering should happen to come upon a person, it has the potential to act as an agent of *kapara* due to the physical, mental and emotional drain.

---

owitz, *Panim Yafot, Parshat Vayikra* 1:4.) *Nefesh*, as we discussed, is understood as being linked to the blood. So when the animal is *shechted* (slaughtered) and its blood is drained out, this is seen as drawing out not only the *nefesh* of the animal, but also the excess *nefesh* (*cheit*) of the person to whom that animal is now connected. (As in, ועי"י הקרבת נפש בהמה תתעלה נפשו; ibid.) In effect, it is a technique for drawing out the person's excess *nefesh* without having to spill any of their own blood. Once the person has been purged, now there is blood that theoretically contains that person's excess energy/*nefesh*. So that blood is sprinkled on the Altar, the otherwise wasted energy "put back" into the system as it were. Hence, *cheit* is not simply purged, but rather its energy is "recycled" for the benefit of the *Klal*, the people.

[25] See p. 81, also Note 25, p. 94, regarding money as being part of the *nefesh*.

[26] See p. 56, on the concept of "*chol.*"

[27] See Rambam, *Hilchot Teshuva* 1:11–12.

Tefila Bimkom Korban

In addition to other methods of *kapara*, there is of course *tefila*, prayer. *Tefila* is understood today as being *"bimkom korban,"* in place of *korban*, sacrifice.[28] In the basic sense, this means that while there is no *Mikdash*, the *tefilot* act as a substitute for morning, afternoon and evening *avoda* in the *Mikdash*.[29] But it is not simply that *tefila* acts as a placeholder for *korban*—it also approximates the *function* of a *korban*. A *korban* is that which a person offers, gives, draws from his or her *nefesh*, either for corrective purposes (*kapara*, as with the *korban chatat*) or out of *simcha* (as in the *korban shlamim* or *korban todah*). Likewise, when one uses words and emotions to express his or her innermost desires and wants, joy and pain, awe and gratitude, regret and resolve to change, this too constitutes a needed "giving." *Tefila* thus has the capacity effect *kapara*, to restore and vitalize the *nefesh*.[30]

וְלֹא לִידֵי נִסָּיוֹן וְלֹא לִידֵי בִזָּיוֹן

and not in the hands of a test, and not in the hands of degradation

---

Nisayon – a Test of Identity

A *nisayon* (from the root נסה) is a test, a trial or a proving. It bears a linguistic similarity to the word *neis* (from נסס), meaning banner or flag/flagstaff.[31] A banner is an identifier, as in the phrase *"Hashem nisi"* (*"Hashem* is my banner," i.e., "I identify with *Hashem*").[32] To tie together the concepts of a trial and a banner, a *nisayon* could perhaps be thought of as a test of one's identity, in effect asking the person: "To whom or what do you hold your allegiance? Whose banner are you really under?"

---

[28] As is learned out from the *pasuk:* וּנְשַׁלְּמָה פָרִים שְׂפָתֵינוּ, "And our lips will compensate for bulls" (*Hoshea* 14:3).

[29] *Shacharit* and *Mincha* correspond to the *Tamid*, brought twice daily in the *Mikdash*, and *Ma'ariv* corresponds to the overnight burning of the remaining fats and limbs. (See *Brachot* 26b, which also cites the opinion that the three *tefilot* correspond to *Avraham*, *Yitzchak* and *Ya'akov*.)

[30] As the Midrash states, אין לנו קרבן לכפר עלינו אלא תפלה (*Otzar Midrashim, Ma'asim*, p. 354).

[31] See entries for נסה and נסס in the *Etymological Dictionary of Biblical Hebrew*, M. Clark. Note that the word *neis* meaning "miracle" is a late-Hebrew term, deriving from נס as a "sign" (see *Brown-Driver-Briggs Lexicon*, entry for נס/נסס). The notion of *neis* as a miracle does not appear in Tanach.

[32] See *Shemot* 17:15.

In the *bracha* we express the hope that we not be put to the test, that our identity and allegiance not be challenged. True, challenge can be a catalyst for growth. It often makes us stronger people. But in the same way that a person should not go out of their way to seek out *yisurin* (hardships) so as to gain *kapara*, so too we want to avoid situations of *nisayon* where there is a high risk of coming to the hands of *aveira, cheit* or *avon*, as we expressed previously in the *bracha*.[33]

Fences and Economy of Energy

A person may look at traditional Judaism and ask, *Why all the fences?* That is, why does Rabbinic Judaism go above and beyond what the Torah asks by piling prohibition on top of prohibition? The primary concern is that people not come to break a Torah command.[34] In addition however, it can be seen as a fulfillment of our *bracha* in the sense of not putting a person unnecessarily into a position of *nisayon*. It is a *bracha*, a good thing, not to have to endure tests of our identity, if only from the standpoint of economy of energy. It takes energy to get through a *nisayon*. When something is pulling us away from our preferred banner/identity, it requires an expenditure of energy to counteract that pull. And if we succumb, end up actually getting pulled in, it has the potential to exert an even greater pull the next time around.[35] A fence is thus a way of conserving precious life-energy so that it can be spent on more productive and worthwhile pursuits.

That said, there is the potential here for *"ein ledavar sof,"* for there being no end to the making of fences, to the point where it reaches an absurd degree. The idea is not to lock oneself in a room—or take on excessive *chumrot* (stringencies)—in the attempt to remove any and all obstacles and challenges. Rather, each of us must be honest with ourselves and determine what kinds of challenges are normal and healthy for us, part of the human experience, and which ones are simply best avoided.

Bizayon and Devaluation

The word *bizayon* (בזיון), "degradation," is from the root *baza* (בזה), meaning to spurn, despise, degrade or disgrace. A *bizayon* takes place

---

[33] As the Talmud states, לעולם אל יביא אדם עצמו לידי נסיון (*Sanhedrin* 107a).

[34] See Bartenura on *Avot* 1:1: יעשו סייג לתורה' גדר שלא יבא ליגע באיסור תורה.

[35] As it says, עברה גוררת עברה (*Avot* 4:2)—one *aveira* drags along the next *aveira* with it.

when something of high value is treated as if it has little or no value.[36] The word also bears a relation to *bazaz* (בזז), to spoil, rob or plunder.[37] To be degraded in the sense of *bizayon* is to have one's dignity plundered, to feel that one has been robbed of his or her value as a person by being despised and spurned in the eyes of others.

The plain meaning of the *bracha* is that we express the hope not to experience *bizayon*, not to be devalued by others or be robbed of our dignity. However, perhaps the desire not to come to the hands of *bizayon* might be understood as similar to not coming to the hands of *aveira*. That is to say, we do not wish to "commit" a *bizayon*, to degrade anyone or anything, to take something of high value and treat it as if it lacks worth. Indeed, every waking minute of life is a gift of tremendous value, to be savored and enjoyed. Our lives and the lives of others should never be undervalued, stripped of their worth. Hence we say, "*lo liydei bizayon.*"

וְאַל תַּשְׁלֵט בָּנוּ יֵצֶר הָרָע... וְדַבְּקֵנוּ בְּיֵצֶר הַטּוֹב

and may the destructive inclination not dominate within us...
and attach us to the enlivening inclination

Yetzer Tov and Yetzer Hara

The word *yetzer* (יֵצֶר) stems from the root *yatzar* (יצר), meaning to impart shape by applying pressure.[38] *Yetzer* can refer either to a physical form[39] or to that which forms or shapes a person's thoughts and actions—i.e., their "inclination." The tradition understands people as having two distinct paradigms within consciousness which shape the way we are inclined to think and act. These are the *yetzer tov* and the *yetzer hara*, typically translated "good inclination" and "evil inclination." The good inclination is generally defined as that which brings us closer to Torah and *mitzvot*, and the evil inclination as that which brings us further away.

---

[36] As it says, וַיִּבֶז עֵשָׂו אֶת הַבְּכֹרָה (*Bereshit* 25:34). Why use language of *bizayon*? Because Esav did not merely "reject" his birthright—he devalued it, as evidenced in his rhetorical question two *psukim* earlier: "What worth is this birthright to me?" I.e., it had no worth, no value, in Esav's eyes.

[37] See entries for בזה and בזז in the *Etymological Dictionary of Biblical Hebrew*, M. Clark.

[38] See p. 99, on the concept of *yatzar/yetzira*.

[39] See *Yeshayahu* 29:16, referring to formed pottery.

In the same way that we seek not to fall into the hands of *aveira* and *nisayon*, we also hope not to be dominated by the influence of the *yetzer hara*, but instead to have the *yetzer tov* dominate, as the Talmud says:

לעולם ירגיז אדם יצר טוב על יצר הרע, שנאמר, רגזו ואל תחטאו

"A person should always agitate the yetzer tov against the yetzer hara,
as it is said: 'Be agitated and do not sin'."[40]

The Maharsha[41] brings up an intriguing point regarding this statement in the Talmud. He says that typically *rogez* (agitation in the sense of "shaking with anger") is something that we associate with the *yetzer hara*, not with the *yetzer tov*, since anger tends to lead us to rash and impulsive action, resulting in *cheit*. Yet here the Talmud is suggesting that a person "get angry" in order to dominate over the *yetzer hara*. He says that clearly here, anger is actually a *good* thing. Point being, it is incorrect to think of "good" and "bad" as being fixed or absolute designations. Rather, they are heavily context-dependent, whereby what is bad in one situation can be good in another, and vice-versa.

The Trap of Tov and Ra

Likewise, there is a tendency to say that the *yetzer hara* stems from instinctual proclivities and physical drives, whereas the *yetzer tov* is spiritual, driven by conscience, the sense of right and wrong. However (as exemplified above), there are times when one's more "base" emotions and instincts are unquestionably *good*. And clearly, to dismiss physicality as inherently "evil" is not true to life, nor is it true to Torah. Furthermore, spirituality is hardly a guarantee of goodness. There are those who, with every noble intent and desire to uphold what is "good" and "right," will strap a bomb to their chest and walk into a public thoroughfare. There are those who, with every sense of idealistic transcendence and spiritual motivation, will sit down and devise a plan that involves the murder of millions. And it all *feels* as if it's coming from the *yetzer tov*. If feels morally, philosophically and spiritually justified.

---

[40] *Brachot 5a*, quoting *Tehilim 4:5*. The *yetzer hara* is connected conceptually to *aveira*. Indeed the phrase וְאַל תַּשְׁלֶט בָּנוּ יֵצֶר הָרַע is based on the *pasuk*, וְאַל תַּשְׁלֶט בִּי כָל אָוֶן, "May no manner of iniquity dominate in me" (*Tehilim* 119:133).

[41] R. Shmuel Eidels (1555–1631), author of *Chidushei Maharsha*, a renowned commentary on the Talmud.

This brings up an inherent difficulty in how we define *tov* and *ra*. Not only are "good" and "bad" highly context-sensitive, but they can also differ very significantly based on the religion or ideology to which a person subscribes. For instance, who is to say what is "murder" and what is a holy act commanded by God? Clearly, it depends on which group you ask, and to which "god" you subscribe. In the Eden narrative, the Serpent tells Chava that when she eats from the Tree of Knowledge she will be "as gods, knowing good and bad."[42] The problem is, every "god," every ideology, has its version of good and bad. That is the trap of *da'at tov vara*.

Etz HaChaim as a Tikun for the Etz HaDa'at

But the *Etz HaDa'at Tov VaRa* is not the only tree in the center of the Garden—there is also the *Etz HaChaim*. True, the Torah seems to imply that since Adam and Chava's expulsion, we lack full or direct access to the Tree of Life. However, we can recognize life, savor it, and hold it as a guiding principle. We can embrace the will for Life. That is precisely the Torah's strategy for evading the trap of good and evil, for effecting a *tikun* (rectification) of the *Etz HaDa'at*. It is to tie "good and bad" to the Life principle, as the famous *pasuk* suggests:

רְאֵה נָתַתִּי לְפָנֶיךָ הַיּוֹם
אֶת הַחַיִּים וְאֶת הַטּוֹב וְאֶת הַמָּוֶת וְאֶת הָרָע.
"See, I have placed before you today
the life and the good, and the death and the bad."[43]

The Torah here explicitly associates "good" with "life," and "bad" with "death." Meaning, what is "good" is that which *enlivens*, which fosters life and vitality, and what is "bad" is that which *deadens*, which diminishes life/vitality. So, one cannot say that something like anger is absolutely "wrong." It is wrong when it fails to serve Life, when it deadens rather than enlivens, when it is destructive rather than constructive. It just so happens that anger very often manifests destructively, which is

---

[42] See *Bereshit* 3:5. As to the translation "as gods," see Targum Onkelos and Ibn Ezra, both of whom take the word "*elohim*" to be the plural, common form. (Onkelos translates *elohim* to mean "*ravravin*/rulers" and Ibn Ezra says "*malachim*/angels.") The plural form is suggested by the phrase "*yodei tov vara*," where *yodei* is plural, and it is unclear whether it refers to Adam and Chava or to the word כֵּא-לֹהִים.

[43] *Devarim* 30:15

why it is generally cast in a negative light. In the same way, moral right-eousness and idealism are not absolutely "right." They are right only when they result in the preservation, enrichment and increase of Life.

The same goes for all "virtues" such as truth, justice, liberty, cour-age, modesty, humility, patience, compassion, love, and so on. In Torah terms, these are not "good" in any absolute sense. Yes, they are good when they foster Life, when they serve to enliven—and they often do. But when they do not, they lose their worth. For instance, there are times *not* to tell the truth, *not* to be compassionate, *not* to be humble, situations where it is evident that if we were to uphold the "virtue" it would run counter to life and well-being. And one who pursues them in such in-stances, at the expense of Life, is following a kind of idolatry.

Notions of "good and bad" are like *elohim*, rooted in the *Etz HaDa'at*. Torah however is rooted in *Hashem* and the *Etz HaChaim*.[44] In Torah, it is the *Etz HaDa'at* which is meant to serve the *Etz HaChaim*, not the other way around.[45] It is the other values which must serve the cause of Life, the *elohim* which must serve *Hashem*, as it says:

הִשְׁתַּחֲווּ לוֹ כָּל אֱלֹהִים
"bow to Him, all gods!"[46]

All the *elohim* must bow to *Hashem*. All delineations of *tov* and *ra* must yield to *chaim*. Morality needs to conform to the Life principle. Likewise:

לֹא יִהְיֶה לְךָ אֱלֹהִים אֲחֵרִים עַל פָּנָי
"you shall not have any other gods before Me"[47]

---

[44] As it says, עֵץ חַיִּים הִיא לַמַּחֲזִיקִים בָּהּ, "[Torah] is a Tree of Life for those who grasp on-to it (*Mishlei* 3:18).

[45] The "*mei meriva*" story (*Bamidbar* 20:1–13) is an example of putting the *Etz HaDa'at* be-fore the *Etz HaChaim*, *tov* and *ra* before *chaim*. Rather than simply give the people water as commanded, Moshe tells the people that they are undeserving: שִׁמְעוּ נָא הַמֹּרִים, הֲמִן הַסֶּלַע הַזֶּה נוֹצִיא לָכֶם מָיִם, "Listen rebels, is it from this rock that we should bring out water for you?" As the Ba'al HaTurim notes here, the only other place in the Torah where the phrase הֲמִן הָעֵץ אֲשֶׁר צִוִּיתִיךָ לְבִלְתִּי אֲכָל מִמֶּנּוּ (המן ה-) ("is it from the") is used, is in the Eden story: אָכָלְתָּ, "Is it from the tree that I commanded you not to eat from that you ate?" (*Bereshit* 3:11). By condemning the people rather than seeking out their welfare/*chaim* as a matter of first priority, Moshe in effect eats from the fruit of *tov* and *ra*. Like Adam and Chava, Moshe is exiled, fated never to enter the Land of Israel. (See also Note 62, p. 54.)

[46] *Tehilim* 97:7

[47] *Shemot* 20:2

No other values must come before the value of Life. As we spoke about earlier, even the *mitzvot* themselves are subject to the *chai bahem* principle, *meshubad* (subservient) to Life, so that any *mitzva* that contravenes life is negated, as the Sages say:

וחי בהם, ולא שימות בהם

"'And live through them', [meaning that] one should not die through them."[48]

Giving Up One's Life

The question is, if the Life principle comes above all, what do we make of the Talmudic stipulation *"yehareg ve'al ya'avor,"* that we should allow ourselves to be killed before committing an act of murder, idolatry or forbidden sexual relations?[49] Isn't it clear from this idea that the Torah holds certain things to be of higher value than "life"?

The answer is that the Life principle is not only about "being alive" as opposed to losing one's life, nor is it only about the life of the individual. Life (with a capital "L") encompasses all the myriad factors that serve to "enliven"—physical and emotional well-being, creativity, joy, fulfillment, and so on. It includes the well-being and advancement of the society as well as the individual. It also takes into consideration the effect that our actions have on others, as well as the impact our actions today will have on the well-being of future generations. In other words, "Life" certainly includes, even primarily so, the life of the individual, and a person has the right—indeed the *mitzva*—to guard his or her life to every extent possible. However, there are certain limited circumstances acknowledged in the Torah tradition that have the potential to bring about such a profound degradation of Life (in the wider sense of the term), that giving up one's life rather than commit such acts is in fact a highly "yea to life" expression. It is an elevation of Life that extends beyond the self, and beyond the here and now.

---

[48] *Yoma* 85b; see also *Sanhedrin* 74a, *Avoda Zara* 27b and 54a. Also see *Meshech Chochma* on *"chai bahem"* (*Vayikra* 18:5), who explains: פיקוח נפש דוחה כל התורה, that saving a life pushes off any command of the Torah. See also p. 85, on the *"chai bahem"* principle.

[49] See *Sanhedrin* 74a. These are commonly referred to as the three "cardinal *aveirot*." They in fact correspond to three of the Ten Commandments: Do not have other gods, do not murder, and do not commit adultery (a subcategory of forbidden sexual relations).

Investing Energy for the Long-term

Even in everyday situations, the challenge is to think bigger, longer term, beyond the moment. As the Talmud says:

זה יצר הרע, שראשו מתוק וסופו מר

"This is the yetzer hara, whose beginning is sweet and end is bitter."[50]

Yes, there is absolutely a place for pleasures that are transient and fleeting, and indeed they often do add to the "sweetness" of life. After all, we need to live in the moment, connect to the Life in each moment, rather than simply live for the future (or live in the past). However, when the present comes at the *expense* of the future, when the life-energy derived now by a particular action is far outweighed by the life-energy that stands to be *lost* in the future based on that action, this is what the tradition refers to as being pulled by the *yetzer hara*. The inclination is "evil" insofar as the net result is destructive to Life. It is also a *bizayon*, in the sense of taking something of the greatest value, the highest *kedusha*—one's life—and degrading it, devaluing it, embittering it.

The Life principle can thus be understood as being comparable to the following rule, expressed in terms of *kedusha*, which is brought in multiple places in the Talmud:

מעלין בקודש ולא מורידין

"We may raise the level of kedusha, but not lower it."[51]

One does not take something of high *kedusha* and downgrade it to a lower level—such *kedusha* may only be brought "up" an additional level. In the same way, Life is something never to be degraded or diminished, but rather to be continually added to, expanded and elevated.

---

[50] *Yerushalmi Shabbat* 14:3; see also *Vayikra Rabbah* 16:8. The *gemara* is cited by Abudraham, commentary on *Birchot HaShachar*.

[51] *Yoma* 12b, *Menachot* 39a, *Zevachim* 18a, *Megila* 9b.

וּתְנֵנוּ הַיּוֹם וּבְכָל יוֹם לְחֵן וּלְחֶסֶד וּלְרַחֲמִים
and position us—today and every day—for elicited-favor,
for just-kindness, and for undeserved-compassion

The Magnetism of Chein

The word *chein* means favor, grace or charm. It is often used to describe the attribute of a person, one who is graceful or charming.[52] But *chein*, as used in our *bracha*, can also mean the favor or grace that is *given* to another. *Chein* (חן) stems from the verb *chanan* (חנן), meaning to grant favor, bestow grace. And indeed there is a connection between *chein* as an attribute one possesses, and *chein* as something one receives from another. Namely, a person with the "trait" of *chein* possesses the kind of character, appearance and/or manner which elicits the "giving" sort of *chein*, which provokes a favorable response from others. One who has *chein* is able to be "*motzi chein*"—he or she can win the grace of others, "bring it out" of them.

In addition, there is a relationship between *chein* and the verb *chana* (חנה), to "encamp," pitch one's tent, settle, stop moving and connect oneself to a particular location.[53] Someone with *chein* has the capacity to trigger a connection, to cause other people—whose attention is moving, wandering—to stop and focus. The person radiates a certain energy and vitality to which others desire to connect and thereby take part in that vitality. Thus we might think of the attribute of *chein* as a kind of "magnetism," drawing people to attach to a source of life-energy. And that same *chein* draws vitality from others—it induces others to want to give, offer their favor, grant clemency, and so on.

Chein, Chesed and Rachamim

In the context of the *bracha*, the order is *chein*, *chesed* and *rachamim*. *Chein* (grace) is what a person receives as a consequence of who they are and what they radiate outward. This does not mean they are "deserving" of favor, but rather that they have positive qualities which *elicit* favor. *Chesed* (kindness) is more neutral, based not on the qualities of the recipient but rather on the general recognition in society that if someone else

---

[52] As in, אֵשֶׁת חֵן תִּתְמֹךְ כָּבוֹד (*Mishlei* 11:16) and שֶׁקֶר הַחֵן וְהֶבֶל הַיֹּפִי (Ibid., 31:30).

[53] See entries for חָנָה and חָנַן in the *Gesenius Lexicon*.

has a need or lack, it is proper and just, the right thing to do, to sustain them, help fill their needs. (Hence there is a connection between *tzedaka* and *chesed*.[54]) *Rachamim* (compassion) is what one receives *despite* themselves, when the *din* (judgment) would otherwise come out against them, and they are deemed undeserving. Therefore, *rachamim* is a function of the giver's sheer desire to give, a desire for life above all.

What we are saying then is ideally we hope to achieve *chein*. We hope that we possess the kind of positive qualities, vitality and charm, which draw favor. Failing that, we hope for *chesed*, that at least we are neutral enough that we can petition from the standpoint of justice and decency, to be given help because it is the right thing to do. If worse comes to worse however, and we are negative to the point where we cannot even garner *chesed*, we will settle for *rachamim*. We hope that the desire for *din*, to act toward others only in accordance with what they deserve, is surpassed by the desire for *rachamim* and *chaim*—to give for no other reason than the desire to sustain life, i.e., regardless of deservingness.[55]

That is all from the recipient's point of view. From the standpoint of the giver, the opposite order is arguably preferred. The best and highest place to give is out of *rachamim*, pure desire for life. The next is to do so because it is just and proper, as an act of *chesed*. Last is giving from *chein*, where it is only due to the person's magnetism and charm that a giving response is triggered, implying that someone else in the same situation, but without the *chein*, would not have received the gift.

In addition, *chein*, *chesed* and *rachamim* can be looked upon in the sense of the three-phase developmental process.[56] *Chein* is Phase One, characterized by natural charm and *chiyut/chaim*. *Chesed* is Phase Two, characterized by the reliance on people's sense of *tov* and *ra*, *din*, right and wrong.[57] *Rachamim* is Phase Three, distinguished by the prevailing desire for and consciousness of Life. *Rachamim* also conveys the idea of

---

[54] As in: רֹדֵף צְדָקָה וָחָסֶד (*Mishlei* 21:21) and עֲשֵׂה עִמָּנוּ צְדָקָה וָחֶסֶד (*Avinu Malkeinu tefila*).

[55] As it says in the *tefila* following the *Akeida* in *Shacharit* and before *tekiat shofar*: יִכְבְּשׁוּ רַחֲמֶיךָ אֶת כַּעַסְךָ וְיָגֹלּוּ רַחֲמֶיךָ עַל מִדּוֹתֶיךָ, "May Your *rachamim* extinguish Your anger, and may Your *rachamim* prevail over Your [other] attributes."

[56] See p. 167, discussing the Three-Phase model.

[57] Note that this characterization of *chesed* is relational, meaning it applies to the *chein-chesed-rachamim* sequence. In other sequences such as *chesed-gevura-tiferet*, *chesed* is in the first position, and it is *gevura* that takes on the *tov/ra* characterization.

"*rechem*," the womb—that which not only sustains life but has the ability to create *new* life, achieving a level of *chaim*/vitality that surpasses the original state.[58] Phase Three and *rachamim* can thus be seen as representing a "rebirth" for humankind.[59]

בְּעֵינֶיךָ וּבְעֵינֵי כָל רוֹאֵינוּ
in Your eyes and in the eyes of all who see us

Integrity and Groundedness

The previous phrase in the *bracha* expressed our desire to be granted *chein, chesed* and *rachamim*. We now specify that we hope to evoke such favor and compassion not only "in Your eyes," but also "in the eyes of all who see us," meaning from fellow human beings.[60] Classical commentaries link this part of the *bracha* to the following *pasuk*:

וּמְצָא חֵן וְשֵׂכֶל טוֹב בְּעֵינֵי אֱ-לֹהִים וְאָדָם.
"*And find favor and good understanding in the eyes of Elokim and humanity.*"[61]

The Sages cite this *pasuk* among others when stressing that a person must be upright and well-regarded, not simply from the perspective of "*shamayim*" (i.e., in the "ideal" sense), but also by the people around us.[62]

To have *chein* "in the eyes of *Elokim*" might be thought of as *chein* from a more objective standpoint, meaning to possess the positive qualities of the sort that would make a person favorable, at least "on paper." Of course, it is possible to be a person of high moral fiber, character and personal development, one with qualities that "should" make a person likable and elicit favor in the eyes of others, but somehow people do not

---

[58] A similar pattern can be seen in the *Sim Shalom bracha* of the *Amida*, where *chein, chesed* and *rachamim* are parallel to *shalom, tova* and *bracha* respectively. *Shalom* is the natural state of equilibrium and vitality, similar to *chein*. *Tova* is similar to *chesed*, that which sustains us during a period of *tov* and *ra*. And *bracha* is like *rachamim*, relating to *ribui* and *rechem*, proliferation, where life is increased far beyond what it was at first.

[59] See p. 131, on the concept of *techiya* and humanity's future rebirth.

[60] This idea is echoed in the *pasuk*, וַתְּהִי אֶסְתֵּר נֹשֵׂאת חֵן בְּעֵינֵי כָל רֹאֶיהָ, "And Esther was one who carries favor in the eyes of all who see her" (*Esther* 2:15).

[61] *Mishlei* 3:4. See R. Yehuda Bar-Yakar and Abudraham on *Birchot HaShachar*.

[62] See e.g., *Tosefta Shekalim, Perek* 2, quoting וִהְיִיתֶם נְקִיִּם מֵה' וּמִיִּשְׂרָאֵל (*Bamidbar* 32:22), and וְעָשִׂיתָ הַיָּשָׁר וְהַטּוֹב בְּעֵינֵי ה' (*Devarim* 6:18) which is interpreted: הטוב בעיני שמים והישר בעיני אדם. See also: אדם צריך לצאת ידי הבריות כדרך שצריך לצאת ידי המקום (*Mishna Shekalim* 3:2).

see it. So we likewise seek *chein* "in the eyes of *adam*." On the other hand, we know all too well that one can be charming and charismatic, winning favor from people right and left, yet be sorely lacking in character and integrity. So we also desire to have *chein* "in the eyes of *Elokim*," in the more objective sense.

The *pasuk* likewise speaks about "*sechel tov*," being seen as possessing good sense, insight or understanding. To have *sechel tov* in the eyes of *Elokim* could be thought of as achieving a correct objective understanding, coming closer to the truth. But of course, one can discover the most profound of truths, yet for the life of them they cannot get others to see it. So we hope for *sechel tov* "in the eyes of *adam*." On the other hand, one can be lauded as a beacon of great wisdom in the eyes of people, but it is simply a result of the person's charisma and ability to captivate an audience rather than their possessing actual truth-content or good sense. So we desire not only to be *perceived* as having good understanding, but also to actually *possess* genuine *sechel tov*, to be aligned with truth, to formulate ideas that are sensible and wise.

The question is, why isn't it enough to have *chein* and *sechel tov* in the eyes of *Elokim*, to be a person of character and integrity, of truth and understanding? Why should we care whether or not people *recognize* it? We might offer several answers to this. To begin with, on a very practical level, we are sometimes put into situations where we have to rely on people's benevolence, and being well-regarded by others can make all the difference in terms of our success. Second, we are not expected to be robots. It is *human* to want to be recognized and appreciated, both for our character and for our ideas.

Further, getting other people's feedback is crucial. If we expend effort in the area self-development and yet find ourselves the object of scorn rather than *chein* in the eyes of people, this might be a sign that we need to reevaluate ourselves and our efforts.[63] Similarly, if we develop an idea that appears to us to be the very epitome of truth, and yet people do not see the *sechel tov* in it, it could be that we need to rethink the idea. Perhaps we have been "inside our own head" for so long that we have lost perspective and could use a bit of constructive critique. If all we do is preach "truth" with an air of absolute certainty, without the humility

---

[63] See p. 144, on using people's perceptions of our words and actions as a "litmus test."

to listen to and learn from others, that is arguably the very *opposite* of what it means to be truth-seeking. Rather than desire continual development and refinement, the goal becomes having oneself "be heard." Such a person is in fact referred to as a "fool," as it says:

לֹא יַחְפֹּץ כְּסִיל בִּתְבוּנָה, כִּי אִם בְּהִתְגַּלּוֹת לִבּוֹ.

"A fool does not desire discernment, but rather to display his own thought."[64]

Finally, to care about how others perceive us and our thinking is essential because it emphasizes the fact that we live in a world of *people*, a world of relationships. Ideas, beliefs and principles are important, it goes without saying—but *people come before ideas*. When they do not, we end up with ideologies and "isms" that take on lives of their own—where schisms and polemics divide us, and we cannot bear one another "on principle," where allegiance to the "ideal" eclipses the lives and needs of individuals, and where we create the possibility of ideas worth *killing* for. That is the danger of *da'at tov vara*, the realm of "right" and "wrong" thinking. When it becomes detached from *chaim*, disconnected from real people and their lives, it all too easily degenerates into killing.

To live in the world therefore requires us to seek not only *emet* but also *shalom*. It is to say that ideas and truth are only so important, because at the end of the day, we must face one another, talk with each other, work things through together, and live as neighbors. We also laugh together, grieve together, share real moments of life together. It is these moments that remind us that all the ideas, beliefs and principles by which we define ourselves—and indeed thoroughly immerse ourselves in on a daily basis—are really just a shell, an outer veneer. Remove that, and we find a far greater *human* dimension that lies beneath. It is a dimension that is no less "true," no less of a "principle" to live by. Indeed, it is the *Life principle*.

Having *chein* and *sechel tov* in the eyes of *"adam"* might then be understood in relation to *"adama"* (earth), i.e., as that which keeps us "grounded," down to earth. While we pursue integrity and truth for their own sake, and even do so with great passion and determination, at the same time we ground that pursuit in our connection with people. Rather than sit in ivory-tower isolation, we filter our own ideas and ex-

---

[64] *Mishlei* 18:2

perience through our relationships. This enables us to achieve a healthy balance of theory and practice, living in the realm of ideas as well as in everyday reality—and in so doing, we better enable the success of *both*.

בָּרוּךְ אַתָּה ה' הַגּוֹמֵל חֲסָדִים טוֹבִים לְעַמּוֹ יִשְׂרָאֵל
*Be expanded, You Hashem, Who fully-transmits
beneficial sustaining-kindnesses for His people Yisrael*

Gemilut Chasadim – Weaning off of Chesed

The word *gomel* (גומל) means to fully transmit or give over to another, whereby the other side has received all that is needed. It is related to the verb *gamal* (גמל), to wean or ripen, where the child/fruit has received sufficient direct nourishment from the parent/tree and is ready to separate, become independent.

"*Gomel*" can be used in the negative sense of doling out a full punishment,[65] as well as in the positive sense of *gemilut chesed*, the act of giving. Regarding the latter, to be *gomel chesed* means to transmit everything that the person needs, such that ideally he or she is now able to separate from the source of support and achieve independence.[66] So while it may sound counterintuitive based on the colloquial usage, the phrase "*gemilut chasadim*" does not imply the "continuation" of *chesed* so much as it does the *cessation* of *chesed*, an end to the need for *chesed*.

Rising to the Challenge of Conscious Independence

This is the spirit of the final *bracha* in *Birchot HaShachar*. On the one hand, it expresses our recognition and gratitude for the unending *chesed* we experience daily and without which we would not survive. But on the other hand, it relates the anticipation of a day when we will be "weaned" as it were and achieve independence. It looks forward to a time when we are "*mitkayem*," when we can stand on our own, as a result of our own efforts, not be so needy or dependent.

---

[65] As in, וַהֲשֵׁבוֹתָ לוֹ גְּמוּלוֹ בְּרֹאשׁוֹ (*Al HaNisim tefila* for Purim).

[66] This is similar to the Rambam's description of "levels" of *tzedaka*, whereby the highest level is to give to a person in a way that they will no longer be in a position of need, such as helping them to find a livelihood (see *Hilchot Matanot Ani'im* 10:7). This kind of *tzedaka* is *gemilut chesed*, an act of kindness used to wean a person off of perpetual need.

Indeed this is a natural part of growing up. The goal for a child is to mature, thrive, succeed and achieve independence. This success gives a parent "*nachat*" —they can now rest well, contentedly, knowing that their child is able to make it on their own. The fact of independence does not break the connection between parent and child—on the contrary, it *deepens* that connection. Because not only does it enable the relationship to progress beyond one of fulfillment of "needs," but also as the child becomes a parent and engages in his or her own creative activity, there is now a level of shared understanding and experience that was not present before.

Each time we awaken in the morning and regain consciousness, *da'at*, it hearkens back to the primordial story of our eating from the *Etz HaDa'at* and subsequent separation from the *Etz HaChaim*, our source of nourishment. This was a separation that came with great bitterness and pain. However, it was also a crucial step toward our maturation and independence, and as a result we now stand equipped with *da'at*, conscious awareness—the *tzelem Elokim* itself. We carry within ourselves the very power of creation. It is therefore our intent and greatest hope that we rise to the challenge, use this power wisely, overcome our destructive inclinations, and forge the way toward a redemptive future where our great creative potential is harnessed for the benefit of all.

Amen
אמן

When *Birchot HaShachar* (or any *bracha*) is said aloud, those listening respond *"Amen."*

אָמֵן
I hereby affirm / May it be so / Activate!

Amen – Hold Steady, Firm and True

The word *amen* derives from the root *aman* (אָמַן), meaning to hold steady or support continually, implying something that can be fully relied upon. Similarly, an *omen/omenet* (אמן\אמנת) is a foster parent or nurse, one who "faithfully supports" the life of a child. *Omnot* (אמנות) are doorposts or pillars, whose job is to hold a structure steady. A master craftsman or artist is called an *uman* (אומן), owing to the reliability and expertise of their work. Also related are the words *emet* (אמת), being true/faithful to someone or something, and *emuna* (אמונה), reliability, faithfulness, holding steady or firm.[1] *Amen* thus implies "affirmation" in the literal sense of "make firm," to solidify or concretize, and it also acknowledges reliability, that something holds true and steady.

Three Types of Amen

The Talmud lists three usages for the word *amen*:

אמר רבי יוסי ברבי חנינא,
אמן בו שבועה בו קבלת דברים בו האמנת דברים
"Rabbi Yosi son of Rabbi Chanina said:
'Amen' implies oath-taking, acceptance of terms, and giving support."[2]

---

[1] See p. 34, on the concepts of *emuna* and *emet*.

[2] *Shevuot* 36a

The first two categories have specific *halachic*/legal ramifications, whereby uttering *"amen"* makes an oath or contractual terms go into effect. The word *amen* in this context is a performative statement, a word that initiates a new status quo.[3] One example in the Torah of this kind of *amen* comes in the series of "blessings and curses" which *Am Yisrael* is enjoined to accept upon entering the land of Israel, as in:

אָרוּר מַכֵּה רֵעֵהוּ בַּסָּתֶר וְאָמַר כָּל הָעָם אָמֵן

"[The Levites will say,] 'Be cursed, he who strikes his neighbor in stealth,'
and all the people will say, 'Amen'."[4]

Answering *"amen"* to such a statement is to accept a certain reality upon oneself, upon the society, so that it becomes binding and impactful within the national consciousness. *Amen* gives the preceding statement *"kiyum,"* makes it stand, establishes it. Again, this applies to oaths and contractual conditions.

The third scenario the Talmud mentions for the use of *amen* is "giving support," which relates to *tefila*. A person says *"amen"* to a *bracha* as a means of affirming the truth of what was stated, or to express the hope and desire that the *bracha* be true, come to pass.[5] So for instance, the conclusion of the *bracha* of *Elokai Neshama* states: "Who returns *neshamot* to dead bodies." Saying *"amen"* to this *bracha* can mean an affirmation that yes, our consciousness is faithfully restored every morning following the "quasi-death" of sleep, or it can communicate the fervent desire that our *neshamot* be restored in a future era, such that death gives way to everlasting life.

---

[3] Also known as a "speech act," a performative statement or utterance is something that, when said, ushers in a new status—legal, social or otherwise. The term "performative utterance" per se comes from the writings of philosopher John L. Austin, but the concept has existed and been in use for millennia. Any statement that begins "I hereby declare" is a performative utterance. An example in Jewish tradition is הרי את מקודשת לי, "You are hereby betrothed to me." Likewise, the word *"amen"* can be used to imply, "I hereby accept upon myself the aforementioned oath/conditions."

[4] *Devarim* 27:24. The Talmud (*Shevuot* 36a) cites a similar *pasuk* in the curses as an example of *kabalat devarim*, accepting contractual conditions. Regarding *amen* as the acceptance of a *shevua*, an oath, it cites the *parsha* of the *sota* (*Bamidbar* 5:22).

[5] See Rashi on *Shevuot* 36a, who says: שיהא רצון שיהא אמת כן, "that may it be [*Hashem's*] will that it be truly so."

Amen as Kiyum HaBracha

There are those who view saying *"amen"* to a *bracha* to likewise constitute a performative statement, in the same way it does regarding an oath
or a contract—i.e., imparting *kiyum*, bringing the *bracha* "into effect" as it
were. According to Rabbeinu Bachye,[6] of the three categories of *amen*, it
is specifically *amen* said in response to a *bracha* that he identifies with
"kiyum," where uttering *"amen"* is what activates the *bracha*.[7] He then
cites a statement from the Talmud:

גדול העונה אמן יותר מן המברך

"Greater is the one who answers 'amen' than the one who utters the blessing."[8]

Why should the person who answers *amen* be considered greater?
Rabbeinu Bachye likens it to *eidut* (testimony), where the second witness
is the one who gives *kiyum* to the *eidut*, makes it stand as legally binding.
Regarding *brachot*, the person who makes the *bracha* is like the first witness, and the one who answers *"amen"* is like the second witness, creating *eidut* and thereby activating the *bracha*, affirming it—i.e., making it
stand firmly as a reality within consciousness.

Fig. 39   Bracha, Amen and Kiyum in consciousness

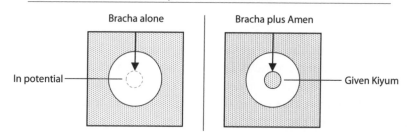

---

[6] R. Bachye ben Asher (mid-13th century–1340).

[7] As he says: אמן קבלה, אמן שבועה, אמן קיום (Rabbeinu Bachye on *Shemot* 14:31). See also
Radak (on *Tehilim* 41:14, בָּרוּךְ ה' אֱ-לֹהֵי יִשְׂרָאֵל... אָמֵן וְאָמֵן) who says, אמן לשון קיום.

[8] *Nazir* 66b (the very end of the tractate). The Talmud however cites different opinions
on this matter, and the *rishonim* and *achronim* likewise differ as to who has more "merit,"
the one who recites the *bracha* or the one who answers *"amen,"* which has a number of
ramifications in practical Halacha.

Amen – Will into Action

Answering *"amen"* can thus be seen as a means of "activation." It is taking an intent, plan or desired outcome, and initiating it through a spoken command, like saying: "Run the program!" "Start the flow!" "Make it so!" It is a statement of execution, bringing a plan to fruition. In this sense, *amen* might be understood as a statement of *malchut*—initiating the transmission of an idea, so that it reigns, holds influence within the consciousness of an individual, a *kahal* (congregation), or *Am Yisrael* as a whole.

There are times when the process of activation/transmission bears repeating, as the *pasuk* says:

בָּרוּךְ ה' לְעוֹלָם אָמֵן וְאָמֵן

"Be propagated, Hashem, to the reaches of time/space—be so, and be so![9]

The phrase *amen ve'amen* is understood by some as adding emphasis, as in, "May it *really* be so."[10] Others however understand *amen ve'amen* as conveying our desire that the *bracha* be activated again and again, as in "be so, and be so again," or "keep running."[11] In this sense, the phrase *amen ve'amen* echoes the word *"le'olam,"* expressing continuousness.[12]

Throughout the book, we have looked at the *brachot* we say in the morning as articulating the desire to infuse our consciousness—as well as the world around us—with Life. The word *amen* is about going the next step, taking that wish or desire, and committing ourselves to make it so, to actualize it, concretize it, internalize it, make it manifest in our actions. It is about transforming the will for Life into reality. That is the word *amen*.

---

[9] *Tehilim* 89:53

[10] See e.g., *Metzudat David*, ibid. (also on 72:19), which says, וכפל הדבר לחוזק, that the repetition of the word *amen* is intended to "strengthen" the matter.

[11] See Radak (on *Tehilim* 41:14), who says, אמן ואמן, קיום וקיום.

[12] Indeed, in all three *psukim* in Tanach that contain the phrase *amen ve'amen* (*Tehilim* 41:14, 72:19 and 89:53), the *pasuk* also contains לעולם or ועד העולם מהעולם.

To end, a personal *tefila*:

Yehi ratzon—
May our will and desire be for Life.
May it infuse our every waking day with gratitude,
our interrelations with benevolence and uprightness,
our pursuits with a sense of creative purpose,
and in so doing, may we experience bracha, shalom and simcha—
all the concrete expressions of Life—in ever greater abundance.

Amen ve'amen!

List of Figures

Acknowledgements

I begin by thanking my great teacher, mentor and friend, Professor Joe Levinson. Anyone who can say that in their lifetime they found a true teacher—in whose "tent" they could spend long hours discussing, learning, stretching the mind, expanding and growing—is extremely fortunate. I count myself as one of those people. For the past twenty years, from just about the time when I first came to Israel to learn Torah, I have been close with Dr. Levinson and his wife Linda, who have been like second parents to me. Where I have come in my concept of Torah, including and especially my focus on "*chaim*," I owe in large part to the good Doctor. He is indeed a person who lives, breathes and exudes *chaim*. I so treasure our friendship and look forward to sharing much more life—and many more *chidushei Torah*—together. A lifetime of gratitude goes to you!

One bittersweet part of publishing this book is the fact that my parents, Peter and Charlotte Behrendt, *z"l*, are not here for me to hand them a copy. I wish I could have given them that *nachas*. I miss them both tremendously, and I thank them for the outstanding *midot* they taught me in the sincerity and generosity with which they conducted their lives, and the boundless love and support they always provided to me and my siblings.

Thanks go out to my brother Larry, with whom I've shared many meaningful discussions on Judaism (and a host of other topics) and whose thoughtful insights I value beyond measure, and to my sister-in-law Stephanie Hammer, whose enthusiasm has helped get me remotivated about this project on many occasions! To my sister Judy and brother-in-law Dave Baraff, for being so supportive, for discussing ideas, and whose deep connection—including so many shared laughs and fun times—I count as one of the greatest highlights of my life. To my sister Leah, who—by opening me up to Judaism and welcoming me into her world—made this book possible and enabled the wonderful life I now have here in Israel, and to my brother-in-law Zev Kops for his ever-inspiring Torah and *derech eretz*.

An enormous *"todah"* to all my teachers and friends who contributed to this book, either in processing ideas, teaching me Torah or reading the manuscript. These include Dr. Rabbi Natan Lopes Cardozo, Rabbi Joel Zeff, Rabbi Daniel Channen/Pirchei Shoshanim, Dr. Rabbi Yisrael Gottlieb, Rabbi Harry Greenspan, Greg Silverman, Rabbi Doron Kornbluth, Andye Friedman, Evan Steele, Rachely Schloss, Meir Kanal, Dr. Roni and Channa Shweka, Fred Leibowitz, Chaim Scheff, Baruch Sirota and all the "Thursday Group" regulars, also Dovid Neiburg, Rabbi Natan Slifkin, Rabbi Danny Myers, Rabbi Yonatan Kolatch, Rabbi Dovid Kaminetsky, Dr. Rabbi David Montag *z"l*, Gershon Hellmann, Eli Shine, Moshe Braun, Michael Cohen, Stuart Schnee, Michael Rose, Bryan Edgar and Daniel Manevich, as well as Aharon Botzer/Livnot U'Lehibanot, Rabbi David Aaron/Isralight, and my Rebbeim at Yeshivat Darche Noam.

Thanks to my extended family, nieces and nephews, brothers and sisters-in-law, aunts and uncles, all those friends who are like *mishpacha* to me (you know who you are!), and particularly to my mother-in-law, Donna Rader, who calls me "son" and who I genuinely feel like a son to. Your constant cheering on and support are very important to me!

A special word of thanks goes to my publisher, Urim Publications and Tzvi Mauer, whose patience has been superhuman! Thank you for all your meticulous, generous help on this project, from start to finish.

Thank you to my boys, Daniel, Ilan, Bentzi and Yeshaya. Each of you inspire me in your own unique and wonderful ways, and fill my life with incredible *simcha*. I feel like the luckiest *abba* in the world.

Finally, to my wife, Kerry, I can't begin to express my gratitude for everything you've done to help make this book happen. The countless hours I spent researching, writing and editing (and then editing some more…) were made possible because you gave me that space. It was a gift, pure and simple, and I know it came with a lot of extra work and sacrifice on your part. Thank you for that, and for all the joy, energy and gusto, deep fulfillment and friendship, that you bring to my life every single waking day!

Index

About the Author

David Bar-Cohn holds an M.A. in Clinical Psychology and maintains a part-time psychotherapy practice. He also works in music and video production, and is the creator of the "Rebbetzin Tap" children's musical video series. His immersion in Torah/Judaism began at Livnot U'Lehibanot in Tzfat, followed by Yeshivat Darche Noam/Shapell's in Jerusalem. He later received *semicha* in *issur v'heter* through Yeshiva Pirchei Shoshanim. A native of Los Angeles, David now lives in Ramat Beit Shemesh, Israel, with his wife, Kerry, and their four sons.